A WILL FOR THE MACHINE

A WILL
FOR THE
MACHINE

Computerization, Automation,

and the Arts in South Africa

◉

Mark Sanders

THE UNIVERSITY OF CHICAGO PRESS

Chicago and London

The University of Chicago Press, Chicago 60637
The University of Chicago Press, Ltd., London
© 2026 by The University of Chicago
Published 2026
Printed in the United States of America

35 34 33 32 31 30 29 28 27 26   1 2 3 4 5

ISBN-13: 978-0-226-84460-2 (cloth)
ISBN-13: 978-0-226-84461-9 (paper)
ISBN-13: 978-0-226-84462-6 (ebook)
DOI: https://doi.org/10.7208/chicago/9780226844626.001.0001

The University of Chicago Press gratefully acknowledges the generous support
of New York University toward the publication of this book.

Library of Congress Cataloging-in-Publication Data

Names: Sanders, Mark, 1968– author
Title: A will for the machine : computerization, automation, and the arts in South
    Africa / Mark Sanders.
Description: Chicago : The University of Chicago Press, 2026. | Includes
    bibliographical references and index.
Identifiers: LCCN 2025019306 | ISBN 9780226844602 cloth | ISBN 9780226844619
    paperback | ISBN 9780226844626 ebook
Subjects: LCSH: Automation—Political aspects—South Africa | Automation—
    Moral and ethical aspects—South Africa | Labor supply—Effect of
    automation on—South Africa | Discrimination in employment—South
    Africa | Apartheid—South Africa | Arts—Political aspects—South Africa |
    Computer poetry | Computers in literature | Computers in art
Classification: LCC HD6331.2.S6 S36 2026 | DDC 331.110968—dc23/eng/20250721
LC record available at https://lccn.loc.gov/2025019306

♾ This paper meets the requirements of ANSI/NISO Z39.48-1992
(Permanence of Paper).

Authorized Representative for EU General Product Safety Regulation
(GPSR) queries: **Easy Access System Europe**—Mustamäe tee 50,
10621 Tallinn, Estonia, gpsr.requests@easproject.com
Any other queries: https://press.uchicago.edu/press/contact.html

Contents

Figures

Introduction

Dumani mishini yezinkomponi,
Nidume ngesokusa lize lishone.

(Thunder away, machines of the mines,
Thunder away from dawn till sunset)

B.W. VILAKAZI, "Ezinkomponi" ("In the Gold Mines")

And it was no more than that: to read the meaning of these structures,
you must go inside and see what piece of work is performed there.

NADINE GORDIMER, "The Witwatersrand: A Time and Tailings"

Black and white, indistinct, the photograph shows seven human figures stooped before a cylindrical object taller than they are. Above it looms another object with seven points, like claws, pointing down toward it. It is some species of heavy machinery, and the ones stooping before it, one infers, are workers assisting in its operation. A machine with its operators—a quintessential image of the age of industry. This is the photograph, taken deep under the earth's surface by David Goldblatt, that appears on the front cover of *On the Mines*, a book that he co-authored with novelist Nadine Gordimer.

Published in 1973, *On the Mines* may be the most important attempt, in its time, to capture, in high artistic image and word, what mining in South Africa was and what it had been a generation before. The word *on* in the phrase "on the mines" is a play on words. In a South African idiom, "on the mines" is a commonplace statement of location. One may work *in* a mine or *at* a mine, but when one speaks generally of mines as sites of labor, capital accumulation, or unique social organization, both below- and aboveground, one says "on the mines." For being commonplace, however, the phrase is by no means lacking in suggestion. The *on* as it is used in the title also proposes an essay: *on*—or *about*—the mines, specifically the gold mines, the economic foundation of modern South Africa. A tableau is produced by Goldblatt and Gordimer in which machines and their users are, as might have been expected by readers exposed to mining house publicity or committed to an aesthetic of socialist realism, integral features. What was probably less expected is that *On the Mines* does not give its tableau to the eye—or the mind's eye—without reservation. Goldblatt and Gordimer make plain, in image and word, the racial division of labor in South African gold mining and the social, economic, and political disparities attendant on it. Yet *On the Mines* is not quite documentary, and it is not socialist realism. Writer and photographer maintain a reserve.

The writer states synoptically that "between two and three hundred thousand black men a year have worked the mines of the Witwatersrand. They always far outnumbered the twenty to forty-two thousand white miners, technicians, and administrators. . . . The men have come and gone over more than half a century. They left behind them their great part in the complex of men and machinery whose momentum has powered the most diversified industrial state on the African continent. They took away a pittance in money and possessions."[1] Gordimer vividly gives the social concomitants of this racial division of labor.[2] But when it comes to describing "men and machinery" in operation, the surface of what is seen confronts the writer in its opacity. Gordimer is justly celebrated, in South African letters, for writing "history from the inside."[3] Accordingly, when she notices that mine buildings, built of galvanized iron, conform in size and shape to the machines they are built to house, she realizes that "to read the meaning of these structures, you must go inside and see what piece of work is performed there."[4] What the writer finds on the inside is a scene of labor on the verge of vanishing as steam power gives way to electricity. Before her are men—a white winding-engine driver and his black assistant—but it is the machines themselves that act on her senses and prompt a deciphering of social relations: "Yet these were the real beauties, on the Property: the great machines. . . . Theirs was an aesthetic expressing the reality of the place, the work, the daily human experience."[5]

Gordimer's impressions and commentary allude to, and anticipate, the photographs in "The Witwatersrand: A Time and Tailings," the first of three sections in *On the Mines* and the only one to which Gordimer contributed. Like her sentences, Goldblatt's photographs also do not admit of an ease of mediation—a self-evident translation of what is seen into what is spoken, of image into word. Heralded by Gordimer's essay, and given captions, the photographs speak to the theme of "Time and Tailings"—of a place that once was, of which only remnants and ruins are left (tailings are what remain after the gold has been extracted from the ore-bearing rock). In these pictures, abandoned works and buildings are what speak. There is only a single portrait. In the landscapes that predominate, human beings are infrequently present. They are there only when what remains—a tailings dump or the veranda of a house—calls for them to work. This is in stark contrast to the third section, "Mining Men," a series of individual and group portraits of miners and managers.

But it is Goldblatt's images in the middle section of *On the Mines*, "Shaft Sinking," that profoundly defy the idea that, looking at them, you have before you anything quite amounting, as Gordimer puts it, to "the reality of the place." Nothing, or practically nothing, emerges with the clarity for which photography, as a technology of reproduction, is known and celebrated. Shapes and outlines are ablur. You can make out men and machines, but neither are clearly delineated. The surface of the photographs is disturbed enough that it—and not what is depicted—is what most powerfully strikes you as a viewer. In contrast to nearly every other photograph in *On the Mines*, this series places the medium of photography, in all its materiality, in the foreground. Goldblatt did not use a flash or introduce any lighting of his own. His exposure times were long, his aperture settings wide. His camera was struggling for the light just as a living thing might struggle for air. The negative, exposed in this way, takes on a character known as graininess. A photochemical reaction, it represents, within the frame of the book, an aesthetic effect achieved through what a conceptual artist would call restriction: no flash, no additional light. If the scene before you speaks, its words are indistinct. There is, so to say, more sound in these photographs than sense.

But the deficit of light in the shaft and the artist's decision not to add any are not the only reasons for the unusual way in which the surface of these photographs is realized. Although not actually commenting on how his photographs were made and why they look the way they do, Goldblatt affords us details so that we can find out for ourselves. As he explains, in the shaft that is being sunk, water and dust fill the air. "Water rains ceaselessly onto the shaft bottom," he writes. The bottom of the shaft is where Goldblatt is with his camera, alongside the shaft sinkers: "up to seventy-two Basuto with a white Sinker and Sinker's Helper."[6] The water that falls from the rock, Goldblatt explains, is subterranean. After blasting with explosives, "light filters gently through the settling haze." And then "drilling starts. . . . Water, to dampen the deadly dust raised by the drills, fogs the atmosphere so that all is clothed, incongruously, in soft mist."[7] A photograph a few pages later shows "machine men fogged in dust-damping water" (figure I.1).[8] What light there is down below is obstructed, and also refracted, by the water and the dust. This affects the photograph. Not mottled graininess exactly, the surface effect is rather of a shimmer, as light of a certain spectrum travels through the particles in the air, overexposing areas of the negative. The disturbed surface of the printed photographs thus both obscures the image and reveals a fact: water and dust are, in the mine shaft, elements as much as light and air. But that second revelation depends, to an extent, on words.

Prefacing the series of eleven photographs in "Shaft Sinking," Goldblatt provides a meticulous description of the work that is being done.[9] The photograph on the book's cover is from this series. Its caption reads, "'Lashing' or loading a kibble" (figure I.2). The word *lashing*, in its sense of loading—or loading with a shovel—comes from the Zulu verb *ukulayisha*. This verb itself is a loanword from Dutch or Afrikaans, in which the verb *laai* means "to load." On the mines, the verb *layisha*—meaning to load or to lash—is also in the lexicon of Fanagalo or Fanakalo[10] (a command language to which Gordimer alludes).[11] Having made this historically contingent linguistic detour, the word makes its way from Dutch into English. Naming the clawed machine that appears in several of the photographs in the series, the caption to one of them refers to a "cactus grab." Goldblatt's preface supplies the rest: The workers are shoveling the blasted rock left by the cactus grab into the giant metal bucket known as a kibble, which will be hoisted onto the stage, the platform suspended above them that transports debris, equipment, and workers to and from the surface.

As Jeff Guy and Motlatsi Thabane explain, shaft sinking was a highly

Figure I.1. Photograph by David Goldblatt, "Machine men fogged in dust-damping water, 1969." © David Goldblatt. Courtesy the David Goldblatt Legacy Trust and Goodman Gallery.

Figure I.2. Photograph by David Goldblatt, "The cactus grab has dumped the last load of big rocks in the kibble, now the men clear the smaller rocks from the bottom, lashing the kibble with shovels. President Steyn No. 4 Shaft, Welkom, Orange Free State, 1969." © David Goldblatt. Courtesy the David Goldblatt Legacy Trust and Goodman Gallery.

invested event—a nervous time for shareholders. Sinking a shaft committed vast amounts of capital on which no return could be expected until after the shaft was sunk and mining operations commenced.[12] In the mines of the Orange Free State, where the Anglo American Corporation and other companies took their operations after the mines of the Witwatersrand were exhausted,[13] and where Goldblatt took these photographs, the new shafts were sometimes more than a mile deep and took almost two years to sink.[14] Goldblatt's naming of the shaft sinkers as "Basuto" (or Basotho) is consistent with what is known about the ethnicity of the mine workers—men from Lesotho who specialized in this type of work. Both the mining houses and the Basotho miners evinced a myth of manual labor.[15] That myth styled the lashers and rock drillers as the main protagonists of a process that, although never completely mechanized, by the 1950s had been transformed by the introduction of the cactus grab.[16] Mining house publicity of the 1980s, however, tended to downplay these technological advances. It posited a past in which manual labor was dominant in order to emphasize the urgency of mechanization at a time of growing labor organization among black workers.[17] The photographs that Goldblatt took may thus be read as anticipating, in some sense, the relative obscuring of the machine in the frequent items on shaft sinking that appeared in the years after his essay in *Optima*, Anglo American's in-house journal.[18] By letting the photographic medium infuse the image, to the extent of obscuring it, the photographs prompt the viewer to question what they are being shown.

The reticence about the machine is interesting. Although evident in the mystification of manual labor by the mining houses, which is not quite the same as the workers themselves asserting their manual prowess in oral history, this reticence is not general in high artistic production. B. W. Vilakazi (1906–47), whom Gordimer names as a pioneer in mine literature, begins his 1945 poem "Ezinkomponi" by directly addressing machines. "Dumani mishini yezinkomponi / Nidume ngesokusa lize lishone," Vilakazi writes. "Thunder away, machines of the mines, / Thunder away from dawn till sunset," as A. C. Jordan translates.[19] *Izinkomponi* are literally the mine compounds where black African workers live. Just as the compound (thought to come from the Malay *kampong*) names the mine by synecdoche,[20] in Vilakazi's poem, machines are what stand for the mines. Although one can translate

"Ezinkomponi" as "On the Mines" (Jordan renders it as "In the Gold Mines"), the Zulu locative prefix *e-* does not, strictly speaking, admit of the essayistic *on*, the preposition on which the title of Goldblatt and Gordimer's book plays. That does not, however, make Vilakazi's poem any less of an essay. An industrial invocation of the muses, the machines "bring to my mind,"[21] the poet writes, images and a narrative of labor migrancy and loss of land. It is for this vision, above all, that the sound of the machines is significant.[22] Human labor is described as workers with their tools—*ipiki* (pick), *ihalavu* (shovel)—descend into the mines.[23] Named by loanwords from English and Dutch (*ihalavu* comes from *graaf*), the tools are as foreign as the machines: "It is far, / It is far away where you were moulded."[24] But that foreignness is less significant than the future of which the poet warns the machines—a time when they will be controlled and exploited by black people: "Rumble softly, O machines; / Be pleased to hear what we have to say / Lest we have nought to say for you / On that far-off day, that unknown day, / When it shall be said of you irons / That you are the slaves of us, black men."[25] The word that Vilakazi uses for "slave" is *isigqili*, a term that, in contrast to *isisebenzi*, which Jordan translates as "labourer,"[26] is unequivocal in denoting forced servitude. Summoning the machine, and calling it to account, this poem is anything but a paean to manual labor.

Although beset by a grainy and shimmering photographic surface, the machine in Goldblatt and Gordimer's *On the Mines* insists on being noticed. Taken through a curtain of water, a haze of dust, and under low light, the photographs in "Shaft Sinking" call for a deciphering that reads the photograph for what it depicts and for its surface: What is it of? And what makes it look the way it does? The same could be said of the polluted water aboveground when it reflects the polluted sky. "But sometimes," Gordimer observes, "it became perversely, suddenly, the parody of picture-postcard beauty. The dust put a red filter over the suspended sun; the step-pyramids and cones were repeated, upside down, in the lakes of dead water."[27] Gordimer unfavorably compares these "chemically-coloured reflections of sunsets" to the "reality of the place" as expressed by the "great machines."[28] But perhaps the novelist is too hasty in formulating the antithesis, since the recipient of the imagined postcard would need her correspondent's commentary on the back for what lay behind the beauty. The clue lies in the phrase "upside down." Marx and Engels famously compared the workings of ideology to the camera obscura,[29] the optical device from which the camera got its name. The camera obscura produces an inverted image, which is then placed right side up — by the artist. Gordimer is correct that you have to go "inside." And Goldblatt *does*, into the dark chamber of the physical space of the new shaft — and, like Vilakazi, into the verbal space of the language of the miners. Although not literally inverted, the images that he brought back call for, and reward, interpretation. Their style must nevertheless have affirmed the sophistication of his patrons' artistic taste. For they were secure enough in their hold on public opinion — or on shareholders' — to accept five of the photographs from the series, including "'Lashing' or loading a kibble," for *Optima* in 1969. They had published Gordimer and Goldblatt's essay and photographs, "Time and Tailings," the year before.[30]

In the third series of photographs in *On the Mines*, "Mining Men," Goldblatt brings up into the light of day members of the dramatis personae from "Shaft Sinking." It is as if, drawn aloft on the "stage," they are being asked to take a bow: "Basuto shaftsinkers seeking work, President Steyn No. 4, Welkom, 1969"; "Masotho shaftsinking Machine Man. President Steyn No. 4, Welkom, 1969"; "Spanner Man. Carletonville, 1970"; "Butch Britz, Master Sinker. President Steyn No. 4, Welkom, 1969"; "Sinker's Helper. President Steyn No. 4, Welkom, 1969." The portraits in this section also include "B. Falk, mine captain. City Deep, Johannesburg, 1966"; "Time Office Clerks. City Deep, Johannesburg, 1966"; and "Chief Draughtsman and Sampler. Mine offices, Consolidated Main Reef Mines, Roodepoort, September 1967" — as if filling out the infrastructure aboveground that allows the mine to function: management, organization, recordkeeping, communications. As if to complete the tableau, much as a nineteenth-century novelist would depict both low and high — one thinks of the Montsou colliery in Émile Zola's *Germinal* — there appears, a few pages before the end of the book, between photographs of a white miner and the sinker's helper, a portrait of "Harry Oppenheimer, mining house chairman. Johannesburg, 1966." Oppenheimer is seated in a leather armchair in a three-piece suit, his face and hands lit from his right, chiaroscuro.[31] The hierarchy is complete; the purpose of sinking a shaft becomes as apparent in image as it is in words,[32] and, to the well informed, the identity of the artists' patron, who sits uncomfortably for his portrait, is revealed.

The Villagers, an entertaining show about white mine personnel and their families from the early days of SABC television in the late 1970s, sometimes cuts to scenes of black mine workers and their white supervisors underground. More frequently, scenes are set in management offices, with "head office" coming up frequently in characters' conversations. But in high artistic South African image and word, head office and chairman are neither often nor easily connected with workings underground. A notable exception is in *Mine*, a 1991 animated film by contemporary South African visual artist William Kentridge. In *Mine*, Soho Eckstein—the magnate caricature whose name evokes that of the early Johannesburg mining capitalist Hermann Eckstein—makes an imaginary descent from his bedroom directly into the depths of a mine by depressing the plunger of his coffeepot. In the next frame, the plunger becomes the lift that transports workers down into the mine. Intercut with its descent are images of a rock drill with an African rock driller at work. Passing through a workers' barracks, the lift evocatively ends its journey by releasing its passengers into what resembles the famous image of the slave ship *Brooks*. Subsequent frames show Soho at his desk, with a ticker tape machine that emits a mass of workers, who turn into a tailings dump, and what looks like a Benin bronze head with a miner's headlamp. Kentridge's visual sallies are audacious. But even the cut in *Mine* from the chairman's bedroom and office to the mine is a short cut. Verisimilitude would call for attention to the nodes that connect and mediate between underground operations and head office.

In *On the Mines*, the "Time Office Clerks" personify part of what is typically overlooked in the representations of mining that dominate South African artistic and scholarly representations of work in its industrial-era organization. I refer to the mine bureaucracy with its *mabalanas*, or African clerks, and the mine offices that report to head office.[33] Yet even in Goldblatt's photographs of offices on the mines, in contrast to those he took of underground workings, machines are sparse. In "Chief Draughtsman and Sampler," there is what looks like a mechanical adding machine on a desk. In the other photographs taken inside offices, however, apart from a telephone in "B. Falk, mine captain," there are only paper aids to memory, reckoning, and communication. Although she vividly evokes social life, black as well as white, Gordimer only mentions mine administrators in passing.[34]

By 1968, however, and certainly by 1973, when their book was published, it was the mine office, perhaps more rapidly than the under-ground workings during that era,[35] that saw the introduction of new machines for automation. These machines were computers. Other mining companies appear to have been ahead of Anglo American in the automation of the office by the introduction of computers.[36] Having launched an initial investigation of computerization in 1959,[37] Anglo opted to "hasten slowly."[38] By 1962, the company had introduced two electronic computers—one for processing dividend warrants, the other for technical calculations for its Nchanga Consolidated Mines in the copper belt in Northern Rhodesia.[39] By 1964, Northern Rhodesia had become Zambia, and a group data processing unit at Kitwe served the computing needs of several mines. In the same year, Nchanga re-placed its punch card machines with a computer to handle the payroll for nineteen thousand employees at four mines.[40]

Mining's increasing use of machines makes it an irresistible point of reference for any study of mechanization, automation, and the re-sponse of creative and performing artists to those changes in the or-ganization of the labor process. This is as plain to see in Goldblatt and Gordimer's *On the Mines* as in Vilakazi's "Ezinkomponi." But comput-erization in the 1960s is different from, say, the introduction of the rock drill in the 1890s or the cactus grab in the 1950s. As a technolog-ical advance, it is not limited to mining or, for that matter, any single sector of the economy. Although the mines were early to computerize, computerization represents a set of technological changes that were pervasive. The same is true, historically, of the office as a meeting point of labor and technology. An office, strictly speaking, falls into a differ-ent category than a mine or a farm or a factory. It is adaptable to each workspace. In that sense, the countinghouse, the *comptoir, kantoor,* or *inkantolo,*[41] is the forerunner of the "universal machine"—which is how Alan Turing famously described the computer.

Nobody would profess to dislodge gold mining from its central place in South African history or challenge the consensus that the im-peratives of mining capital were constitutive of modern South Africa.[42] Although I frequently turn to mining, my book is not about technology in any single sector of the economy. By turning toward a set of techno-logical changes that eventually spanned almost all sectors, I wish in-stead to bring into narration a different facet of that modernity. Partly discernible in statistics showing changes in the labor market and from pronouncements by the government, this aspect comes clearest in the imagined worlds of the country's writers and artists. As the trajectory of my reading of *On the Mines* anticipates, I refer to the rise in importance of clerical and office work and other kinds of white-collar work. Although studies of capitalism in the United Kingdom, Europe, and the United States emphasize their decisive role, those types of work are relatively neglected in South African historiography and social science. They boast nothing comparable to Siegfried Kracauer's *The Salaried Masses: Duty and Distraction in Weimar Germany* (1930) or C. Wright Mills's *White Collar: The American Middle Classes* (1951).

As an account of technology and labor in the office and allied workspaces, my study relates to the growing body of research on the history of technology in Africa.[43] But this emerging field has scarcely addressed how literature and the arts mediate local understandings of technology. This is where my study offers its particular contribution. Even South African literary history has nothing of the ambition of Leo Marx's *The Machine in the Garden: Technology and the Pastoral Ideal in America* (1964) or the body of techno-criticism that it inspired.[44] My emphasis is on the era of computerization. Technological changes in South African mining practices have been studied extensively,[45] and computerization has received excellent scholarly treatment for its role in apartheid governance.[46] But the assumptions about labor and race that informed responses to the technological changes brought about by mechanization in earlier phases of industrialization in South Africa have not been shown to bear, as they do, on computerization and automation. When writers and artists engage with these developments, they sometimes do so in ways that are oblique and opaque. They also emphasize perspectives underrepresented in historiography. One such perspective is the idea that technology has its own agency or effectivity within a historical totality.[47] Another is the idea, discomfiting to some, that humans and machines share more in common than meets the eye.

These perspectives emerge, notably, when the workers who use machines are women. By the 1960s, when the mining companies were computerizing in order to automate their offices, although mine clerks were almost all male, women were the emerging majority among office workers in South Africa. Although still a small minority compared to those women classified under apartheid as white, Coloured, or Indian, black women were a significant growing number among office workers. Their ascendence meant that, in certain circumstances, women became a factor, ideologically and actually, in asserting and challenging the racial division of labor that was one of the hallmarks of apartheid. The fact that these women used machines meant that mechanization and automation also became factors in the long struggle in South Africa over the racial division of labor.

Although far from transparent—like the images by Goldblatt and the scenes sketched by Gordimer in words—the record of women using machines in offices (and elsewhere) is there to be read. As C. Wright Mills had to concede, the ascendency of the "white-collar people" is unspectacular and eludes notice.[48] Yet the record of these women remains in published labor statistics, in official pronouncements, and in expressions of middle-class and working-class aspirations. Bringing that archive into visibility, I show how certain texts, artworks, and instances of performance place workers at the center of questions of automation and the racial division of labor.[49] This centrality of the worker is no longer a given. The most highly automated machine that we use—the smartphone—is not utilized *at work* alone, and it is not viewed as a replacement for its user *as worker*. As I show, a contemplation of laboring with machines in books by South African novelists Miriam Tlali and J. M. Coetzee gives way, in the animated films of William Kentridge and the experimental puppet theater of Handspring Puppet Company, to a vision of what machines and humans share—in different senses: ontologically, physically, socially, ethically. This brings into view theories about the human-machine organizations that evolve in their interaction.

One body of theory comes from the observation that the worker adapts to the machine. In *On the Mines*, this adaptation is visible in Goldblatt's photographs of a "machine man" and a "spanner man." In older parlance, dating back to the introduction of rock drills in the gold mines in the late nineteenth century, when one worker operated the drill and another steadied the drill and changed out the "jumpers," or drill bits, the designations were "machine boy" and "spanner boy."[50] Like those "boys," the "telephone girl" of the same era was a worker similarly adapted to her machine. An interest in women's bodies emerged historically as labor organizations and politicians drew attention to the harmful effects of machine use on women workers. Just as it did for men who worked in the mines, organized labor rep-

resented women who operated the telephone exchanges before automation. The new machines were not solely mechanical. When, like the
telephone, they combined mechanism with electricity, the interest of
organized labor and politicians extended to the effects on the worker's
nervous system—which was understood, physiologically, in terms of
electricity, in ways that anticipate those relating to human-computer
interaction.

This is the context in which the Labour Party member for Troyeville, Morris Kentridge, spoke up in parliament in the 1920s for the
telephonists—as telephone operators were called in South Africa.
Like the history of computerization that is its more recent context,
this history is indispensable for making sense of important departures
in South African art making and writing. Not all the writers and artists
I write about summon attention to women and their labor situation as
directly as their political representatives. It is sometimes the case, however, that when they figure forth the machine and its inner workings,
they make it possible to write women into South African modernity
in ways that scholars have neglected. The epistemological horizon of
Morris Kentridge's labor politics flickers as an afterimage seventy years
later when his grandson, William Kentridge, brings the telephone operators onto the screen in his stop-motion film animation. The longer
history of ideas of which the idea of nervous strain was a part resurfaces
with the rhinoceros puppet-automaton of Handspring Puppet Company. At the farthest end of the artistic continuum of human-machine
interaction, human and machine merge. I refer to the cyborgs of fiction by Willem Anker and Namwali Serpell—in whose work insect
and machine also merge. These imagined near-future scenarios are not
quite "posthuman";[51] although machines have a certain autonomy, and
there is a case to be made for decentering the human agent,[52] the story
that they tell, and that I tell in turn, is one in which the hopes and fears
of human beings play a key role.

The last two writers I have mentioned, and perhaps Serpell in particular, are also inheritors of the legacy of colonial feminist author
and theorist Olive Schreiner. Her novel *The Story of an African Farm*
(1883) is a tale set in the agrarian times that were just giving way to
the accumulation of capital at the diamond diggings that would usher
in the era of capitalist modernity when gold was discovered on the
Witwatersrand three years after the publication of her novel.[53] In her

novel, the young Waldo Farber constructs a scale model of a sheep-shearing machine that, after a tragic turn of events, is never manufactured. Schreiner likens Waldo's machine to a work of art. If we read Schreiner's favorite author, Ralph Waldo Emerson, from whom Waldo receives his name, this was still a time when the "fine and the useful arts" had not yet definitively diverged.[54] It is to this notion that William Kentridge, and Handspring Puppet Company, speak in another way. They sometimes seem to be telling us that, if a machine can be a work of art, as in Schreiner, a work of art can also be a machine—or be *like* a machine. This may also be true of J. M. Coetzee's early experiments in computer poetry, if a set of instructions for a machine in the form of a computer program qualifies. We have then come half circle from Schreiner. Although she issued dire predictions of how women would be left unemployed by machines, whereas men would not be, even amid her darkest prophecies of female "parasitism" in *Woman and Labour*, she never gainsaid the idea of the inventor as artist.[55]

In Nuce

I make two types of findings in *A Will for the Machine*—of relevance in history and in the history of literature and the arts. These findings are interlinked. From the 1950s, critical discussions of automation, in the United States and elsewhere, build upon a foundation of older ideas about mechanization. If mechanization referred to the use of machines in the production process generally, then automation came to refer to the use of machines designed to regulate their own operation. Such machines could also control the operation of other machines. Although the term *cybernation* was sometimes used to refer to automatic control performed by computers,[56] I employ the more familiar general term *automation*, which, when it emerged into common usage, did not refer only to computerized control.[57] As the first Industrial Revolution gave way to the second,[58] and automation became synonymous with the computer, however, the evaluative terminology that grew around mechanization and labor remained relatively stable. The machine substituted for the worker. The idea that a machine could take the place of a worker, or workers, governed the value assigned to automation by representatives of business, organized labor, and government.[59] Just as the steam engine once had, the computer came to stand for their hopes, their fears, and a more nebulous intimation of possibility, of a radical break. It informed their sense of crisis—whether of profitability, employment, or national policy.

In South Africa, the idea of automation as substitution received a peculiar turn. In the late 1960s, the state assumed a major role in economic policymaking as it endeavored to direct the gains of the post–World War II economic boom toward an ultimate elaboration of apartheid. Under continued white minority rule, there would be total territorial separation of the races: residential segregation in the towns and cities, control of African migration to urban areas, and a system of pseudo-independent black ethnic-national Bantustans on a national scale. This is often referred to as "grand apartheid."

Customary relegation of certain categories of work to black Africans had been a feature of the colonial labor market from the beginning. Statutory reservation of certain categories of work for white people dates back to at least the 1890s. It is possible, therefore, to speak historically of a racial caste system. But in the 1960s, as more Africans found employment in industry and commerce, there was an intensified effort to separate the races *by* workplace or, if this was not feasible, *in* the workplace. It is with this goal in mind that apartheid technocrats and ideologues turned their attention to mechanization and automation. Machines would, in their view, substitute, not for black workers, but for white, who were in short supply. This marked a contrast to what had happened half a century before. Then, as a response to a shortage of black workers, mechanization by the gold-mining companies displaced white workers. Organized white labor rose up as a result. But in the 1960s, the idea was not to render white workers redundant. Rather, it was that white workers—specifically white male workers—would be redeployed. This was so that they could do work that, as dictated by labor needs and the labor market, would sooner or later have to be done by Africans and Coloureds. This argument was made by apartheid ideologues with reference to industry, agriculture, and commerce. A corollary to their thinking was that, in order to relieve the labor of white men, more white women would need to be encouraged to enter the labor force. In the light of studies from other developing countries, they saw this being facilitated by the introduction of machines in factories as well as offices. The view of the government and its ideologues, especially in the late stages of the apartheid project, did not necessarily coincide with that of capital, although it still attempted to accommodate the political demands of organized white labor. White unions were in favor of job reservation and against the deskilling seen as part of the reorganization of work through a proliferation of semi-skilled jobs.

In the office, during this period, automation was on the rise. Long essential equipment for the office, the typewriter, the adding machine, and other mechanical devices, such as the addressograph, were beginning to be replaced by computers, at least at larger concerns. The history of computerization in South Africa is not well documented, understood, or critically analyzed. I therefore begin my book with a brief account of this history against the background of apartheid thinking about automation. This takes me into the general topic of office work, which is also neglected in South African historiography, although it is occasionally represented in literature. There, mechanization and automation do not necessarily bring about the outcome envisaged by the ideologues.

What we discover, reading the work of Miriam Tlali and others, along with the labor statistics of the period, is that, contrary to official proscription, African women were being employed in offices by white-owned businesses (African men had long been employed as mine clerks, in fairly large numbers, and in smaller numbers also in the offices of white-owned businesses). Although their ranks, statistically speaking, were small, what this shows is that, even in the late 1960s, office work offered educated African and Coloured women a path into upward mobility. By the 1980s, when the mother of comedian Trevor Noah found work as a secretary,[60] this path was an established one.[61]

One can draw further conclusions. Historically, women workers have repeatedly brought about changes in an existing division of labor. By the late apartheid era, office work had become the domain of women. It therefore was possible, for a brief time, for black women in white-collar jobs to be at the vanguard of social change. Although this change in employment patterns has been recognized by some economic historians, an awareness of the historical trend has not greatly affected commonly held assumptions about the working lives of black women toward the end of the apartheid era. What we also discover, reading Tlali, is that, among these women, there is a demand *for* the machine. This is because certain office machines alleviate the tedium of routine office tasks, just as an electric sewing machine facilitates women's economic independence through home industry. They are not perturbed by the prospect that machines are, or could be, substituting for workers. Their view is rather that, if a machine is introduced, then one's working conditions improve, and if a machine is acquired by oneself, then, as owner of the means of production, one can appropriate fully the surplus realized by one's work. This view contrasts, historically, for example, with that of unionized mine workers, both white and black, who resisted the mechanization and automation proposed by management.

Although one character in her subsequent novel *Amandla* (1980) scoffs at the notion that a "true middle class [exists] in a place like Soweto," whereas another declares that "there's no such thing as a middle class . . . whatever inequalities seem to exist, are false,"[62] and her later stories in *Footprints in the Quag* (1989) align her with the poor, Miriam Tlali may be unique in South African literature in having created and preserved a record of how some educated middle-class African women found a path into upward mobility in the 1960s and 1970s. These women neither adhered to customary and legal strictures on employment, which formed the background of some of the more extreme apartheid views on mechanization and automation, nor maintained the view often held by organized labor that, given that the machine substituted for the worker or deskilled them, the introduction of machines by owners and management was to be opposed. Despite the obvious differences between them, what most clearly links Tlali to other South African writers and artists who respond to mechanization and automation is how what she describes deviates in both these ways from what one might expect as a response to these conditions and assumptions. In the works of J. M. Coetzee, William Kentridge, and Handspring Puppet Company, we find that, although certainly shadowed by the implication of the machine in apartheid thinking, and at times, to be sure, hospitable to received notions of mechanization and automation as substitution, their works point in different directions. This is apparent as they alternate between representations of the figure of the worker and the inner workings common, at some level, to the worker and the machine. Turning toward human-machine interaction in its perceptual and affective phenomenality, they reveal facets of mechanization and automation that, being more intimate but less frequently represented, are all the less palpable.

In Outline

I begin chapter 1 by showing how, addressing a conference of experts on automation and computerization in 1969, an apartheid government minister speculated about how the introduction of computers might help bring more white women into factory and office work, thereby freeing up the labor of white men and helping stem the increased employment of Africans in skilled work. The ultimate goal of "grand apartheid" was to slow the migration of Africans to the cities and, if that was not possible, to keep the urban workplace as segregated as urban residential areas and schools. The meaning of automation was thus keep-white, bar-black, continuous with long-standing policies and practices of racial "job reservation" in skilled and semiskilled work.

As I show in the second section of my chapter, however, by the late 1960s, this was an unachievable fantasy—as black Africans, Coloureds, and Indians, and, increasingly, black women, were being employed, not only in factories but also in offices at white-owned concerns. This change in employment patterns was a result of the same economic boom that made it possible for the state to imagine putting the idea of "grand apartheid" into practice. This trend is evident from official labor statistics but is given remarkable narrative form in Miriam Tlali's novel *Muriel at Metropolitan* (1975), set in the late 1960s, a work of office fiction virtually unique in South African literature. The novel describes job reservation and pay discrimination—statutory as well as informal—and also comments on the organization of the office in which Muriel works. Notable is the protagonist's appeal for increased mechanization in order to relieve the tedium of routine tasks.

The reality was that, in the offices of white-owned South African businesses, by 1965, there were already more machines, or there would be soon. But because not enough white women could be recruited, their operators were increasingly black and increasingly female. These facts help us recognize that, during this period, office work, because it starts to involve computer use, sheds a great deal of light on other processes of mechanization and automation. And the meaning given to mechanization and automation by the black women in white-collar jobs who were briefly at the vanguard of social change was different from that of the ideologues and management—not replacement of the worker but alleviation of work.

In the rest of chapter 1, I provide an outline of the early history of computerization in South Africa. Discussions of the economics and ethics of this new kind of machine and automation were dominated by the idea of replacement. But as African workers made their voices heard, the debate shifted to how best to alleviate taxing, hazardous, and tedious labor. In other words, human-machine interaction increasingly came to the fore. I conclude the chapter by presenting two case studies of computerization from the early 1960s — the City of Port Elizabeth and Rand Mines — that are microcosms of apartheid civic administration and the southern African migrant labor system in operation. The managers who introduced the machines were thinking mainly in terms of efficiency, which meant that they considered how they would affect office employment. But they also provide a preview to how computers were used in state labor controls, militarization, and securitization in the 1970s and 1980s, the subject of excellent research by Edwards and Hecht, as well as Breckenridge, upon which my work builds.[63]

In chapter 2, I continue to show how, among urban African women of Tlali's class and generation, there was a general will for the machine. From there, I develop parallels, not typically entertained, between Miriam Tlali and J. M. Coetzee as authors of office fiction. Tlali's work is little known outside of South Africa, and Coetzee, who won the Nobel Prize in Literature in 2003, is better known for his other works, such as *Waiting for the Barbarians, Life & Times of Michael K*, and *Disgrace*. I open my chapter by drawing significance from the little-remarked fact that, in the first issue of *Staffrider* magazine (1978), a computer-generated poem by Coetzee appeared along with the first installment of an oral history series, Soweto Speaking. For this series, Tlali interviewed various African working people from Soweto. Her column ran for two years, whereas Coetzee's poem was his sole contribution to *Staffrider*. Although computers do not feature in Soweto Speaking, another kind of machine does. Concentrating on Tlali's interviews with women who proclaim the benefits of owning an electrical sewing machine, I also note an ambivalence about writing as being — or not being — proper work. This leads me to a comparison of Tlali's work with J. M. Coetzee's *Youth* (2002), a fictionalized memoir about Coetzee's time in London in the early 1960s. There, the protagonist, John, is similarly ambivalent, albeit not for all the same reasons as Tlali, about writing and its status as work. John's doubts do not prevent him from having qualms, however, about getting a machine to do that work. This is what Coetzee did when, working at IBM in London in the early 1960s as a programmer, he programmed a computer to generate lines of poetry. At the time, computers were only in the early stages of being used to manipulate text; word processing was more than a decade away. With computers not available to the average writer, John feels that he had an unfair advantage.

His notion that computers could put writers out of work I place in the context of discussions of the effects on employment of computerization in the office, already taking place by the late 1950s in the United Kingdom and the United States. Elaborating on Rebecca Roach's work on Coetzee's computer poetry, I analyze in detail a program written by Coetzee in 1963 in FORTRAN II and run on an IBM 1401 computer. I grasped this experiment more fully after experts with the IBM 1401 restoration project at the Computer History Museum in California recreated the necessary punch cards from the copy of Coetzee's program that I provided and, after making a few necessary modifications, ran the program anew on one of the museum's machines. I compare Coetzee's to other experiments in computer poetry and computer art from around the same time, such as American artists Alison Knowles and James Tenney's *House of Dust* (1967), which used a slightly later version of FORTRAN and ran on similar hardware. What virtually all these experiments had in common, even if their creators were probably unaware of each other, was the use of a random number generator, integral to later versions of FORTRAN, to select words at random for predetermined syntactic "slots." Coetzee saw this as an update on the aleatory techniques used by the Surrealists, the Dadaists, and his contemporaries, William Burroughs and Brion Gysin.

In turning toward computer poetry, we have moved from automation in the South African labor process, the meaning of which was highly specific, to more general questions about automaticity. In ancient Greek, *automatos* meant self-moving. The mechanical automata still in vogue in the early nineteenth century were self-moving to the extent that, once set in motion by their exhibitor, they would move by themselves in predetermined ways without further human intervention. This is the sense in which a programmed machine is automatic. Even when a computer selects numbers at random, because it is programmed to do so, its selection is pseudo-random.

Finally, I show, as in chapter 1, how the meaning of the machine—or mechanization and automation—is overdetermined in complex ways. J. M. Coetzee's ambivalence in *Youth* about work, and about working or not working—and writing is not quite work for John—can be related to the protagonist's South African origins and a racial division of labor that makes the conscientious white person wary of eschewing the work disdained historically by his people as fit for black people only. This wariness extends to a general suspicion about avoiding work—which is what John imagines the computer helping him do exponentially. By contrast, the wariness that Miriam Tlali expresses about sitting at a typewriter, of being a writer, comes from a different and gendered logic, in which real work is defined as the preserve of women and men who tap at the keys are idlers.

Transferring my emphasis from word to image, specifically the moving image, in chapter 3, I analyze William Kentridge's film *Stereoscope* (1999). My analysis pursues the implications of the fact that whenever there is a machine, there is, in principle, also a human being using it—what computer scientists refer to as human-machine interaction. World famous for his haunting series of stop-motion animated films based on charcoal drawings known as Drawings for Projection; his shadow-procession installations; his direction of the operas *The Magic Flute*, *Wozzeck*, and *The Nose*; as well as large-scale multimedia performances such as *The Head and the Load*, William Kentridge's work is historically situated in ways that are not always obvious. Following a discussion of animated film as an electromechanical recording and representing technology, I analyze the work of Kentridge in the context of the racialization of labor during and before the apartheid era. As in chapters 1 and 2, I concentrate specifically on white-collar women workers. This time, my emphasis is on telephone operators from an earlier era. As in those chapters, I pay close attention to the artist's biography as it relates to their art making, although, in this chapter, the emphasis is different—not as much individual, as in the case of Tlali or Coetzee, as genealogical.

The eighth film of Drawings for Projection, *Stereoscope* opens and closes with a scene showing a telephone exchange from the time before exchanges were automated. An operator is at her switchboard connecting calls. The cables that she plugs in and unplugs become abstract lines of communication, drawn in blue pastel, that range across the city of Johannesburg. They connect people in different spaces, including the isolated Soho Eckstein, the main protagonist of the films. Like South Africa's office workers, its telephonists are little represented in cultural production and have received no significant scholarly attention. As was the case in other countries, before the automation of the exchanges, the vast majority were women.

What directly links William Kentridge to this sphere of work is that his paternal grandfather, Morris Kentridge (1881–1964), who represented the Labour Party in parliament, is on record, in the 1920s, as having spoken up in the chamber for the telephonists. As his memoirs, *I Recall* (1959), tell us, early in his career, Morris Kentridge was a leading participant in the 1922 Rand Revolt, an uprising of white workers against the state. One of the main reasons for the strike that led to the uprising was that mine management had attempted to relax the "color bar."[64] This was a discriminatory set of rules that, by determining what types of work could be done on the mines by white people and by Africans, respectively, protected white workers from competition. As a member of the Labour Party, which joined the National Party to form the Pact government after the 1924 election, Morris Kentridge continued to press for "job reservation" for white workers until, a few years later, the Labour Party "began to waver in [its] policy of segregation" and to promote the "principle of a national minimum wage . . . based on White standards of life, so that everybody who works must be paid a wage based on a civilised standard of life."[65] As I detail in chapter 3, the Pact government's policy of mandating or encouraging the employment of "civilized labor"—with workers classed as "civilized" by virtue of being paid a certain wage—meant in practice that preference was given to white over black and Coloured workers, especially in skilled and semiskilled work. Morris Kentridge's appeal for the telephonists, who were mostly white, was consistent with his party's position.

Scholars have paid some attention to William Kentridge's relationship to his parents, the celebrated anti-apartheid lawyers Sydney Kentridge and Felicia Kentridge. But his grandfather, who was a strong familial presence, and his political choices have rated scarcely a mention. In 1976, William Kentridge, as a member of Junction Avenue Theatre Company, workshopped and performed in a play that displayed, in critical fashion, a banner with the slogan of the 1922 strikers: "Workers of the World Fight and Unite for a White South Africa." By working in

African trade union theater, in racial terms, William Kentridge made the opposite choice to his grandfather. But what connected them was an advocacy of the worker as indispensable even with advanced mechanization and automation.

Having established this context, and being instructed by Kentridge's view of apartheid as a "rock" that cannot be confronted head-on by the artist, my analysis moves in two interconnected directions. Analyzing what was written in the 1920s about the work hazards for telephonists in *The South African Telephone and Telegraph Review* ("*The Live Wire*"), the South African telephone and telegraph employee association's journal, which draws on the classic Canadian study by Mackenzie King following the 1907 Toronto operators' strike and thus emphasizes nervous strain, I turn from the figure of the worker to what I am calling inner workings: electricity is a medium that human nerves and telephony have in common. The second strand of argument is familial and psychoanalytic: when William Kentridge talks about *Stereoscope* and suggests that his interest in obsolete technologies is related to his childhood curiosity about inner workings, he is alluding to the mother's body. In other words, when William Kentridge shows women at work in the exchange, he is occupied with a number of things at the same time.

In this multigenerational family drama, he is not only performing a delicate *Aufhebung* by canceling the white supremacy upheld by his grandfather while preserving his assertion of the worker in a time of mechanization. In his revelation of underlying mechanisms, he is also symbolizing in his art a relation to his parents: his mother as an object of infantile curiosity and his father, who, as an eminent man of law, personifies the Oedipal prohibition on access to the mother. In conclusion, I relate that, although Sydney Kentridge is better known for having defended Nelson Mandela at the Treason Trial and for his representation of Steve Biko's family at the inquest into his death, Felicia Kentridge significantly contributed to the legal challenges that led to the dismantling of the laws discriminating against African workers by restricting their free movement in the country.

In chapter 4, I turn to how the puppet theater engages with automation and computerization in a context where their meaning depends on a racialization of labor by analyzing how Handspring Puppet Company adapted Georg Büchner's *Woyzeck* (1836). Best known internationally for its production of *War Horse*, first staged in 2007, Handspring's work, dating back more than thirty years, is celebrated among puppeteers and scholars of puppetry. In its adaptation as *Woyzeck on the Highveld* (1992), which William Kentridge directed, Woyzeck becomes an African migrant worker in Johannesburg in the 1950s. The result is a kind of avant-garde workers' theater. I concentrate on Handspring's adaptation of the famous scene in which Woyzeck and Marie, his beloved, go to see a performing horse and hear a fairground barker proclaim its talents. In an audacious African transposition, Handspring makes the performing horse a puppet rhinoceros. In Büchner, the Barker dares the audience to deny that, like the horse, a human being is anything more than a calculating machine, an idea that Büchner himself abhorred. In the puppet play, however, in which the manipulation is visible, the living creature is, literally, a machine, dependent on the puppeteers for its motion. I observe how Handspring alternates between the figure of the worker—so central to South African artistic production—and the shared mechanics—so graphic in the medium of puppetry—that make it possible for humans and machines to interact. In this case, the machine is a puppet. In so doing, I develop my observations from chapter 3 about early twentieth-century telephony and its significance for William Kentridge as a precursor to the technological convergence of computing and telecommunications that brought us the internet and the smartphone and also as an example of an earlier electromechanical convergence that led to the invention of film.

As in chapter 2, when analyzing Coetzee's computer poetry, I moved from the specificity of the automation of labor to more general questions of automaticity that exercised the creators of computer-generated art, I explore here how puppetry leads us to reflect on whether the automatic is purely self-moving or whether it depends on a program that is set in motion by another. This time, it is not the randomness of the computer's selection that complicates the decision as to what is self-moving or not but rather the conversion of the movement of the puppeteer into that of the puppet. Although skillfully activated by them, this transformation depends on an abstract system of conversion not under the puppeteer's control.

In the second part of chapter 4, I thus turn toward Büchner's near contemporary, Heinrich von Kleist, whose "Über das Marionettentheater" ("The Puppet Theatre"), published in 1810, is one of the most

famous reflections on puppetry. I approach Kleist's text through literary theorist Paul de Man. He interprets as anamorphic the transformation of the movement of the puppeteer into the movement of
the puppet because straight lines are automatically converted into
curved ones. I go on to propose that anamorphosis connects Handspring's puppetry not only with William Kentridge's view of computers but also with Coetzee's early experiments in computer poetry. For
Kentridge, using a computer mouse or keyboard to produce an image
on a monitor is like what happens when, in classic examples of early-
modern anamorphic image making such as Holbein's *The Ambassadors*,
a distorted image resolves itself into a regular one. For Coetzee, as with
other pioneers in computer poetry, word is converted into number in
order for the machine to print it out as word. In the abstract sense suggested by de Man of a "system of transformation" between puppeteer
and puppet,[66] a sense beyond the turning of one image into another,
this regulated automatic conversion of word into number into word is
anamorphic.

More generally, then, for an artist in an era of computerization to
engage with anamorphosis as an artform or metaphor is to comment
on how users of computers and smartphones produce images and
words and sounds through the mediation of a machine. The machine's
workings in no way resemble what its user keys into it and sees or hears
coming out of it. Nor would they be intelligible to them even if those
workings were visible or audible. When Gordimer brings to mind in
On the Mines how the artist places the camera obscura's inverted images right side up, thereby alluding to Goldblatt's camera, it becomes
evident that, even in media that came before digitization, processes
of mediation may have been scarcely intelligible. One could perhaps
have accompanied Goldblatt into his dark room to see "machine men
fogged in dust-damping water" develop, but how many of us would
have been able to describe with any accuracy the photochemical reactions that made the photograph materialize before our eyes? Yet when
computerization renders systemic a limit to what is sensible and intelligible, it is not the camera obscura or photography that becomes
its figure. In the art making that I analyze, that distinction belongs to
anamorphosis. It stands there as the phenomenal counterpart to digitization.[67] One can, in other words, discern in Handspring's practice
something in addition to the alternation of the figure of the worker

and their inner workings. When de Man calls the "system of transformation" the "text that spins itself between" puppeteer and puppet, we are ready to posit a poiesis or "making" of a different order, reducible neither to one nor the other. With computers, this making involves an automatism. With art that mimics the machine in its automaticity—as does any puppet performance—the automatism is demonstrated as it is effected. In the work of these artists, this is perhaps where the difference between the machinelike artwork and the machine lies.[68] In making this argument, I engage with a recent book by Premesh Lalu, who argues that key works by Handspring, Kentridge, and Jane Taylor figure an "undoing" of apartheid—in the sense that they reveal apartheid to have instituted an automaticity at a perceptual and cognitive level, in which racial categories are applied without reflection.

I conclude my book with a brief discussion of two recent works of southern African speculative fiction and one from China. The works from southern Africa emerge from a world in which the meaning of the machine—specifically the computer—is no longer restricted to the labor process. I show how these works, nevertheless, render visible the use of machines in the global division of labor, for example in manufacturing. The history of computerization in the Global South is not everywhere the same. India and China have traveled paths different from South Africa and from each other. Drawing a brief comparison between these countries, I analyze a literary work that describes the invention of the computer in a form for which there is no known historical example. At this limit of the actual, meaning is what presses itself into the foreground. This allows me to restate the main theoretical contention of my book: to know the meaning of a technology—and thus what that technology was or is—depends on knowing the conditions under which it emerged.

1

The Meaning of Automation

What is the meaning of automation? Yes, the meaning—not the definition, which, although one finds disagreement about its precise scope and encounters technical and colloquial senses of the word, circulates and is accepted as common coin. With the growing use of computers in industrialized countries by the 1950s, the need arose for a clear distinction between automation and mechanization. Whereas mechanization denotes the use of machines generally, automation came to refer specifically to the use of a machine to control or regulate its own use, as well as that of other machines—for example, in a factory or power station. Examples of automation from before the 1950s remind us that computers were, as John Diebold, author of the influential *Automation: The Advent of the Automatic Factory* (1952), explained to the United States Congress in 1955, first conceived of as being a subset of electronic closed-loop control systems, also known as servomechanisms.[1] Advances in the control of antiaircraft guns used in World War II are frequently cited as an example.[2] Norbert Wiener, whose name is synonymous with information theory and cybernetics, called the rise of automatic control a "new industrial revolution which . . . consists primarily in replacing human judgment and discrimination at low levels by the discrimination of the machine. The machine appears now, not as a source of power, but as a source of control and communications."[3] For Wiener, this was not necessarily a boon for workers.[4] When definitions of automation like this emerge, not all "automatic control" entails computerization. This remains true, although automation has tended to become synonymous with computerization and, as an offshoot, robotics. A less exact distinction than Wiener's from the same time says that, whereas mechanization is the use of a machine to do manual work, automation involves using a machine to do mental work. Given the imprimatur of the Euro-American metropole, such definitions circulated widely and informed and influenced academic and political discussion far and wide. A South African study of automation from the early 1970s includes references to the definitions in *Automation and Technological Change*, the report of the 1955 congressional hearings.[5] South African discussions about automation also refer to a 1964 US congressional report.[6] But these definitions emerge from a time and place where meanings are fluid. Even for experts, "automate" is still a novel and unfamiliar verb,[7] and popular views about automation are, to some extent, being shaped by imaginative literature.[8] Wiener himself uses the term *automatization*.[9] When a definition emerges, it emerges in a definite context. The meaning of any word is thus, at least to begin with, idiomatic. In the case of automation, that idiomaticity is because it depends on ideas about work: what work is to be done, who is to do it, and for whom that work is to be done. These things, which are not everywhere the same, and may lead to invention and innovation, determine the tool or machine to be used.

"The Scarce Type of Labor"

In his opening address to the third national conference of the South African Council for Automation and Computation (SACAC), held in Pretoria in October 1969, Minister of Economic Affairs Jan Haak cited a study from Japan that showed how women entered the labor force in dramatically greater numbers during a period of mechanization and automation. Addressing the concerns of labor organizations, Minister Haak proposed that white women in South Africa might do the same:

> It would be shortsighted of the broader workers' group to oppose automation that furthers the more intensive and efficient utilization of the scarce type of labor. We in the Republic can least of all afford it, in view of the probability that, in the foreseeable future, skilled Whites will remain a bottleneck [*knelpunt*] to a greater or lesser degree. A new effect of increased automation and mechanization is naturally that the demands that are made of specific groups of workers drastically change in many cases. In this connection, a study that was recently undertaken

in Japan in connection with the employment of women is of great importance to us. The "Women and Minors' Bureau" of the Japanese Department of Labor found that in the majority of the 4,000 establishments that were studied, the number of women increased during the period 1958 to 1963. It was precisely in this period that the rate of technological innovation was at its highest. In 20% of the enterprises women were placed in positions that did not exist before, or that were filled exclusively by men. The changed working conditions that came into existence through automation and mechanization thus made the replacement of men possible. A similar development in South Africa can have important and useful consequences for us. In recent times reference has often been made to the underemployment of women in South Africa, and if we can create more positions in our industries through automation through which men become available for other tasks, then we will indeed have made great progress. It is not only manufacturing that is affected by automation. The influence on the office worker is just as strong.[10]

Those who subscribed to apartheid thinking understood the underemployment of women in the context of a shortage of white labor. In a 1965 article in the popular Afrikaans women's magazine *Sarie Marais*, Erika Theron appealed to employers to facilitate part-time work for married women. A respected Stellenbosch University professor of social work, Theron received her doctorate from Stellenbosch for her study of female factory workers in Cape Town in the 1940s. She is perhaps best known for leading a commission of inquiry that in 1976 recommended various reforms in state policy affecting Coloured people, including direct parliamentary representation for Coloureds.[11] In the article published in *Sarie*, Theron observed,

> Like other countries in the Western world, South Africa has a shortage of "manpower." Yet on the other hand there is a surplus of "woman-power" that is available part-time, but is not fully utilized.... Although it does not prevent them from accepting work outside of the home, many married women have a kind of guilt feeling. On the other hand, we also find nowadays, especially where so much is being said about the shortage of white "manpower" in our country, that some women are even apologetic because they are "only housewives" and are not active in the community in a voluntary capacity or for remuneration.[12]

As Theron notes, norms around working outside the home were changing. But white women, especially the white Afrikaans-speaking readers of *Sarie* who felt guilty about taking a job, may still have been feeling the force of an ideological imperative to reproduce the *volk* that predates the call for a mobilization of white "womanpower."[13] That force would, for instance, not have been felt by Coloured women, who were never interpellated by Afrikaner-nationalist ideology.[14] Although this contrast suggests something specific about how the demand for reproductive labor was racialized in South Africa, competing demands for women's reproductive and productive labor are a feature of advanced and developing capitalist economies generally. They surface during this era in the sphere of office work. Whereas, after World War II, in the United Kingdom, women office workers still tended to be younger and unmarried, in the United States, a rising demand for office labor led more married women to enter the workforce.[15]

A photograph accompanying Theron's article, in the style of the themed fashion spreads typical of *Sarie* in those days, depicts two young white women discussing something at a desk featuring an IBM typewriter, with a white man in a business suit on the telephone standing behind them. This suggests that *Sarie* views Theron's appeal as relating specifically to office work.[16] One can also infer from her appeal to married women that the demand for clerical workers was not being met from among the young white women traditionally employed in South African offices. In other countries, shortages of labor are sometimes explainable by uninterrogated assumptions about the gendered division of labor.[17] But in South Africa, as in the United States at various times, the relevant assumptions were racial. Apartheid thinkers perceived a shortage of "white manpower" in the 1960s because they wanted to keep certain types of work white—at least in those businesses owned and run by white people and serving a white clientele. A growing domain of labor in the 1960s, clerical work was one such type. That is why, even as businesses could no longer find white women to do certain kinds of work in the office, apartheid ideologues made appeals for white "womanpower" and not for the labor of black Africans, Coloureds, and Indians.[18]

A few minutes before drawing the SACAC delegates' attention to the Japanese labor study, Minister Jan Haak had made a veiled reference to why black people could not be asked to help meet the "shortage of skilled manpower." On the one hand, he observed, automation may not always be necessary in South Africa because "it is one of the few industrialized countries in the free world with a relatively large complement of unskilled labor at its disposal."[19] "On the other hand," Haak continued, "we have in South Africa our own unique long-term political policy and objectives that can possibly result in short-term economic bottlenecks. One of the economic bottlenecks is a shortage of skilled manpower. This problem can be alleviated in different ways. Some methods that are being proposed are not acceptable for social and political reasons, whereas others, such as accelerated immigration, necessarily have a long-term character."[20]

What are the methods that are not acceptable for social and political reasons? One would be the employment of Africans by white-owned businesses in white communities to perform skilled work. Another would be training enough black people to do such work. Minister Haak speaks for a government that, although it could never entirely prevent white people from employing Africans as clerical workers, for example, was extremely effective in making sure that its education policies distorted the labor market by reducing the number of Africans who could apply for those jobs.[21] The effects of racial disparities in education on employment were not unique to South Africa in the 1960s. In the United States, radical black activist James Boggs observed that industrial automation—or "cybernation," automatic control by computers—was "eliminating 'Negro jobs'" because, in contrast to white workers, black workers did not have the technical training required to work in "these highly developed industries."[22] In South Africa, however, the idea was to turn automation into a force to ensure that black people were not hired in certain positions to begin with. This was unlikely to happen in factories, which, by the 1950s, had begun to depend on black workers. But white-collar occupations, which were not yet as dependent, still represented an opportunity for the ideologues of apartheid. For them, the meaning of automation and computerization was ultimately keep-white, bar-black.

Both Haak and Theron call on white women to enter the workforce because the demand for white labor was unmet. Theron does not consider technology as a factor that could alleviate a shortage of white workers. But Haak does when he explains to the country's experts in computerization and automation that the goal of keeping-white and barring-black could be realized by the introduction of machines. Like the government's education policies, machines would accomplish this goal in an indirect way. An unstated subtext is that direct means, such as labor legislation, could never have helped swell the ranks of white workers. More machines, Haak argues, would mean more jobs for women. If white women took these jobs, then white men could be employed in other positions. The net result, the logic ran, was that if black workers were not needed, only or mainly white workers would be hired. But that scenario is at odds with what was actually taking place in South Africa in the 1960s and 1970s. For a more complete picture, we turn, first of all, to fiction—and a portrait of office work. In this period, the office was a sphere in which mechanization and automation offered measurable benefits. It is thus a place in which, in South Africa, the meaning of automation, at the nexus of women's work and apartheid strictures on work, comes starkly into relief.

Office Fiction

Published in 1975, Miriam Tlali's *Muriel at Metropolitan* is set in the late 1960s.[23] Employed as a typist at Metropolitan Radio, a white-owned furniture store in Johannesburg with a mainly black clientele, an African woman is, before long, assigned other, more responsible, clerical tasks. When this happens, the white women already working at the store object:

> The two senior white women tried to reserve certain jobs for themselves and to allocate the more mechanical ones to me, such as folding letters and statements and putting them into envelopes, and printing addresses on statements with the addressograph machine. I would accomplish these tasks in no time and find myself idling. There were approximately 4 000 customers. The white staff could not cope with all the work requiring skill and thinking. I was there and I could do it. I had proved that I could type anything as well as they could, if not better. The boss was not blind to the fact, so he called upon me to do more and more of the seemingly complicated work. He was not going to employ someone else while I was there.[24]

The word *reserve* is significant, alluding to the South African practice, and policy, of reserving certain occupations for white people (and, specifically in the Western Cape, for Coloureds). In mining, a color bar had existed since the 1890s. In 1911, it was given statutory form by the Mines and Works Act. The Industrial Conciliation Act (1924) strengthened the hand of white labor organizations by instituting a framework that allowed them to "determine the racial allocation of jobs within an industry."[25] Other laws allowed the government to restrict black employment even further.[26] In response to the increased demand for semiskilled labor because of the rise of manufacturing after World War II, which forced white workers to compete with lower-paid Africans and Coloureds, an amendment to the Industrial Conciliation Act passed in 1956 gave the minister of labor the authority, under Section 77 of the act, to reserve jobs for white people, over and above restrictions already agreed to between white workers and employers.[27] Not typically noted is that Section 77 also privileged other non-African workers, the provision having been regarded by the Department of Labour as "a protective measure for the Whites, Coloureds and other Non-White groups against racial competition." Coloured and Indian workers thus also used Section 77 to protect their interests against Africans.[28] Before it was scrapped as the government implemented the recommendations of the Wiehahn Commission (1979),[29] Section 77 had been applied less frequently than its opponents had feared.[30] Arguably, for white organized labor, which remained an important political constituency of the National Party until the early 1970s, Section 77's importance was mainly symbolic.[31] This may also have been true of the so-called Coloured labor preference in the Western Cape, which was effected principally through "influx control" measures applicable to migrant Africans, with other labor controls instituted in the 1960s failing due to an increased demand for labor in the region far exceeding the number of Coloured people looking for work.[32]

This is, of course, not to say that the laws and regulations in question did not act as a deterrent to employing Africans.[33] The prospect of impending legislation, even if it was not enacted, could also affect the decisions of employers.[34] And because the law did not prohibit employers from not hiring Africans, Coloureds, and Indians, de facto job reservation existed wherever white employers could find the white workers they wanted and wished to pay them the higher wages that they commanded. Black people had always done the bulk of unskilled work, but finding enough white people to do semiskilled work became almost impossible by the 1960s as demand rose and education levels among white people improved.[35] The market for skilled workers was also changing, as, for example, a shortage of white applicants for clerical jobs led to the employment of Coloureds, Indians, and Africans.[36]

But the practices of white-owned businesses varied considerably—as the new typist at Metropolitan Radio discovers. A demand for labor exists, and the boss employs a black woman to do work that white women do not want to do—and then, when a demand for labor that involves relatively greater skill arises, employs her over the objections of those white women. They can appeal to the law to prevent her from using the same toilet as they do and from working in the same office space—they do the former but not the latter—but they cannot actually use the law to prevent her from doing skilled work.[37]

This, in a nutshell, is what takes place in the 1960s, as the demand for clerical workers rises with the long postwar manufacturing boom that ended in 1973.[38] In the late 1960s, there is a large increase in white women doing office work, but it does not meet rising demand. According to the biennial Manpower Surveys, from 1965 to 1971, there was an increase from about 170,000 to about 249,000, or about 46 percent. The total number of clerical workers in South Africa rose by about 39 percent over the same period (1965: 354,576; 1971: 492,106).[39] In 1971, there was a shortage of about 3,800 white female clerical workers, whereas in 1965, it was 2,700, a rise of about 41 percent. This shortage may have been even more serious had Coloureds, Indians, and Africans not been employed in far higher numbers than before. Muriel is only too aware of the apartheid fantasy of doing without black workers—she contemplates a general strike—and punctures the fiction of black people not being assigned skilled work.[40] Accordingly, the labor statistics show the employment of Coloureds and Indians, and, to a lesser extent, black Africans, as clerical workers rising even more dramatically than that of white women. In 1965, about 14,300 Coloureds (10,677 men, 3,630 women), about 13,000 Indians (12,222 men, 830 women), and about 31,700 Africans (30,847 men, 913 women), were employed in clerical jobs. The numbers for 1971 were: Coloureds, 24,333, about a 100 percent total increase (15,935 men, 8,398 women); Indians, 29,202, about a 123 percent total increase (25,462 men, 3,740 women); and Africans, 49,126, a 55 percent overall increase (45,766 men, 3,360 women). Muriel's husband, we learn, also works as a clerk.[41] That there were good opportunities for Coloured women is borne out by the labor statistics as well as autobiography; by the late 1960s, a young Coloured woman in Cape Town with only a Standard Seven (ninth grade) can leave her job on the factory floor and rapidly move from one secretarial position to another, each time commanding a better rate of pay.[42] Black women, however, are still a tiny fraction of all clerical workers by 1971—making Muriel's career somewhat atypical, even exceptional. White women, Coloureds, Indians, and Africans, all can be paid progressively less than white men. Pay rises steadily for white and Coloured clerical workers during the period 1966–1970, with weekly earnings for Coloureds in the Cape Peninsula (39%) and for white women on the Witwatersrand (28%) rising more rapidly than for white men on the Witwatersrand and for white women and men in the Cape Peninsula (19%–21%).[43] But wage levels do not act as an incentive to automate the office (as they do in the US),[44] except perhaps, as we shall see, in larger concerns where there exist economies of scale.[45]

The pattern in South Africa is different for another reason. The political incentive to automate to keep the office white through automation, in addition to reserving jobs for white people, including white women, is in conflict with labor demand. It is also in conflict with what labor costs in a racially differentiated and distorted labor market. Taking a longer view, this contradiction needs to be understood within the overarching economic contradiction of apartheid. Because labor productivity rises with education, barring black workers from skilled work, especially by limiting the education and training of Africans to prepare them for such work, is ultimately in conflict with economic growth.[46]

Seeking short-term gain, however, business owners took advantage of the distortions in the labor market. Muriel is underpaid because, as an African, Metropolitan Radio can get away with paying her less than a white employee, even though she evidently has a university education.[47] When Muriel comes to Metropolitan, she has a testimonial from her previous employer, a Mr. Levenstein, who "had conveniently omitted to mention that he had used me for two years as his senior balance sheet typist. He had hundreds of clients, and the arrangements and layout, typing and binding of all the balance sheets was left entirely to me. But I was black, so he was not going to mention it; nor was he going to encourage his successor to pay me for my experience."[48] The meanness of the old employer suggests racism, but Muriel believes that Mr. Bloch, her new employer, would also pay his white apprentice radio mechanics less if their interests were not protected by the "Wage Board, the Industrial Council and the Trade Union." "The non-white workers were," by contrast, "unorganised, and it was difficult to get them more organised as the activities of the few trade unions . . . were weakened by the fact that it was illegal for non-whites to strike. What we were paid, therefore, was a matter which rested almost entirely in the hands of the masters. If he 'liked' you and felt you were a 'good boy or girl,' then he paid you a little more than the others."[49] Muriel is underpaid for as long as she works at Metropolitan.[50]

What about automation? At a small concern like Metropolitan Radio, which employs only three clerical workers, there is, as one would expect in 1967, no computer.[51] Until the late 1970s, in South Africa, computers were only in use at large-scale enterprises (although any number of smaller concerns were contracting with computer bureaus for office-related services).[52] Although Metropolitan utilizes some of the basic office machines already widely used for about half a century—typewriter, addressograph, and adding machine,[53] the sort of devices that come across as old-fashioned by the late 1980s when they appear in William Kentridge's films—there is a reluctance to mechanize further, or to pay for mechanized services, when the human labor the machine would replace is perceived as being cheaper. As Muriel remarks to a fellow worker, of folding letters and inserting them in their envelopes, one of the "more mechanical" jobs that her white coworkers assign to her, "At the last place I used to work, we used to send them to a certain factory where they used machines. It was done in no time. I don't think that Mr Bloch would want to pay for that. He doesn't realise that it costs more this way. Every month approximately four thousand to fold. I think it is a waste of manpower."[54] "There was no proper office," Muriel has already observed, "with convenient, modern, labour-saving, systematic methods of record-keeping."[55]

It could thus appear paradoxical that, when Muriel resigns from Metropolitan, she does not type up her notice but writes it by hand: "I decided to write the letter in my own handwriting instead of typing it. . . . My handwriting had never looked so beautiful. I had at last decided to free myself from the shackles which had bound not only my hands, but also my soul."[56] For Muriel, the typewriter symbolizes her exploitation, and the constraints on her freedom, at Metropolitan, a point that the allusion to enslavement reinforces. That the shackles that she refers to bind her soul probably means that her sense of a possible future was suppressed by her present constraints. Through Black Consciousness, Steve Biko taught his generation to rid themselves of that mental slavery. But what is less clear is that what the typewriter means for Muriel at this moment of self-liberation applies for Tlali to typewriters generally. Nevertheless, as I show in the following, even as other machines, such as the sewing machine, are viewed as emancipatory by the women of Soweto with whom she speaks, the typewriter remains an object of some ambivalence.

If, in these years, the dream of an all-white office was unrealizable because of an availability of cheap black labor that may also have slowed down mechanization and computerization, in the next decade, as those technological trends increased, the demand for semiskilled and skilled labor would only rise further. But, by then, Bantu education had taken its toll, and the demand for skilled labor could not be met. During the boom that peaked in the 1960s, especially as it was coming to an end in the early 1970s, despite pronouncements of apartheid doctrine by the government, there were constant appeals from those studying automation and computerization for the training of more Africans and for improved education generally.[57] By the late 1970s, when computerization had become the general trend in business and public administration, the labor shortage had become acute, especially for programmers and systems analysts. It is possible, on the one hand, to say that this slowed down computerization. On the other hand, one can assert that it helped break down the apartheid orthodoxy (never corresponding to economic reality) that certain work must only be done by white workers—unless it was done in the "Bantu communities"—and the accompanying bar to training more Africans to do skilled work. Identifying a "skills gap," by the early 1980s, appeals were being made from within the computer industry specifically for directing primary and secondary education for Africans toward the acquisition of "basic skills."[58] In the near absence of government action to train Africans, Coloureds, and Indians, major computer companies began to conduct in-house training for programmers and systems analysts.[59]

The story that everybody knows about South Africa is political—with 1976 as the climax of revolt against oppression. The story that

I am uncovering, however, is about changes in the labor market and the way technological advances, despite the dreams of apartheid thinkers, helped bring those about. There is a story to be told in which, although things are beginning to change in the labor market, that change is accelerated due to the increased automation and computerization of office and other work. If the dominant South African story—to which Tlali's novel, with good reason, is typically read as subscribing—is political and social, then the story I am telling is more technological. In the dominant narrative, after Sharpeville, the Rivonia trial, and the repression of black political activity, the 1960s were a dormant time, with the 1973 Durban strikes as the watershed. But the rapid economic growth of the 1960s established conditions for renewed black self-assertion, just as it did for the Bantustan policies, which, for some time, had been rejected as being too expensive. Thus, for a certain period, grand apartheid intensified, just as socioeconomic trends intensified that would make such a system unworkable and give black people the power to reject it.[60] By the mid-1970s, this was obvious, but in the mid-1960s, it was happening in a less overt way all over the country where business was booming. Just as labor statistics for computer programmers and systems analysts began to be collected only in 1973, it took time before the massive change underway was perceived to be systemic. This almost imperceptible historical change seems echoed in *Muriel at Metropolitan*, of which the writer Sheila Roberts, who edited the manuscript of Tlali's book for Ravan Press, notes that "there are no strongly dramatic moments in the narrative, no unbearable tensions leading to climactic peaks. There *are* tense moments of anger and anxiety such as we all suffer at work."[61]

In short, the story I am telling is about how black African labor became more valuable and about how machines, specifically computers, helped make it more valuable. What was new was the role of black women workers in this process of historical change. That is not to say that the economic conditions that helped produce upward mobility for some black people, including these women, especially in the cities, were enough to prevent the crash of 1973 and the sustained economic decline of the next twenty years—conditions that both put an end to the apartheid project and left millions of black South Africans without jobs.[62] Ultimately, although black labor became valuable, it did not become valuable enough—which is another way of saying that productivity remained too low—relative to competitor economies.[63] The stirring epic tale of black women contributing, through their highly skilled labor as "computers" and aeronautical engineers, to American national greatness, at the same time as African Americans fought for their civil rights, which one reads in Margot Lee Shetterly's incomparable *Hidden Figures*, is not paralleled in South Africa.[64] The political struggle against apartheid succeeds, and black women enter white-collar jobs in increasing numbers,[65] but the fall of apartheid coincides with a long period of national economic decline. I am telling a story in a minor key, perhaps with a sense of what might have been had circumstances been different. Yet, at the same time, the lineaments of that story are of enormous significance—and call for careful study, given the paucity of reflection on how, in those years, technological change helped bring about social and political change.[66] And today, when smartphones are ubiquitous, surprisingly little thought has been devoted to the historical effects of computerization and the factors that led to or retarded it.

South Africa also does not have the equivalent, say, of Siegfried Kracauer's *The Salaried Masses*, his celebrated reportage of shop and office workers in Weimar Germany, let alone the impressive historical scholarship on women working in offices in the United States and Great Britain.[67] But fiction can reveal much about the underlying economy of an age—think of Balzac, Zola, Dreiser, even Austen. Tlali's *Muriel at Metropolitan* is an invaluable index for how a worker's ability to command a certain wage—by virtue of whether they are white or African, male or female—can function as a factor in business calculations and state planning as much as it does for the worker. There are not many works of literature set in the South African office. Phyllis Altman's *The Law of the Vultures* (1952) made office work the sign of the thwarted ambition of Thabo Thaele, who leaves rural Basutoland (today Lesotho) wanting to become a doctor—but Thaele loses his position in the second chapter when he is wrongly convicted of theft, and the novel moves on to narrate his career in politics.[68] Its full-scale depiction of office work thus makes *Muriel at Metropolitan* unique in South African fiction and autobiography of the period—which, when it represents work, is more typically set at a mine, or on a farm, or, when the protagonist is female, in a white household.[69] No other author offers anything like Tlali's insights into how, from the point of view of a worker, the country's racially distorted labor market determined what mechanization and automation meant. If, in the 1960s, for the apartheid government, automation meant keep-white, bar-black, then, by the end of the same decade, because of an increased need for skilled and semiskilled workers in mechanizing offices, for business it began to mean make-black. In the 1970s, this trend was magnified when the computer industry specifically undertook to train its own black programmers and systems analysts. Let us now amplify the insights of Tlali's novel into these historical processes by providing a brief account of the history of computerization in South Africa, including two case studies of the early introduction of computers.

A City Gets a Computer...

In August 1963, the office of the city treasurer of Port Elizabeth, a harbor city in the Eastern Cape known for its automobile assembly plants and renamed Gqeberha in 2021, advertised a tender for a new electronic computer.[70] The tender called for a system composed of a punch card input reader, a central processor with large core storage, four magnetic tape units, a fast online output printer, and various additional equipment.[71] With the implementation of PAYE, the national payroll tax withholding scheme, the city treasurer's computing needs had grown beyond the capacity of its ICT 555 punch card computer. Other large public administrative entities, such as the Cape Provincial Administration (CPA)[72] and the Pretoria Municipality, had recently updated their respective systems to the magnetic tape ICT 1500, keeping up with advances in computer technology.[73]

The main tasks to be performed by the new computer related to weekly and monthly city payroll, payments from residents of the "Bantu housing schemes" at New Brighton and Kwazakele (18,000 houses, 30,000 payments per month), accounting and costing, stores, job costing, interest warrants for bonds issued by the city, and electricity, water, and gas billing.[74] With this set of tasks, we see a nexus of public administration designed to make the racially segregated city fiscally sustainable through rents, including rents combined with loan repayments; Kwazakele, the newer and larger of the two African townships in Port Elizabeth, was a "house purchase scheme." We also see how business interests were competing in a still small but lucrative state market.

As council officials evaluated different computers, comparing their capacity, assessing their cost, and deciding whether to purchase or rent, labor was a central consideration. "The introduction of a computer system," wrote G. W. Bullen, assistant accountant (mechanisation), in a report on the IBM 1401 computer prepared for the city treasurer, "was envisaged to extend mechanisation, save staff, improve methods, avoid rising costs, and deal with this city's future development." IBM's proposal fell short of meeting those criteria.[75] A report prepared by Bullen after attending a demonstration of the ICT 1500 computer in Johannesburg, over a year before the tender was advertised, noted that a seventeen-year-old girl with the South African equivalent of a grade-twelve education was employed as an operator: "Data processing systems require less operating staff and, as a point of interest, I must add that the operator employed on the 1500 computer in the Johannesburg I.C.T. training centre is a young girl of 17 years of age. Her educational standard is a second class matriculation. Her duties, which are not particularly arduous, consist of magnetic tape changing (this takes under one minute per tape), setting the system in motion, and checking the stationery as it is processed."[76] The implication was that, given the low level of education and skill necessary to be a computer operator and her gender, the "young girl" would not command high pay. We do not know the race of the employee, although her educational attainment makes her more likely than not to have been white. Yet it seems clear that the City of Port Elizabeth was more interested in keeping its labor costs down than in creating the conditions for the employment of white women, as Minister Haak contemplated a few years later when he referred to the Japanese study that showed more women being employed as automation increased. Given that the city treasurer had already been using a punch card computer,[77] and probably a Hollerith tabulator before that,[78] much of the clerical labor saving achieved through mechanization would already have been realized. This would explain why that is not what is emphasized in these documents. Subsequent estimates for staffing established that, in addition to two additional computer operators, a full-time programmer would be needed, all of whom would work under the direction of a new section head. A need for additional clerical assistance was also identified.[79] Aptitude tests had been conducted by International Computers and Tabulators (ICT) on behalf of the city in order to select trainees for programming from among existing staff.[80] All of the seven eventual trainees, save for one, were male, and, judging by their names, all were probably either white or Coloured.[81] Thus, as various experts were predicting in the 1960s, although automation would replace human labor in the long term, as had happened in the United States, computerization generated more jobs in the short term. There was a recognition of "the difficult staff position in the country at the moment."[82] This would, as we have observed, lead to shortages when those jobs were reserved for white workers (1960s) and when not enough Africans could be found (1970s) to fill them.

In the Port Elizabeth tender file, one finds correspondence between the city treasurer, Frank Jenvey, and the companies vying for the tender. The most extensive is between Jenvey and various representatives of ICT, the company from which the city was already renting a computer, which gave it a foot in the door ahead of IBM.[83] Until the late 1960s, ICT, the company for which J. M. Coetzee worked as a programmer in England after leaving IBM, enjoyed the largest share of the South African computer market. ICL's competitors, Leo, IBM, and NCR, all submitted proposals in response to the Port Elizabeth tender. But ICL's proposal was the winning one, and an agreement was signed on November 27, 1963.[84] Hein Lederman, the managing director of ICL in South Africa from 1960 to 1967, had aggressively pursued the contract. In one of his letters to Jenvey, he offered to cover the travel expenses for a city official to come to Pretoria to study the ICT 1500 newly in use:

> If you feel . . . that a good purpose would be served by one of your Senior officials studying the Pretoria application in all its details, I would be very glad to issue an invitation to your Council to send somebody up to Pretoria at our expense. Clients and/or prospects to travel for demonstrations at the invitation of the supply company seems now to become a matter of course in this country, and I truly agree that this method, if one has something interesting to show, is a quick way of settling doubts in a customer's mind. If you agree with this contention, please do not hesitate to let me know, so that we can make the necessary arrangements.[85]

Although probably not technically an infraction because the offer was made some weeks before the tender was advertised and ICL had submitted its bid, such an offer may have run afoul of the spirit of the conditions of purchase of goods and tender, which stipulated against the offering of "any commission, gratuity, gift or other consideration."[86] Preserved in the archives, in the light of what we witness half a century later—when Port Elizabeth has been the target of scandalous "state capture"[87]—these were modest attempts at influence. Although they were politely ignored by the official responsible,[88] these overtures bring onto the stage a figure who, because of his long career in computers, offers elsewhere one of the few accounts of the early history of computer use in South Africa.

In an interview published in 1978 in the South African trade paper *Computerweek*, Lederman explains that, after emigrating from Germany in 1934, where he qualified as an electrical engineer and was trained to use Hollerith machines, he was employed by South African Railways and Harbours. It had contracted the Hollerith bureau to perform a staff survey (a "bureau" rented out equipment and sold processing time on its machines, usually also providing related technical support services). "At that point," he relates, "there were some 15 tabulators in the Republic—at AECI, Durban Municipality, Cape Town Municipality and such."[89] After working at the parastatal Iron and Steel Corporation (ISCOR), Lederman was hired by the Hollerith bureau, which won contracts from the Railways as well as from the Union Defence Force during World War II. "During the war," Lederman notes, "the authorities brought out the punch card as a payable document for forces dependents." "Teachers," he adds, "were the first to be paid by mechanically signed cheques."[90] After the war, Lederman traveled to the Zambian copper belt, where the Anglo American and Rio Tinto mining companies installed thirty tabulators in four years. He describes how British Tabulating Machinery, which later became ICT (and then ICL) after merging with Powers Samas in 1959, had exclusive rights to sell the Hollerith equipment in the British Empire until 1949, in terms of an agreement it had made with IBM.[91] Various advances are mentioned, such as the HEC 1 and HEC 2, and the "RCA 1500 in 1961 was the start of the proper computer age in SA reckons Lederman—one of the first really big contracts was for 10 systems for Railways which meant a revenue of around R60 000 monthly."[92] This was also the computer that Lederman sold to the City of Port Elizabeth in 1964.

No history of computerization in South Africa exists in the form of a single ready reference. As a prelude to analyzing further the *meaning* of computerization and automation in discourses of the state and in the arts, I am outlining an account that, because of the sources on which it relies, hews closely to the preoccupations of the computer industry and its clientele.[93] Excellent critical work has been done by Keith Breckenridge on the use of computers for South Africa's biometric identification system,[94] and Paul N. Edwards and Gabrielle Hecht have made a sophisticated analysis of the "technopolitics" of computerization in South Africa during the 1970s and 1980s as the international anti-apartheid movement campaigned for divestment from South Africa by IBM and the other major computer companies.[95] But for basic information about developments in computerization—dates, places, names, trends—it is necessary, in addition to opening up forgotten folders of archival documents and obscure ring binders with SACAC conference proceedings, to glean what one can from periodicals published by professional organizations, in-house magazines put out by the computer companies, trade papers, and yearbooks, as well as general business magazines. From these sources, one can confirm and augment Lederman's observations.

Although the protagonist of J. M. Coetzee's *Youth* is mistaken in believing that there were no computers in South Africa when he is trained as a programmer at IBM in the early 1960s,[96] that was indeed a time when the number of computers in South Africa could still be counted. In the "status-gadget-conscious world" of business,[97] their names and model numbers were invoked like those of expensive luxury motor cars. Noting in 1960 that IBM had recently rented a computer to the Inland Revenue Department in Pretoria, *Financial Mail*, South Africa's main business magazine, observed that "an organisation must have a considerable amount of work available before either renting or buying a computer can be considered. Sanlam, the CSIR [Council for Scientific and Industrial Research], the Durban Municipality, the Cape Provincial Administration, Iscor, the Railways, and General Motors each use one."[98] CSIR got its "ZEBRA" computer in 1958.[99] Sanlam, one of the country's two largest life insurance companies, had acquired its Burroughs 205 computer in the same year, whereas its main competitor, Old Mutual, installed its own in 1960—a "British-made Perseus Ferranti costing £350,000."[100] By 1965, about one hundred computers were in use, according to Lederman's estimate.[101] This made South Africa a relative latecomer: "Australia had 254 in April this year (77 in 1962). The world's total is estimated at something over 30,000, though the lack of information from behind the Iron Curtain makes accuracy difficult. United States: over 22,500."[102] By the end of 1969, South Africa would have 407 large- and medium-sized computers, and in 1974, 650.[103] As microcomputers started to be "a positive flood" by the end of the 1970s,[104] the experts stopped counting.

The online networks for savings banks and ticket purchasing that had become part of the fabric of our lives growing up in the 1970s first emerged in the mid-1960s. In 1966, Johannesburg Building Society would bring into operation the first civilian—assuming that the military probably secretly built one earlier—online computer system in South Africa.[105] South African Airways would introduce an online booking system in 1970,[106] and Computicket, which remains the country's largest theater, cinema, and sports ticket seller, made its debut in August 1971 as "the first fully centralised and integrated computerised box-office system in the world."[107] The company made use of an IBM 360/40 owned by Sigma Data, the computer bureau with which it partnered in the beginning.[108]

Those online networks had also begun to weave another, darker, part of our lives' fabric. According to Jack Clarke of IBM, South Africa, "our Government at the Department of the Interior is installing a real time population register with terminals in all registry offices. . . . Once again, [like the online banking and airline booking systems supplied by IBM,] it is certainly the most advanced system of its kind in the world."[109] By then, IBM's equipment was also being used by the South African Defence Force for data processing and management—of, for example, the system of military conscription to which all white men of my generation were subject.[110] IBM was not alone in profiting from apartheid. Even as it showcased ICL's training schemes for black employees, *Datarama*, the company's in-house magazine, proudly announced its sale of computers to the administrations of the Ciskei, Transkei, and Bophuthatswana Bantustans.[111] By 1972, however, with ICL as its sole competitor, IBM had garnered 67 percent of the government market for computers and 58 percent of Railways' business.[112] These business arrangements would soon make IBM, which had overtaken ICL as the market leader in South Africa by 1968,[113] one of the main targets of the anti-apartheid divestment campaign and of the US embargoes "forbidding computer exports to SA Defence, Police, Atomic Energy and Administration Boards in late 1977."[114] The "Administration Boards" enforced "influx control." There were, in response, a few attempts at local manufacturing and assembly,[115] but South Africa remained dependent on imports, especially of components.[116]

Amid these rapid developments in computerization in business and the state, there were also experiments in what is nowadays called the digital humanities. Computer-aided analyses of the French *nouveau roman* and of San rock art were described in the *South African Computer Bulletin* and in the Computer Society's successor journal, *Systems*.[117] The computer-aided stylistic analysis of one of Samuel Beckett's stories carried out by J. M. Coetzee was thus part of a broader wave.[118]

...And So Does a Mining Company

My second case study from the early days of computerization in South Africa comes from the mining industry and confirms some of the assumptions that arise from the Port Elizabeth file. At SACAC's inaugural conference in 1965, P. C. Pirow, who later served as vice president of SACAC, described in great detail the acquisition, in May 1962, by Rand Mines of a British-made Leo III computer. Rand Mines was one of the largest gold-mining companies in South Africa. Speaking to this gathering of specialists, Pirow described the computer system of the company he worked for in technical terms — but also addressed some of the relevant labor issues.[119] The background is South Africa's racial capitalism and the administrative mechanisms that kept it running.

If the Port Elizabeth file reveals something about a segregated city with an expanding African population, the Rand Mines case study takes as a given the existence of a migrant labor system that drew black African mine workers from all parts of southern Africa. The labor force at the mines served by the computer was overwhelmingly African, with sixty-four thousand African compared to about eight thousand white employees.[120] The computer was used principally for pay and stores, although scientific and other tasks were also performed.[121] "Native pay" was particularly complicated due to the way workers' contracts, incentives, and deductions worked. It was here that the computer came into its own:

The computer programmes cater for all Natives who are paid on a 30 shift, full ticket basis, except certain ward boys and trainee hospital orderlies who are deemed to work a seven-day week. Mabalans [clerks] and other monthly paid Natives are also excluded. For the "full ticket" Natives, the computer performs the following tasks:

(a) Determines when the Native has completed his ticket of 30 shifts and proceeds to calculate pay and print a payslip.
(b) Calculates the components of gross pay from the basic data (overtime hours worked, shifts absent, etc.) notified by Native time office (gross pay includes basic pay, service increment, convalescent and surface acclimatizing pay, Sunday and overtime pay, special holiday, drilling and First Aid bonuses, paid leave and sick pay . . .).
(c) Reads in at periodic intervals the amount of incentive bonus to be paid to each Native.
(d) Calculates the necessary deductions from the Native's pay, allowing for the minimum net pay provision, and automatically reduces the balance of the deductions outstanding.
(e) Calculates the deferred pay to be deducted in accordance with the Native's territorial category and/or expressed wishes, and accumulates each Native's deferred pay credited to date.
(f) Automatically increases the Native's mine rate when he has the required service.
(g) Calculates the terminating payment for Natives who are discharged and prints a terminating payslip.
(h) Maintains the Native's pneumoconiosis record.
(i) Maintains the Native's accident record for Rand Mutual Assurance, and calculates any ex gratia accident payment.
(j) Records the Native's intelligence and leaderless group ratings, education, date of birth and length of service and prints details on request.
(k) Prints schedules of deferred pay deductions taken from Portuguese East Africa Natives.
(l) Deducts the annual Nyasaland tax and prints a schedule of such deductions.
(m) Every six months, prints a consolidated record of the Native's work and pay for the previous six months, as his permanent printed record.

(n) Accumulates and prints statistics required by the Mines Department, the Chamber of Mines, Rand Mutual Assurance, Rand
Mines mine management, etc.

(o) Prints accumulated payroll and control totals for auditing purposes.

(p) Reports errors in the data submitted by the mine and rejects suspect data and also reports certain information for administrative
control.[122]

Rand Mines viewed computerization as helping to further the goal
of simplifying and standardizing the "Native payroll" by reducing the
separate components of gross pay from fifteen to seven.[123] In this tabulation of input, processing, and output, the fundamental element is a
standardization attendant upon the term *Native*. The word is used, of
course, as a racial category to refer to black Africans. It may even be that
Native is being used in contradistinction to *Bantu*, which had, by the
mid-1960s, become the term used in the apartheid government's official discourse to refer to black Africans. For mine management, what is
important is that *Native* denotes a category of labor, the cost of which
is, historically, a crucial factor in the profitability of the gold mines.
Low wages for the "Native" subsidize far higher wages for the "European." The latter worked mainly in a supervisory capacity, whereas
the former were mainly manual workers, some of whom operated machines. This wage arrangement—a settlement favoring white workers
achieved in the early twentieth century through white trade unionism
allied with white supremacist politics—informed the economics of
mining until the 1970s, when African wages began to rise. It was not
until the 1980s rise of black trade unions, the largest of which was the
National Union of Mineworkers (NUM), and the political influence
of white workers decreasing that the arrangement was fundamentally
challenged.

Although it lent itself to computerization, the economic standardization implied by *Native* was not itself a product of computerization.
As Rosalind Morris observes in her illuminating commentary on an
East Rand Proprietary Mines cash book from 1906, her part in a book
collaboration with William Kentridge, who produced a series of drawings, a standardization was in place much earlier. Columns were printed
in the cash book for "Native Wages" and "Chinese Wages," with indi-

vidual recipients usually unnamed, whereas pay for white employees was listed under "Sundry Persons" and the recipient's name typically recorded.[124] The 1906 cash book presents an interesting snapshot in time. Due to a labor shortage following the Anglo-Boer War, more than sixty-three thousand Chinese indentured workers came to South Africa between 1904 and 1906.[125] As I discuss in more detail in chapter 3, a little later, mechanization was considered as an alternative solution to a scarcity of African labor.[126] The Chinese workers, like the African workers, are subject to a standardization as labor units that contributes to the calculability and predictability of overall labor cost for a mine.

One can see from Pirow's report how, more than fifty years later, in a vastly different world, a standardization of *Native* in terms of unit labor cost remains the basis for mine accounting. If the sheer size of the African workforce engaged in manual labor justifies investment of capital in a computer, standardization is what makes "Native pay" amenable to computerization in ways in which the compensation of other categories of African worker does not correspond. Pirow refers to "certain ward boys and trainee hospital orderlies." But, interestingly, he also refers to "mabalans," or *mabalanas*, the black mine clerks, who, he tells his audience, are paid on a monthly basis.[127] They numbered nearly two thousand across the entire industry in 1943. Represented by a staff association founded in 1920 known as the Transvaal Native Mine Clerks' Association, which was recognized by the Chamber of Mines and won wage and housing concessions on their behalf, they represented a different class stratum within the African workforce. The *mabalanas* were an educated elite with a different set of interests from mine workers, with whom they never really made common cause.[128] Although Pirow does not spell it out in his address, they are also the ones who would be most vulnerable to attrition following the introduction of the computer in order to reduce administrative overhead.

Much of what the Rand Mines computer is programmed to do stems from the standardization described. "Native payroll" in its simplified form includes variables typical of any pay scheme: shifts or hours worked, gross pay and net pay, derived from factors such as overtime worked and variables such as bonuses and deductions, as well as incremental payment increases and termination payment (a–d, f–g). It also reflects factors that, from the point of view of mine management, complicate efforts at stabilizing cost or increase the cost of administration.[129] The system of labor migrancy, as it functioned in the 1960s, in which large numbers of workers were recruited from Nyasaland (present-day Malawi) and Mozambique, explains the "annual Nyasaland tax" (l) as well as the references to "deferred pay to be deducted in accordance with the Native's territorial category" (e, k).[130] The latter are remittances paid to workers on returning to their home country—at the end of their contracts—a system that had operated since at least the early twentieth century.[131] As (e) indicates, it was possible for a worker to make deductions voluntarily. More significant, for what they tell us about how the migrant labor system functioned, were the compulsory deductions. In the case of Mozambique, labor recruitment was governed by the South Africa-Mozambique Convention, which in 1928 updated agreements dating back to the days of the South African Republic. Renegotiated several times, by 1962, the convention was authorizing the mines to recruit up to one hundred thousand workers per year in southern Mozambique.[132] The 1928 agreement stipulated a contract time of twelve months, mandating the deduction of half a miner's average daily wage in deferred pay.[133] Historically, miners' remittances have been a crucial source of foreign exchange and injection of cash into the economies of neighboring countries, a dependence that extends from governments to miners' households.[134]

The other complicating factors, for mine management, are disease, loss of limb, and death. Pneumoconiosis (h), the irreversible lung disease also known as silicosis or miners' phthisis, caused by inhaling mine dust, killed or disabled large numbers of miners—few of whom were compensated.[135] The tabulation includes nothing about related payouts, although it reveals that payment, in the case of an accident, would be made ex gratia through Rand Mutual Assurance (i), an insurance trust established by several of the larger mining houses in 1894 and still in existence today.[136] The computer is also used to record some factors, except for the last, not directly related to labor cost, such as the "Native's intelligence and leaderless group ratings, education, date of birth and length of service" (j). African mine workers were subject to tests of intelligence at the beginning of their contracts—a fact recorded in Lionel Rogosin's film *Come Back Africa!* (1959). Evidently, they were also scored for their participation in leaderless group discussion, a method used in occupational psychology to assess leadership potential.

Pirow foresees automation in the more systemic sense described by John Diebold and others, rather than simply, say, of calculation or accounting by a machine.[137] When quantified across a workforce, the indices under (j) would enable managers to identify individuals for further training. Kurt Vonnegut's *Player Piano* alerts its readers to the dangers of such a system, with human potential limited by what a computer has calculated on the basis of values input.[138] Error reporting (p) is a standard data management operation. The last thing to note is that, along with computerized recording and processing of data, the computer is still being used in conjunction with a system of paper record-keeping (a, g, k, m, n, o). This is a direct result of the limitations of the technology: like its contemporaries, such as the ICT 1500 and the IBM 1401, the Leo III did not have a screen, and all output took the form of paper printouts. Until the advent and spread of the networked terminal with its monitor, the most efficient way for a clerk to look up a worker's record remained consulting a paper computer printout stored in a filing cabinet. Automation of the office continued to include digital, mechanical, and a significant number of manual operations.

For "European pay," on the other hand, as with the Port Elizabeth computer, the inception of PAYE was a reason to accelerate computerization at Rand Mines.[139] Pirow had at the outset observed that "jobs for which a computer will be economic, may be divided into two groups: (1) Where a computer may be used as a replacement for labour on existing jobs. (2) Where a computer undertakes jobs that cannot be undertaken by any other means." Without elaborating on the latter, Pirow identifies and describes "Rand Mines applications that fall mainly into the first group, namely pay and stores."[140] He proceeds to detail the staffing of the company specially formed by Rand Mines, with Leo Computers, to manage its computing needs—in addition to twenty programmers working under a programming manager, three operators, one query clerk, two loaders, and ten data preparation clerks.[141] "The staff may seem large," Pirow concedes, "but . . . it is possible for the machine to carry out the work of 50 clerks in six hours running a week. At this rate the machine running 43 hours per week could carry out the work of some 360 clerks."[142] This figure is practically the same as that given in 1960 for Old Mutual's Perseus machine,[143] suggesting a widely circulated industry talking point.[144] It is clear that, like other large enterprises, Rand Mines foresaw tremendous savings in time and labor cost in computerization. "I may just mention," Pirow emphasizes during discussion, "that the reason that the Rand Mines Group went in for automation of the clerical procedures, first was that it was the easiest in which to show direct savings." The contrast is with production, where a saving through "technical advances" is less easy to show.[145] For the programming, operating, and clerical staff, it represents a tenfold saving. Pirow can still tell his audience that, although there has been no retrenchment of existing clerical staff—who are reassigned to tasks relating to the computer—there has also been no need to employ new clerical staff: "by the time the jobs started running on the computer the staff had decreased by roughly two years' turnover."[146] This seems to have been a typical scenario—and one regularly described in a one-sided way that downplays the longer-term effect of computerization on job openings. Pirow does not say what the relevant figure for two years' turnover is, but one suspects substantial job losses over time, given the scale of Rand Mines' operations. Yet, "at a time like the present," Pirow assures his audience, "when it is difficult to find good clerical staff, there is clearly no difficulty in finding jobs to be done."[147] The new programming and clerical jobs generated through computerization, even by 1963, may already have been starting to exceed the number of qualified applicants,[148] given that the boom of the 1960s meant that traditional clerical workers were also being employed in all the offices that were not automating through computers—those like Tlali's Metropolitan Radio, where Muriel would have been happy to hear that dividend checks mailed to Rand Mines' shareholders "are . . . passed through a Burroughs cheque signing machine which operates at a speed of 3,000 cheques per hour, and are then mechanically inserted into envelopes."[149] In any case, this was the situation at least until the end of the boom in the early 1970s and, for programmers, right through to the early 1980s.

As for the online networks that had become an integral part of our lives by the late 1970s, in reply to a question about the prospective use of an "automatic data transmission system," Pirow says, "I do believe, that in about 5 or ten years' time it will be unnecessary to continue the physical process which meant taking the punched paper tapes to the airport in the Free State, flying them here and delivering to the computer daily."[150] He was right, except that the technology would be in use in South Africa sooner than he expected.

Apartheid and Automation

The three SACAC conferences held in the 1960s revealed a contestation over the meaning of automation in South Africa, which continued to infuse SACAC's important study, *Industrial Automation in South Africa*, published in 1972. If Minister Jan Haak could, in his opening address to the 1969 conference, find a way of turning automation toward apartheid thinking, by envisaging the entry of white women into the workforce, in his address to the inaugural 1965 conference, he presented automation as a potential threat to the unskilled jobs done mostly by black Africans. He begins by speaking generally about the possible effects on employment in terms familiar to his audience: reduced labor need in the longer term, although possible increased need for unskilled operators in the short term, and so forth. When he switches to Afrikaans, as was conventional to do in the days when English and Afrikaans were the two official languages, he is not entirely consistent, unless one assumes that there is a bar to having black workers do both skilled and semiskilled work:

> The great number of unskilled workers over which we dispose in South Africa is, however, a problem that must properly be kept in mind. A rapidly developing country like South Africa usually experiences a shortage of skilled workers that in itself serves as an incentive for the introduction of automation. The unskilled worker, that is to say mainly the Bantu and the Coloured, can certainly be trained in automated industry but great care must be exercised that we do not apply automation in our labor-intensive industries, which are so necessary for the development of the Bantu areas and the employment of our great numbers of unskilled workers, since it can in some cases in fact aggravate our labor problems rather than solving them. In South Africa, it is thus under the circumstances desirable that things must be gone about selectively.[151]

Haak, who was then the deputy minister of economic affairs, then says that he does not "oppose the introduction of automation in South Africa. On the contrary, I want to encourage it."[152]

But Haak's listeners were quite capable of decoding apartheid doublespeak. In his presidential reply to Haak's address, Dr. Otto Brune observes that "the task of automation is . . . to relieve humanity from inhuman tasks. That . . . is a burden which a large proportion of our underdeveloped population is carrying. I don't think for example that it is natural for our Bantu to go and work in the dark and intemperate conditions underground nor that it is what they actually like to do. They like to dance, they like to entertain and they even have a taste for art."[153] Brune's racial paternalism nowadays invites unequivocal objection—not to say scornful rejection—but, at this gathering, among conservative white people, it is the mindset from which contestation comes.[154] A return to some version of African tribal life—"in surroundings which they will enjoy more, and in which they will be able to justify themselves economically"—following massive anticipated layoffs due to automation, on top of more than fifty years of proletarianization and a far longer history of land theft, is a fanciful notion. It also presents an extremely weak alternative to the politico-economic master plan being elaborated and implemented by Prime Minister H. F. Verwoerd and his government.[155] Yet, some of what Brune says corresponds to what we gather from *Muriel at Metropolitan*: Automation of office drudge work is highly desirable. The difference is that Tlali's novel gives no sense that the purpose of automation would be to facilitate the scenario contemplated by Brune, who, although once considered a pioneer in electrical circuit theory,[156] has ideas about black people that are horribly out of date.[157] The reality, ten years later, however, was of rising levels of black unemployment—the result not of automation but of a general decline in national economic performance.

In 1973, SACAC published its report *Industrial Automation in South Africa*. The survey, commissioned by the government, was conducted by SACAC in collaboration with the CSIR and called for "an objective, factual report to be drawn up about the present scope and future development of automation in the Republic taking into account the traditional development patterns."[158] We know from the addresses of government ministers at SACAC's conferences that "traditional" does not refer to something that has existed through time. Rather, it refers to the aspirations of apartheid thinkers for a future dispensation that would include the development of particular regions of the country under the political administration of the ethnic Bantustans. This is made clear when the terms of reference of the survey were specified to include, inter alia, "a factual survey to determine the present state and future development of automation in South Africa both in the industrial areas and in the Border Areas." The "borders" in question are not those shared with neighboring states such as Rhodesia, Botswana, and Mozambique but those with the invented "national states" such as Ciskei, Transkei, and Bophuthatswana. So-called border industries were subsidized by the government to decentralize development and slow the migration of Africans to the cities.[159] The period under investigation was 1970–1972.[160] Taking into account the methods used in surveys by the ILO in the 1960s, as well as in studies done in the Netherlands, the United Kingdom, and the United States,[161] the SACAC/CSIR researchers sent postal survey questionnaires to 1,907 "manufacturing establishments" and conducted follow-up interviews with 160 of them.[162] The basic definition of automation that it adopted was consistent with how automation was in the process of being redefined, internationally, in distinction to mechanization: "Mechanization = replacement of manual labour (operations on and transfer of products)[.] Automation = replacement of mental labour (control of processes)."[163] In practice, however, the report acknowledged that "automation cannot be unambiguously defined."[164] If, as I have argued, the *meaning* of automation cannot be reduced to a definition, it remains to deduce from other remarks what automation meant. A first step is to locate automation within the economic trends of the time, specifically the labor market.

How does the report understand its economic context? Noted among its limitations is that "the period during which the interviews were conducted lasted from the middle of 1970 to early 1972, the majority being conducted in 1971. During this period, the South African economy experienced a stagnation in its industrial growth rate, followed by signs of a recovery in 1972. Earlier, there had been a long sustained boom period during which many industrialists had invested in new equipment. As a result, there was evidence of overcapacity in some firms during the survey period. These fluctuations may have affected the views on automation expressed by industrialists."[165]

As for how these conditions influenced the labor market, the researchers observe that "during most of the survey period there was a manpower shortage and this problem was prominent during discussions on automation. However, the economic climate changed, and by the end of the survey a number of economic events eased the shortage, but did not eliminate it."[166] The economic downturn of the early 1970s is also reflected in articles in *Financial Mail* that reported a stabilization of pay levels for computer programmers.[167] Unlike in the SACAC report, this trend is not placed in context, and one would not know, reading these articles in isolation, that the underlying cause was a recession, rather than a change in the basic trajectory in computerization with its attendant effects on the labor market. By the mid-1970s, despite the general economic downturn in the country, there was again a shortage of programmers.[168]

Findings summarized in the SACAC report show that questions of labor saving due to automation were inextricably linked to the racial structure of the South African labor market: "The application of the Physical Planning and Utilization of Resources Act (1967), which restricts employment of Non-White labour in specified areas, caused some anxiety among industrialists. The general uncertainty as to whether this was going to change was very noticeable and was a factor influencing planning for automated plant."[169] This law gave the government the power to "control the establishment of new factories and the expansion of existing factories in urban areas if they required additional African workers."[170] Its goal was to limit African labor migration to the cities by forcing manufacturers to build factories in or near the Bantustans (the so-called border industries).[171] Reference was also made in the SACAC report to the effects of influx control, another more directly coercive aspect of grand apartheid's attempt to stem black urbanization, on the mobility of "Non-White labourers."[172]

Although the survey was of manufacturing concerns, it inevitably also gathered information about clerical work: "A few firms had hoped to save clerical labour by introducing computers but eventually found that they had to employ more staff. However, most firms had expected to employ more staff when computers were introduced. It was noted that many firms had to employ Non-Whites as punch operators because White female operators found the work unattractive and boring. Coloureds are employed for this purpose in the Cape, and Indians in Natal. Also this is a new avenue of employment for Asians on the Witwatersrand. Most programmers are White, presumably because of the high levels of education required."[173] This situation was confirmed by other sources.[174] It fit the pattern established by Mariotti, whereby semiskilled jobs are filled by black workers as fewer white workers are prepared to do them. Black data-capture staff are also "paid less than White staff."[175] The situation corresponds to what Muriel experienced at Metropolitan Radio. In a time of growing demand for labor, although it does not change the general economic outlook, this leads to significant changes in the labor market.

No report on automation in South Africa from this period would be complete without mentioning the shortage of skilled workers and calling for training.[176] It would have been logical to advocate for increased training generally—but this was apartheid South Africa, and the government commissioned the SACAC survey. Nevertheless, it is still shocking to read the report as calling for different training for different race groups: "Improved training facilities in the machinery industry, both for White artisans (to equip them for higher skills) and for Non-Whites (to prepare them for semiskilled operations), could encourage the use of sophisticated automated equipment."[177] The word *operations* is important here since the semiskilled job related to automation is invariably, in the report, that of "operator"—of a machine of some kind. And, increasingly, black and Coloured men were being hired as "operators." "General opinion," the survey finds, "is that Bantu could be used as fairly skilled operators if training is provided to overcome the lack of industrial tradition. This lack of technical training of Non-White operators, in general, is of concern to many manufacturers.... In South Africa, operators are mostly Non-White, as can be seen from the ratios of Non-White to White employees.... Vocational training for Non-White operators is therefore important, but in 1970 there were only 3 651 Non-White students in technical, secondary, trade and vocation schools and on advanced technical courses."[178] The government would train Africans in trades, but only for service in the Bantustans; hence the verisimilitude of Sibusiso Nyembezi's tacit allusion to "separate development" in his Zulu-language manual, *Learn More Zulu*: "Lapha kulendawo yakithi sinenhlanhla enkulu. Kukhona isikole esikhulu semisebenzi yezandla yezinhlobo ngezinhlobo" (Here in this place of ours we have great fortune. There is a big school for manual trades of several different kinds).[179] The expression *indawo yakithi*, which I have translated as "place of ours," could also be translated as "place of those who are of us," which would more clearly extract the grand apartheid ethno-nationalist subtext.

When the SACAC survey refers to trade unions, just as when Haak refers to labor organizations, it means white trade unions. This was before black trade unions were legalized. The white unions, according to management, do not object to automation, except when "its introduction changes the skills required for the job and makes it possible to employ Non-White semi-skilled workers where formerly skilled White workers were used."[180] Again, the common assumption is that, if white people, specifically organized white labor, do not oppose it, then black people can be employed in semiskilled jobs. If white workers do not want these jobs,[181] and black workers want them, it being claimed that "Bantu men gain substantial social status when they are employed at large machines but Bantu women were more attentive when tending automatic machines,"[182] then black people can be employed. At certain junctures, however, the demand for semiskilled labor, and eventually for skilled labor (in computing), exceeds the numbers of white workers who can be absorbed into these jobs. At those junctures, it starts to make little difference what organized white labor wants because economic growth has come to depend on a deracialization of the labor market. By the 1970s, and perhaps even earlier, the "job reservation" that was designed to protect white jobs was largely symbolic.[183]

The report concluded that, ultimately, automation did and would not affect total employment in manufacturing.[184] It observed, however, that mechanization had a "greater effect on the number of operators than the subsequent development whereby automatic control is added."[185] It was almost in passing that the benefits of automation for improving working conditions for black workers were mentioned; evidently it was not a key consideration for the businesses surveyed: "Only a few manufacturers mentioned that they had installed automation to improve the operators' working environment, but it was significant that many more mentioned that they were thinking along those lines now. The improvements had usually been made in hot and dusty conditions where remote monitoring and control could be applied, as in rubber processing plant[s] and foundries. Where chemical fumes made conditions unpleasant, mechanized handling is often used."[186]

This must have meant that manufacturers were responding to what their workers wanted. Increasing numbers of these workers were African. Capital and labor were determining how industry was organized and how machines would play a part in that process. Government policy, embodied in the Physical Planning and Utilization of Resources Act and other laws of grand apartheid, was an obstruction. The discourse on mechanization and automation had thus evolved to produce divergent meanings. One way of looking at this evolution is to observe how the effects on employment of mechanization and automation changed from the 1960s to the 1980s. In the earlier stages of computerization as undertaken by the City of Port Elizabeth and Rand Mines, there were still unanswered questions about how computers would affect employment, the result in part of confusion created by computer companies trying to make a sale and obfuscation by management of the effects on employment. By 1972 and the SACAC report, however, the debate and discourse on automation and computation had settled into a definite pattern. The question, for capital, was no longer "Will machines replace workers?" but "Where will we find enough workers to operate—and program—our machines?" These questions were, inevitably, addressed in ways that were informed by the dynamics of the apartheid labor market, which was a distorted one. Apartheid policy had created a "shortage" of labor.

The meaning of automation in South Africa thus changed accordingly. In the 1960s, from the point of view of government, it meant keeping-white and barring-black in semiskilled occupations. By the late 1970s, from the perspective of capital, it had, in the skilled work of computer programming, started to mean making-black. But it is the years in between that are most revealing. During that time, we witness a change that began at the very moment that apartheid's rulers issued their most ambitious and extravagant ideas relating to the introduction of machines. We see from Miriam Tlali's *Muriel at Metropolitan* how keeping-white, as apartheid thinkers saw it in the 1960s, would have to involve introducing machines to replace or prevent the employment of black people—unless, as a subtext of this techno-political fantasy, more white women could be drawn into the labor force. This was the theory, the government line under late apartheid, from which practice down at the plant, or in the office, clearly diverged. Capital sought profit, and black women and men sought jobs. Increasingly, those jobs involved the operating and programming of machines.

Miriam Tlali was not the only writer to respond critically to these developments. The political wish that formed the background to these developments was, in a different guise, a version of the old South African colonial fantasy of a world without African labor, which J. M. Coetzee describes so well in his essay on idleness in South Africa.[187]

As I show in the next chapter, a thread running through Coetzee's writing is the meaning of work—of white labor, black labor, and the labor of writing. The meaning of work provides a context for making sense of those productions of the young Coetzee that, predating his novels, are neither writing nor not—his computer poetry.

2

Computer Poetry

"Sometimes he sits and types the whole day on an old typing machine."
   "What does he type?"
   "I don't know. Any rubbish. Sometimes letters, love letters."
   "Love letters! To whom?"
   "To us. The other women who are sitting there, selling. He passes the letters over to us behind his wife's back. (We both laugh loudly.) What can you expect? He's lazy. Doesn't want to go and work like other men."

MIRIAM TLALI, "Soweto Speaking
to Miriam Tlali," *Staffrider* 1, no. 2

At almost the same time as Rand Mines began using a computer to automate its payroll and keep track of its migrant workers' contracts, another aspiring South African writer, whose first novel would be published by Ravan Press a year before it published Miriam Tlali's *Muriel at Metropolitan*, programmed a computer to produce poetry. The writer was J. M. Coetzee, and the novel, published in 1974, was *Dusklands*. As Rebecca Roach has shown, there are continuities among Coetzee's computer poems, his later work in computer-aided stylistic analysis, his ideas about linguistic automatism, and aspects of his early fiction.[1] But Coetzee's computer poems first emerged before he embarked on an academic career and before he made a name for himself as an author. He now regards them as belonging to his juvenilia.[2] Still in his early twenties, Coetzee was living in London, where, from 1962 to 1963, he worked as a programmer at IBM.[3] Many years later, he fictionalized his time in England in *Youth* (2002). The story he tells there is remarkable for its emphasis on work. Using a computer to engage in automatic writing brings to the fore an automation of labor. To the relationship between his computer poetry and his literary theory, *Youth* adds insight into how his early career in programming relates to a preoccupation with labor that suffuses nearly all of his writing. It also allows us to make connections, not typically imagined, between Coetzee's writing and Tlali's. In different ways, both writers explore a set of narrative possibilities circumscribed by the laws, political economy, and practices that defined what it meant to work under apartheid. What also connects the two authors is an acute awareness of the machine.

Coetzee and Tlali, however, are even more directly connected than that. When Ravan Press launched the first issue of *Staffrider* magazine in March 1978, it showcased the work of writers' groups from Soweto and other townships near Johannesburg. Striving for national representativeness, it also included work by writers identified as being from Durban and Cape Town. The issue opens with Miriam Tlali's column, Soweto Speaking. As one of three writers listed in the "Cape Town" section,[4] J. M. Coetzee, whose second novel, *In the Heart of the Country*, was published by Ravan in 1978, contributed a text entitled "Hero and Bad Mother in Epic, a Poem."[5]

When I first read "Hero and Bad Mother," I was researching an English Honors paper on South African literary magazines of the 1970s and 1980s. For somebody interested in politically engaged writing, the first issue of *Staffrider*, with its cover photograph of a high barbed wire fence from an unforgettable sequence by Ralph Ndawo of an African boy climbing over it, was an obvious place to start.[6] Although Coetzee's poem's seemingly random combinations of unusual words appealed to me, the poem seemed out of place—an avant-garde experiment among poems, stories, and reportage in the style of protest literature and committed social realism. "Hero and Bad Mother" opens with the following lines: "dusk seeps up the entrail of the seaborn nude / the vegetable sleeps in its circle / the bedroom drowses."[7]

Tlali's Soweto Speaking came with a note from the editors relating her interviews with three working people to her novel *Muriel at Metropolitan*, "based on her own experiences while working at an 'HP' radio store. After the book's appearance, Miriam Tlali was approached by many people who had 'a story to tell, but how do I tell it?'"[8] The editors drew parallels between Tlali and Studs Terkel, whose *Working* (1972) is a classic oral history of working lives and, as the editors observe, "was a new kind of book which turned 'everyman' into an author."[9] Announcing it as a regular feature, the editors invited "all our readers to speak of their lives. Miriam Tlali can be contacted through STAFFRIDER, 105 Corbett Place, De Korte / Bertha Street corner, Braamfontein. Telephone 724-4033."[10]

The editors' reference to Studs Terkel, aimed at encouraging people to tell their stories, takes us into the changing nature of work. One of the things that a reader of *Working* notices half a century after it was published is that the voices in it come from a time when mechanization and automation of certain kinds of work were rapidly increasing.[11] Frequently drawing a distinction between the work of the hand and the machine, testifying to the dangers of working with machinery, and expressing the sense that as a worker, one has been reduced to a machine, computer, or "servomechanism,"[12] the men and women whom Terkel meets sometimes express ambivalence. "Automation?" a Chicago steelworker asks. "Depends how it is applied. It frightens me if it puts me out in the street. It doesn't frighten me if it shortens my work week. You read that little thing: what are you going to do when this computer replaces you? Blow up computers. (Laughs.)."[13]

Although Tlali's is a world without computers, what is striking about the testimony she records in *Soweto Speaking* is that, when it touches on machines, it reveals little of the kind of ambivalence that Terkel found when he spoke with American workers. As in *Muriel at Metropolitan*, there is a demand, even an enthusiasm, for the machine. This is evident when Tlali interviews Mrs. Leah Koae, a dressmaker who began sewing at the age of twelve. "I had great interest in sewing," she tells Tlali. She relates her story after the completion of her "J.C."[14] and training at a school for weaving blankets and rugs in Natal:

I came back to Johannesburg where I found work in a factory— a clothing factory. First I worked in the office doing clerical work. But in my heart I felt I still wanted to sew. You know what it is when one likes to do a thing.

I would be sent to take something into the sewing-room, and when I saw girls sitting at their machines, busy, I would feel the urge to join them. Even the sound of the machines would make me wonder when I would be able to tread on my own machine and sew like them.

I went to a white woman I knew and asked her to teach me sewing by an electric traddle [*sic*] machine. She did. And I have been sewing ever since.

You know what made me go for that tuition? Pay. Weekly pay. You would have to work very, very hard and sew many, many garments per day—but when you get your pay, it would not be worth the amount of labour you put into your work. It was *so* little! One day I sat down and thought seriously to myself and said, *no*. No, I can't work so hard for another person.

I went and bought my own machine. And I stayed at home and worked at home.

—What machine is it, Singer?

—No, Hostess.

—Oh.

And I am still using it even now. All these years. I have been using it sewing for you and your children, haven't I? Yes, I see now that I am still alive like all the other people who go to work every morning. That machine gives me a livelihood. I am still managing with that very machine. I buy food and I pay rent. Now, if you want to see some of the things that I sew with that machine, I'll show you.[15]

Like the computer operator at ICT with her "second class matriculation," Mrs. Koae, with her "J.C.," is qualified for office work. But, as she explains, working in an office at a clothing factory only makes her "feel the urge to join" the other women at their machines. The "sound of the machines" makes her imagine how it would be "to tread on my own machine and to sew like them." For Mrs. Koae, the machine is an extension of her body; what she emphasizes is the action of the treadle that makes it run. Her wondering begins when she hears sounds, which arouse in her an urge to work—which, in one respect, is to be able to produce, at will, more of those sounds. Mrs. Koae's economic reasoning—the independence that would allow her to avoid being exploited as a factory worker—is inseparable from her enjoyment of sewing, and sewing with a machine, which she expresses in such sensuous terms. If the word *machine* is powerfully invested through its repetition, the meaning of the words "my own machine" changes from their first use, when Mrs. Koae is describing factory work, to when she buys a Hostess sewing machine of her own. The "own" of physical interaction with a sewing machine converges with ownership of what Marx called the "means of production." Mrs. Koae is not doing piecework. In the early decades of the twentieth century, demand in South

Africa for sewing machines, adjusted for population size, approached demand in Europe.[16] All over the world, household demand for machines was greater than from industrial manufacturing.[17] Although this demand may have been driven by a call for clothing made at home,[18] as Mrs. Koae's story shows, that demand may not have come solely from the user's own household.

The Singer, synonymous for generations with the sewing machine and with women's work, has also been a sign of poverty and of women who labor to make ends meet: "and my mother whose legs, for our tireless hunger, pedal, pedal, both by day and by night, and I am even awakened at night by these tireless legs pedalling the night and by the Singer, bitterly biting into the soft flesh of the night as my mother pedals, pedals for our hunger every day, every night."[19] This is from Aimé Césaire's *Notebook of a Return to the Native Land*, first published in 1939. Perhaps this is the sort of scene, before her mind's eye, that prompts Tlali to ask, "Singer?" But the picture presented by Mrs. Koae is different. Through her machine, she achieves an integration of work and pleasure, a pleasure that extends to the teasing and gossip that ensue among the women at Mrs. Koae's house when Tlali tries on a dress that she brings out to show her.[20] Work shades into play. Writing history in a minor key, I note how, at the edges of this scene, a familiar landmark appears of history writ large. "The kids are no longer dressing up for Xmas," Mrs. Koae observes. "They changed since the unrests year before last. They no longer celebrate Christmas."[21] This is how 1976 registers in the dressmaker's house.

By drawing our attention to how people talk about work, the editors of *Staffrider*'s preface to Tlali provide a signpost for the reading that I am performing. By contrast, the editors never explained that "Hero and Bad Mother" was a computer poem (and it is not clear that they knew). This Coetzee would disclose later.[22] The juxtaposition of Coetzee and Tlali in its first issue says a great deal about what *Staffrider* uniquely was in South African literary history (a collaboration to begin with between loosely connected white writers and more organized black writers' groups). But I do not want to use that uniqueness to explain away the copresence of their works. Once it is understood in its own context of production, Coetzee's poem says as much about work and its incipient mechanization and automation as Tlali's reportage and fiction. An academic article by Coetzee on computer poetry that he published in 1979 did hint, through the vocabulary in some of its examples, at the means he employed to write "Hero and Bad Mother." But it was not until the publication of *Youth* that Coetzee's readership at large received an account of how he came to write computer poems (a poem published in 1963 in a University of Cape Town student journal was not generally noted until Coetzee scholars began to refer to it).[23] It was only when computer printouts dating back to Coetzee's days with IBM—and ICT, where he worked for eighteen months after leaving IBM[24]—came to light that the extent of his experiments with the art form became apparent.

The protagonist of *Youth* is called John. Coetzee's book places John's computer poems squarely in the context of work, using them to provoke a reflection on art and authorship in an age of automation and computerization. Like Tlali's *Muriel at Metropolitan*, parts of Coetzee's *Youth* are office fiction. But the poems that it describes its protagonist programming a computer to print are literature of the office in a more immediate way. It is as if Tlali's Muriel, who did not work in an office equipped with programmable machines, were to have used the addressograph at Metropolitan to stamp out copies of verse formatted in the three or four lines that a standard addressograph could print—but that is a story that neither Tlali nor anybody else has written. Whereas Tlali owned a typewriter, and wrote using it at her home in Soweto, as well as at the YWCA,[25] neither John nor J. M. Coetzee would have been able to produce their poems without access to a mainframe computer at work. This was true for most authors of computer poems that appeared in the years before the advent of the personal computer and commercially available word-processing software. Coetzee stands out among the authors of early computer poems that we know about. Whereas the others were at universities and research institutes, Coetzee was employed in business; it was at IBM, in 1962 or 1963, that Coetzee (and not his protagonist John, whose experiments take place at International Computers) began his experiments.

As I detail in the next section, John, in *Youth*, guiltily views his use of a computer to produce poetry as making writing into a form of mass production. Like any machine, whether it weaves textiles or generates text, the computer relieves its user of work. John finds this relief morally problematic because it gives him an unfair advantage over his fellow poets. But it represents a more profound problem when it is understood, as it is in Coetzee by implication, as relieving the *white* person of work. Historically, white people in South Africa have avoided doing certain kinds of work. They have also concealed the fact that they have employed, as they once enslaved, brown and black people to do it instead. As Coetzee writes about the disappearance of African labor in colonial pastoral writing:

> Pastoral in South Africa . . . has a double tribute to pay. To satisfy the critics of rural retreat, it must portray labour; to satisfy the critics of colonialism, it must portray white labour. What inevitably follows is the occlusion of black labour from the scene: the black man becomes a shadowy presence flitting across the stage now and then to hold a horse or serve a meal. . . . The constraints of the genre . . . make silence about the black man the easiest of an uneasy set of options. If the work of the hands on a particular patch of earth, digging, ploughing, planting, building, is what inscribes it as the property of its occupiers *by right*, then the hands of black serfs doing the work had better not be seen.[26]

The fact that, in terms of Coetzee's analysis, there is a clear logic that runs from perception to action — "if . . . then" — means that it can be applied, beyond literature, to any discourse governed by such a logic, no matter how perverse. Think of Minister Haak's 1969 opening address to SACAC, in which he speculated that automation would bring more white women into the workforce. Haak discourses at a time when the farm was no longer as central to the economy as were mine and factory and office. Whether the product that the work of the hand gives the occupier a right to is mineral, industrial, or agricultural, Coetzee's analysis suggests that the drive to keep certain occupations white, despite a growing shortage of white workers, is more than simply economic. It has a logic, but that logic exceeds economic reason. The workplace is designated white, but are there white people working there? Instituting a right to property, the logic is, in a word, political.

Countering this political logic in symbolic terms brings about an interesting bifurcation of views on labor automation. As the 1972 report on *Industrial Automation in South Africa* acknowledged, an increase in automation in factories, on farms, and in offices frees workers from hazardous, exhausting, and mindless tasks. This is what Tlali and her social class see in it for themselves. But because, historically, white people have avoided such tasks, and assigned them to black people, the soul-searching white "occupier" may not have had labor relief as his goal. In fact, for him, such relief may be ethically wrong. The first thing that he thinks he needs to do is reverse the "occlusion of black labour from the scene," break the "silence about the black man." Having made plain who actually does the work, the next thing he thinks he needs to do is break with the racial division of labor by performing the work himself. For him, therefore, the meaning of automation is different: it relieves him of doing work that he sees as a form of symbolic reparation. In his mind, the most exhausting work of the hand is to be done by him, not, as with some of Gandhi's experiments of an earlier era,[27] to counter actual mechanization. Rather, it is performed in order to counter, symbolically, the stigma of *kafferwerk, hotnotswerk*—the hard manual work disdained by white people as being for black or Coloured workers[28]—as we witness at the beginning of *Summertime* (2009), the final installment of Coetzee's fictionalized "autre-biography."[29] Having returned to South Africa, John lays a cement slab in his Cape Town yard, performing, as he tells himself, the work that "people like him" have eschewed historically.[30] In convoluted fashion, this act both coincides with and contradicts how automation is being discoursed about by apartheid ideologues: as a measure not for easing work for Africans but for replacing them as workers, or prospective workers, with white people. Whereas Haak's prospective African workers would have been skilled, those imagined by Coetzee's John are, perhaps anachronistically, unskilled. But the main difference between Haak and John is the purpose of their replacement. At an oblique angle to the tortuous adventures of the concept in South Africa in the era when he came of age as a writer, Coetzee's work registers an ambivalence toward automation that is historically motivated and overdetermined.

In the Land of the Poet

Toward the end of *Youth*, John programs a computer at Cambridge University to generate lines of poetry: "Although Atlas is not a machine built to handle textual materials, he uses the dead hours of the night to get it to print out thousands of lines in the style of Pablo Neruda, using as a lexicon a list of the most powerful words in *The Heights of Macchu Picchu*, in Nathaniel Tarn's translation."[31]

In *Youth*, shortly before John programs the Atlas computer to print out the "pseudo-poems,"[32] he comes to an awareness of his position within a stratified division of labor. As a programmer employed by

ICT, which is contracted by Cambridge University, he is, he realizes, a "skilled workman" or "hired hand." He identifies with Jude Fawley, whom Thomas Hardy places at Oxford, as a stonemason and self-taught outsider.[33] In a double rhetorical turn found frequently in Coetzee's fiction and fictionalized memoirs, John's coming to awareness is absorbed with the gravity of a moral lesson.

First John sees himself from a new perspective—which may be that of another protagonist or projected by himself. Given its second turn, that perspective provides the content for a stern, and sometimes hyperbolic, moral imperative:

> From a certain point of view, he is merely one of a team of professional programmers from the computer industry that the Cambridge Mathematics department has hired to implement its ideas. . . . From that point of view, he himself is merely a skilled workman in the pay of the university, not a collaborator entitled to speak on an equal footing with these brilliant young scientists. . . . He is here by luck and nothing else. He could never have studied at Cambridge, was never good enough to win a scholarship. He must continue to think of himself as a hired hand: if not, he will become an impostor in the same way that Jude Fawley amid the dreaming spires of Oxford was an impostor.[34]

There is much that could be said about the way John's psychology works; there is a certain sophistry in his telling himself that he will be an impostor unless he thinks of himself in a certain way when he is content to let the Cambridge mathematicians allow him to save face by not telling him what he thinks he should tell himself.[35] Private anguish is the price that he, like other Coetzee protagonists, pays for the socially necessary fiction, the "whispered agreement."

Why must John think of himself as a hired hand? It is less his psychology than the possible source of the imperative that interests me. For there are strong hints, if not in the designation "skilled workman"—which he could justly claim to share with Jude Fawley—then in "hired hand," of an even steeper stratification of work in which certain workers are employed only when there is a specific, usually temporary, need for their labor. In South Africa, this was the status of the majority of African workers and of many Coloured workers. In England, John experiences discrimination in the labor market that he would have been unlikely to have encountered firsthand in South Africa. A persistent subtext of *Youth* is that, as an expatriate, who may not remain in the country unless he has a job, John receives a practical lesson about white privilege to which he may not have been exposed had he remained in South Africa.

Youth, as Christina Lupton has noted, is a book about work.[36] In her brief suggestions, Lupton concentrates on its contribution to the question of leisure time and its impact on workers' reading habits. For Lupton, who contrasts Coetzee's John with Leonard Bast from Forster's *Howard's End*, who has time to read literature after working hours, *Youth* cannily anticipates the twenty-four seven work pattern of our era, in which clearly demarcated leisure time disappears: John begins by reading in his spare time (IBM), which shrinks as he starts to take his work home with him in the evenings (ICT). This is a compelling interpretation (although it should be noted that there is another turn, which eludes Lupton's distinction between work and leisure, as John begins using his nights to program computers to write poetry).[37] But behind the book's subtle insight into changes in the working day, there is something else—concerning the division of labor and the protagonist's growing awareness of it.

A conflict relating to work suffuses *Youth*: John *must* work—but he *won't* work. Ostensibly, he *must not* work, in order to be a writer, a poet.[38] John therefore avoids working, pretends to work, and, in certain instances, when he is actually working, works more than he has to. For John, work is complicated: it is never simply work. As *Youth* shows us, the imperative to work involves John's identification with his father, who was for some time out of work and whom John thinks must then have pretended to go to work.[39] "He is not going to be like his father," he tells himself.[40] The urge to work also involves a will not to be dependent on his mother, who, for example, sends him sheepskin mittens from South Africa when he complains about the London cold.[41]

But he also must work because, if he does not have a job, he will have to leave the United Kingdom. And that is how he comes to experience the effects of discrimination in the labor market; to be sure, he had to apply for a work permit to work at IBM, but he had no trouble landing the job, and it is only on reflection that he seems to realize that IBM might have needed to make a special case for him, and he later reproaches IBM for informing the Home Office that he is unemployed.[42]

When *Youth* connects the automation involved in computerization with the division of labor, it does so obliquely. Work displaces writing—unless John is writing computer code—but, more generally, the work of the hand, including writing, is being displaced by machines through automation and computerization. Certain kinds of work are starting to be done by machines and computers, and certain kinds of workers are being put out of work. Such is the logic of technological change, a logic in which he realizes that his experiments with computer poems implicate him. Finding it hard to write—his poetry and short stories fall flat—he programs a computer to generate lines of verse, and this, in turn, raises questions about the work of writing and authorship.

A series of questions address the effects of technological change on poetry and the other arts:

> Is it fair to be using mechanical aids to writing—fair to other poets, fair to the dead masters? The Surrealists wrote words on slips of paper and shook them up in a hat and drew words at random to make up lines. William Burroughs cuts up pages and shuffles them and puts the bits together. Is he not doing the same kind of thing? Or do his huge resources—what other poet in England, in the world, has a machine of this size at his command—turn quantity into quality? Yet might it not be argued that the invention of computers has changed the nature of art, by making the author and the condition of the author's heart irrelevant? On the Third Programme he has heard music from the studios of Radio Cologne, music spliced together from electronic whoops and crackles and street noise and snippets of old recordings and fragments of speech. Is it not time for poetry to catch up with music?[43]

The drift of these questions is to position the computer within a history of mechanization of writing, in which, as a stage in the evolution of printing, it is an advance over, say, the typewriter. Early mainframe computers did not have visual display monitors, meaning that their output was available only in the form of a printout. It is this feature that allies the Atlas computer with the typewriter, even if, as John knows, it "is not a machine built to handle textual materials."[44] Word processing comes later. What makes a computer different from other printing machines, however, is that it can be programmed to select by itself the combinations of words it prints out. Although this is not explained in *Youth*, the programs that Coetzee himself wrote tell the computer to generate combinations that, although produced in lines with a recognizable syntactical structure, are random.[45] A programmed machine works automatically in the sense that, while a program is running, no human intervention is required. Whether or not we believe that computers think, while the computer is executing this particular program, its operator is relieved of the cognitive labor of selection. In this way, the most experimental of art making is continuous with the labor process, where the replacement of the worker by the automatic machine exercises workers and management alike.

This continuity explains how John arrives at his next set of observations and questions. What his experiments have in common with the Surrealists and William Burroughs is random selection. The difference is that he has at his disposal a computer, meaning that he can produce far more of these random selections, and do so at far greater speed, than the Surrealists could by manually drawing pieces of paper from a hat or Burroughs could by cutting and splicing.[46] Implied is that the products of Burroughs's and the Surrealists' experiments were of lesser quality than the work of contemporary writers—"other poets"—and "the dead masters." But with a computer printing out "thousands of lines,"[47] there is a chance that some of them will be as good, or better than, those produced by poets who "write from the heart." Hence the question, "Do his huge resources . . . turn quantity into quality?" As American poet Howard Nemerov acknowledged in a 1967 essay,[48] the logic behind this question is not entirely fanciful; what Coetzee himself did when composing "Hero and Bad Mother" was select a small number of phrases from the lines printed out by the computer. Those were the lines that Coetzee found interesting.[49] And, in his earliest known computer poem, in *The Lion and the Impala*, he selects computer-generated phrases, edits them, and combines them in a new syntax.[50]

John's first series of questions relates to the mechanization and automation of the writing process, without precluding the possibility that the productions of a programmed computer might be equal to, or better than, those of human poets. The next pair of questions, however, address the implications of his experiments from a different perspective—even if it is not clear what, if any, moral lesson he will draw from it. "Yet," John asks himself, having heard experimental music, "might it not be argued that the invention of computers has changed the nature of art, by making the author and the condition of the author's heart irrelevant? . . . Is it not time for poetry to catch up to music?"

John's reflections ally him with computer artists of the 1960s, many of whom also saw computers as having changed the nature of art and authorship. The underlying argument thus changes: what is relevant now is not that he is a worker but that he is an author—or aspires to become one. And because being an author involves not as much labor as public recognition, which is arguably all that it essentially involves, being an author is of a different order than being a worker.[51] In that sense, the author does not even have to be an artist—if being an artist means writing "from the heart." He can even appropriate the work of other authors. The question of labor is displaced. John realizes, against the grain of his previous assumptions, that because "the computer poems," which are also "the Neruda poems," bring him notoriety beyond the world of the little magazine, they are enough to make him an author: "He sends a selection of his Neruda poems to a friend in Cape Town, who publishes them in a magazine he edits. A local newspaper reprints one of the computer poems with a derisive commentary. For a day or two, back in Cape Town, he is notorious as the barbarian who wants to replace Shakespeare with a machine."[52] The joke is supposed to be on Cape Town, on the provinces, and on John's seeking after provincial fame, but what it also shows is that John is getting wise to what it really means to be a "poet" in an age of modern publicity.

This is perhaps *Youth's* last answer to the question of what John learns in England, the ultimate turn of its irony in relation to its epigraph from Goethe: "Wer den Dichter will verstehen / muß in Dichters Lande gehen."[53] If the poet is not simply a worker, but is an author by virtue of being publicly recognized—whether because of a readership, through notoriety, or simply because of copyright law and legal deposit[54]—it may be that whether he wrote what he wrote himself or appropriated it from Pablo Neruda, or even whether a computer generated the poems, is irrelevant to what it means to be a poet. The question of whether the use of "mechanical aids" is "fair" is relevant only to the extent that writers are like other workers. That John even poses the question in this way shows that he is naive. It also shows, paradoxically, that, just as his labor as a writer is replaced by that of a machine, he has

inadvertently discovered how to elude the division of labor governing his professional sphere by becoming an author. If, in the rhetoric
of *Youth*, John's realizations tend to turn into moral imperatives, then
here such a turn is conspicuously absent. In the realm of authorship,
where fairness to other writers is out of the question because fairness
is a criterion that applies to competition among workers, it is left un-
clear what criterion might inform such an imperative. More typically,
as in the case of Miriam Tlali, who struggled to make a living from her
writing,[55] the antagonists were not other writers but publishers, with
whom proceeds were shared.

Poetry on the Mainframe

Coetzee was not the only one programming computers to write poetry.
Was he aware of similar experiments dating back to the 1950s in the
United Kingdom, Germany, and the United States? In his comprehensive study of early computer poetry, C. T. Funkhouser refers to these
experiments as a "predominantly disconnected movement, without
central figures or theories."[56] Just as Funkhouser overlooks Coetzee's
computer poems, which were published only in South African magazines, it is quite possible that Coetzee did not know what other digital
experimentalists were doing. He has never referred to other computer
poets, although, many years after his first experiments, he was keeping
up with academic work in poetics and stylistics on the use of computers for the automatic generation of sentences, some of which was based
on Noam Chomsky's ideas about generative grammar.[57] A result of
this reciprocal lack of reference is that, in the minds of most scholars,
South African arts remained until recently largely disconnected from
the international avant-garde response to computing. One of the goals
of my book is to change the received scholarly view.

Whether or not Coetzee knew about what others were doing when
he first began to program computers to write poems, what we can see is
that certain features of how his programming works are similar to what
others were doing. Whether the artist used a computer to manipulate
sounds, graphics, or words, the use of a pseudo-random number generator had, by the 1970s, practically become standard practice.[58] With
computer poetry, a random number generator would be used to extract
words from a computer's memory, where they had been stored by the
programmer at addresses corresponding to specific numerical values.

With each iteration of the random number generator, something is printed out—a word, a series of words, with or without patterning—depending on what format the computer had been programmed to produce, subject to the capabilities of its hardware. For what is regarded as one of the earliest examples of the form, dating from 1959, the German computer scientist Theo Lutz drew his vocabulary from Kafka's *The Castle*. He used a random number generator, as part of fifty lines of code, to help produce the resulting combinations:

NICHT JEDER BLICK IST NAH. KEIN DORF IST SPAET.
EIN SCHLOSS IM FREI UND JEDER BAUER IST FERN.
JEDER FREMDE IST FERN. EIN TAG IST SPAET.
JEDES HAUS IST DUNKEL. EIN AUGE IST TIEF.[59]

Coetzee gave a first account of his experiments in "Computer Poem," a two-page article published in *The Lion and the Impala*, a University of Cape Town student journal, in 1963. There he is strikingly tongue in cheek, compared to the anguished reflections in *Youth* about authorship. The piece also gives no hint of the dissatisfaction with IBM that John feels in *Youth*, unless the elision of the company name when he mentions the computer he used, and its location, is to be read as such a sign and not as a maintaining of discretion and an accumulation of cachet through reserve: "This [is] a poem generated by the 1401 computer at 58, Newman St., London, W.1. and edited by me."[60]

POEM (EX COMPUTER)	POEM (EDITED)
Dawn Birds Stream	Dawn, birds, a stream, a calm morning.
Calm-Morning	You stand among the trees alone and tense.
You) Stand-Among	
Forest	You have cried.
Alone Tense	You spend the nights away from me,
You) Cry	Terrified, rapt,
You) Spend-The-Nights	Among owls and black men,
I) Away-From	Hoping for violence.[61]
Terrified Rapt	
Owls Blackmen	
You) Hope Violence	

Coetzee describes "the programme (written by me) which generated the poem" as "comparatively speaking, primitive," adding that "without some editing the poem would be, simply, boring."[62] He then indicates how a "more sophisticated programme would do most of the work now done by the editor."[63]

you lie	Action-present
On the Bed	Place
Alone	Manner
You stood once	Action-past
You think	Action-present
In the bedroom	Place
Gloomy	Manner
Hopeless	Manner[64]

Although neither of Coetzee's programs is reproduced, and neither apparently survives, what the respective results show is an evolution in his programming. The first poem, "ex computer," appears to have been generated using a program that formats input—a list of words—according to "types," in this case grammatical parts of speech or combinations thereof. From these types, the computer selects at random in order to arrange the words in new sequences. This reading is suggested by the apparent recurrence of types in lines five and nine, and possibly also in lines ten and eleven. Without seeing more of the poem, and in the absence of the word list or program, however, it is impossible to be certain of this.

What the second program did is explained more clearly. "The poem consists of eight statements based on the elementary paradigm illustrated" by the lines quoted previously. If I understand correctly what Coetzee means by "based on the elementary paradigm," then the program tells the computer to format input by type—there are four types—and to format output by repeatedly combining the types, selection from within which is random, in a regular order—as would resemble a natural language or simulate poetic speech in a natural language. On this reading, although the words or phrases within each type are randomly selected, in what order the types are selected from would be invariable: 1, 2, 3, 4, 1, 2, 3, 3. After each eight lines, the program would repeat the random selection, moving through the types in the same order.

This is the type of computer poetry that Funkhouser calls "slotted poems," meaning that the output places the parts of speech into "slots" that simulate the grammatical regularity of natural language.[65] Coetzee summarizes the result, introducing a play on the word *editor* relevant also for his later *Staffrider* poem: "The computer is provided with the vocabularies, the structure of the poem and its programme, which tells it among other things to go on generating poems until its vocabularies are exhausted, i.e. until all possible poems with the given structure and words have been written. The editor now wades through what has been printed (in this case 2100 poems at the rate of 75 poems per minute), makes his selection, reduces it to standard form, and sends it to the editor."[66]

The only surviving program from Coetzee's time at IBM—as far as we know—exists in the form of old computer printouts preserved at the Harry Ransom Center at the University of Texas.[67] Because these printouts also include the database of words used by Coetzee and the resulting poems, it is possible to be precise about how the program worked. As Robert Garner, who heads the Computer History Museum's 1401 restoration team in Mountain View, California, informed me, Coetzee's program was written in FORTRAN II, the language used to program the IBM 7090 computer, which was the larger and more powerful of the two mainframe computers in the machine room at Newman Street, the smaller being the 1401.[68] This would mean that, if Coetzee began his poetry programming for the 1401, as he notes in *The Lion and the Impala*, when he ran his program at the end of May 1963, on what may well have been his last day of employment at IBM,[69] he was using the 7090. This surprises Robert, by training a hardware engineer, given the cost of processing time on the 7090 and its power as a state-of-the-art scientific computer, used those days by NASA, for example, in its space program.[70] In addition, as Robert points out, the 1401 offered advantages for text manipulation over the 7090. It was able to handle words of more than six letters—hence the longer words in the verses published in *The Lion and the Impala*. In the mainframe era, however, others were employing the 7090 for purposes not anticipated by its designers. In 1962, American digital artist Michael Noll used Bell Laboratories' 7090 to produce graphics with a microfilm printer.[71] Whereas Noll wrote his own randomizing subroutine, Coetzee appears to have used one that was newly part of the FORTRAN II library (or inbuilt functions of a programming language).

On May 30, 1963, Coetzee programmed the 7090 to generate 120 lines of poetry that would be printed out by the 1403 printer on the green-and-white-striped continuous stacked paper used with IBM systems. Here are the first few lines:

YOU	STAND	/	INTO	MOULD	/	WONDRG
WE	MOVE	/	INTO	MOULD	/	SAD
YOU	LIE	/	WITH	LEAVES	/	PENSVE
I	MOVE	/	BY	ROCKS	/	DREAMG
I	STAND	/	AMONG	ROCKS	/	SAD
THEY	STAND	/	AMONG	SKY	/	COLD
YOU	STAND	/	IN	TREES	/	ALONE[72]

The first thing to note is that, compared with the two samples discussed by Coetzee in *The Lion and the Impala*, this program is arranging the words in discrete lines, instead of breaking the line to make the words come out in a continuous scroll. Reflecting this evolution, Coetzee titles his program "Line Generator."[73] Syntax that was evidently manually typed as a feature of the data input is now being generated automatically. Instead of repeatedly printing one "type" below the other in a regular order, they are arranged from left to right in that order, introducing a line break after the program has iterated randomly through the five types. Another thing to note is that text generated by an IBM 7090 or 1401 computer on a 1403 printer, or similar system, is always in capital letters. You can see this also in Alison Knowles and James Tenney's *The House of Dust* (1967), which was programmed using FORTRAN IV and subsequently run on a Siemens mainframe computer.[74] Other elements of the system also appealed to Knowles, who later recalled that the "folded paper had these beautiful green lines. It was the old computer paper. Very fine, very lovely."[75] Finally, from Coetzee's word list, prepared for the IBM 7090, one notices that he had to shorten any words longer than six letters, as its memory was designed to store six-bit words, with each letter taking up one bit of memory—hence the truncated words "WONDRG" and "PENSVE." As Rebecca Roach, who has written about Coetzee as a computer programmer, has observed, this necessity is alluded to by the character Magda in *In the Heart of the Country* when she runs out of stones and must elide letters from the words in her messages to the sky beings.[76] If Coetzee had written his program for the 1401, however, he would have been able to get the 1403 printer to print out words of any length.

Here is Coetzee's program, as transcribed by me:[77]

```
                LINE GENERATOR
        DIMENSION WORD(1000), SENT(5), FACT(6)
C       ALLOWS MAXIMUM OF 1000 WORDS OF 5 TYPES PRODUCING 5-WORD LINES
        A=0.
        FACT(1)=0.
B       BLANKS=606060606060
B       ASTER=545454545454
        DO 101 I1=1,6
        I2=12*I1
        I3=I2-11
        READINPUTTAPE 5, 901, (WORD(I4), I4=I3,I2)
   901 FORMAT(12A6)
B       B=WORD(I3)
        CALLBOOL(B,ASTER,A)
        IF(A)101, 102, 101
   101 CONTINUE
   102 READINPUTTAPE 5, 902, NLINES, (FACT(I5), I5=2,6)
C       READ IN NO. OF LINES OUTPUT AND OF WORD TYPES
   902 FORMAT(I4, 5F4.0)
        NPRINT=56
        DO 201 J1=1, NLINES
   202 IF(NPRINT-56)203, 204, 201
   204 WRITEOUTPUTTAPE 6, 903
   903 FORMAT(1H1)
        NPRINT=0
   203 J2=1
   206 CALLRNDOM(RNDNO)
        INDEX=FACT(J2) + (FACT(J2+1)-FACT(J2)) * RNDNO + 1.
B       B=WORD(INDEX)
        CALLBOOL(B,BLANKS,A)
        IF(A)207, 206, 207
   207 SENT(J2)=WORD(INDEX)
        J2=J2+1
        IF(J2-6)206, 208, 201
   208 WRITEOUTPUTTAPE 6, 904, SENT
        NPRINT=NPRINT+1
   904 FORMAT(1H ,A6,1X,A6,3H / ,A6,1X,A6,3H / ,A6)
   201 CONTINUE
        CALLEXIT
        END(1,1,0,0,0,1,1,1,0,0,0,0,0,0,0)
```

In order to understand how this program works, it helps first to understand the hardware on which it was designed to run. FORTRAN II was developed for use on a system that used punch cards for data input and magnetic tapes for data storage and generated output on a printer. At the heart of the system were the magnetic tape drives, with the essential peripherals being the printer and punch card reader.

There was no screen. Also essential was the key punch machine, at which a punch operator would manually enter the program and data onto punch cards. Key punch machines were, however, not wired to the mainframe. Usually, punch operators, who were typically young women[78] — or, by the late 1960s in South Africa, black men[79] — would work in a separate room away from the heat and noise of the mainframe. The system acquired from ICT by the City of Port Elizabeth was set up in the same way.[80]

Because FORTRAN was designed for the punch card, the input conforms to the lines and columns of the card. Robert Garner patiently explained to me how you can see, from the printout preserved at the Harry Ransom Center, that Coetzee's data is arranged in five lines of a certain number of words each. Robert shows me how each of these lines corresponds to five rows, each filling the seventy-two columns used in FORTRAN on a standard eighty-column punch card. On punch cards used for program statements, column one is used for the *C* that denotes a comment or the *B* that appears to denote a Boolean expression,[81] whereas the first five columns can be used for program statement numbers. In FORTRAN, the sixth column is always left blank.[82] This explains the spacing in the left-hand margin of the printout, in which a *C* or *B* appears at the leftmost edge, with the statement numbers three spaces in and blanks between them and the statements themselves. As somebody new to coding, I find this correspondence unexpectedly literal, quaintly "analog." But, as Robert went on to explain, just about everything else follows from this patterning.

The data is loaded onto the magnetic tapes twelve words at a time, and these words are stored in memory as numerical values that correspond to the position of the words on the punch card. Arrays are stored backward.[83] Thus subject pronouns are 12–1 (there are only four, but the program ignores blanks), verbs 24–13, prepositions 36–25, place nouns 48–37, and adverbs 60–49. Coetzee's program tells the computer to store values within these numerical ranges at separate memory locations. This is what establishes the types, from which the computer, in turn, randomly selects in order to produce its output.

```
206 CALLRNDOM(RNDNO)
    INDEX=FACT(J2) + (FACT(J2+1)-FACT(J2)) * RNDNO + 1.
```

Iterating through the types, the randomization function is set up to multiply a value no larger than that of the initial end index of each type by a random number between zero and one to generate a value that will correspond to the memory address for a word of that type. An interesting feature of this process is that numbers exceeding the end indices of each type are generated, but, because this computer hardware is designed to work with integers and not floating-point digits, the number 12.7, for example, computes as 12. All aspects of format for input and output are specified in separate program statements; what today would largely be done automatically, using database software, is being set up manually, one line of code following another.

Other features of the program are also worth noting. As a high-level computer language, 7090 FORTRAN was formalized as a set of programming statements of thirty-eight types in natural language,[84] which would then be converted automatically into instructions in machine language to control the hardware. Historically, this conversion is the task of the "compiler," first developed by Grace Hopper in the early 1950s.[85] Because FORTRAN had an inbuilt compiler, the IBM 7090, for example, could be programmed without the user having to have a knowledge of machine language. As other programs preserved at the Harry Ransom Center show, this was not so when programming the Atlas 2 that Coetzee used in Cambridge for his subsequent experiments in computer poetry.[86] Some of the programming statements in FORTRAN, such as "READINPUTTAPE" and "WRITEOUTPUTTAPE," are intuitively clear to anybody with a passing familiarity with the relevant hardware and how it worked. But other program statements, such as "DO," which is the statement for iteration, and the "IF" statement, which specifies conditions for a change in the controlling program statement, are idiomatic to FORTRAN.[87] Like the asterisk, which signifies multiplication, "DO" retains its meaning in some of the programming languages that succeeded FORTRAN. Coetzee's program ends with a FORMAT statement specifying the output, with A6 denoting a variable of six characters—materialized in ink on paper as the poem's individual words, with 1H and 1X indicating single spaces and 3H instructing the printer to reproduce the forward slashes and whitespaces exactly as they appear in the statement:

```
904 FORMAT(1H ,A6,1X,A6,3H / ,A6,1X,A6,3H / ,A6)
```

When I spoke with new-media theorist Nick Montfort about my research, he was adamant that I needed to learn to code. Using his book as a guide,[88] I learned enough Python, a contemporary programming language, to adapt the code that Nick had used in his reimplementation—using a different programming language to produce similar output—of one of Coetzee's computer poems from the ICT years.[89] I found reimplementing "Line Generator" to be quite enlightening, bringing into relief the differences between Python and the older language. Whereas FORTRAN II requires that the user program the computer to read data, from punch cards, into specific locations in memory (input) on tapes, and to write it from those locations (output) into other locations and/or print it, with formatting programmed at each stage, in Python, several of the steps may be omitted because they are built in. For instance, you type all the data in the relevant format into the program itself. Of course, there are no punch cards, and, because nowadays our computers have screens, there is no need for a printout—although, of course, using the PRINT command, a remnant of the days when a printer delivered output, will display the output on the screen. In short, what I found was an increase in automation. I had not yet come across the term *automatic programming*, or the generation of computer code by another program. The compiler is an early example.[90]

But adapting Nick's code, with the help of my own rudimentary knowledge of Python, seemed too easy. Another way of saying this is that my reimplementation did not give me the insight I was after into the relationship between early 1960s computer technology and digital art. As David Link, who has recreated what may be the oldest known example of literature generated by programming a digital computer,[91] declares, describing his *Poetry Machine* (2001), "A technology cannot be described without one putting it to use. Programming a poetry machine and reflection about it cross-fertilized and interpenetrated each other. The theoretical text, which at the same time served as construction manual, was tested experimentally in its transposition through programming. . . . Programming takes the place in theory of the example."[92]

The Computer History Museum has two working 1401 computers, painstakingly restored and maintained. Having discovered that the 1401 was the same mainframe computer on which Coetzee had begun his experiments at IBM's Newman Street office, I was eager to see whether Robert and his team would be able to revive Coetzee's "Line Generator" on one of their machines. Michael Albaugh, whom Robert had consulted on the finer points of what turned out to be 7090 FORTRAN, took up the challenge of preparing Coetzee's software to run on the 1401. Doing so demands uncommon expertise, given that the relevant hardware and software are nearly half a century old and no longer in use. FORTRAN itself is rarely used today. After making some minor changes necessary for it to work—such as introducing a newer random number generator after the original one could not be identified—Michael keyed in the punch cards that would be fed into the card reader and read onto the mainframe's magnetic tapes. In June 2019, the 1403 printer at the Computer History Museum printed out a series of new poems from J. M. Coetzee's "Line Generator."

THEY	WANDER	/	THRUGH	MOULD	/	SOLTRY
WE	CALL	/	ON	ROCKS	/	HOPING
I	WANDER	/	THRUGH	ROCKS	/	ALONE
YOU	RUN	/	WITH	LEAVES	/	HOPING
THEY	CALL	/	INTO	MOULD	/	PENSVE

What Michael's recreation—or "port"—showed me was how, as with other computer art produced on mainframe computers in the 1960s, what the programmer does is transform a given medium through the adaptation of a given technological or material support. The words *medium* and *support* are terms introduced by Rosalind Krauss to describe how William Kentridge employs the technology of film—specifically stop-motion filmic animation—to serve as the support for drawing.[93] It is worth noting, however, that early computer scientists also came to terms conceptually with the idea of a machine that could be adapted to do things not initially anticipated by its designer. Although most existing machines, including the first computers, were designed for specific tasks—think of Enigma, which was devised by the British during World War II to crack secret German codes[94]—in principle, the computer was what Alan Turing called a "universal machine." As Turing wrote, "The existence of machines with this property has the important consequence that, considerations of speed apart, it is unnecessary to design various new machines to do various computing processes. They can all be done with one digital computer, suitably programmed for each case. It will be seen that as a consequence of this all digital computers are in a sense equivalent."[95] Computer programmers made Turing's idea into a reality. The adaptation of technological supports such as film and slide tape by Kentridge and James Coleman, respectively,[96] and the experiments of others with other supports, thus parallels the universalization of the machine through computing. The relationship between avant-garde art and computerization can be expressed, historically, in different ways, depending on what one compares. Lev Manovich, in a typically bold formulation, points to parallels between twentieth-century movements in art and in computerization and new media: "Not only have new media technologies—computer programming, graphical human-computer interface, hypertext, computer multimedia, networking (both wired-based and wireless)—actualized the ideas behind projects by artists, they have also extended them much further than the artists originally imagined. As a result these technologies themselves have become the greatest works of art today."[97] According to Manovich, the computer scientists who invented new media technologies "are the important artists of our time, maybe the only artists who are truly important and who will be remembered from this historical period."[98] Equally, had somebody like Olive Schreiner's Waldo Farber seen his sheep-shearing machine into production, and Emerson's plea for the "useful arts" taken up,[99] that inventor's name might one day have entered the annals commemorating the achievements of nineteenth-century artists.

Manovich writes with the benefit of hindsight. In the 1960s, none of the "new media" that he lists was in use, apart from computer programming. That is the method that Coetzee and others used to transform the technological supports of their day. An especially dramatic example of how a mainframe computer could be adapted to unanticipated ends is how, around 1970, Ron Mak produced "chain music" by programming a 1401 to make the 1403 printer—which makes a distinctive sound—play recognizable tunes like "The Blue Danube Waltz." Similar projects were realized by others.[100] In a more fundamental way, although nowadays we take this for granted, the mainframe computer programmed as a random number generator, and designed to manipulate numbers, and do so automatically, is adapted to work with text. When Theo Lutz produced his "stochastic texts," there were "researchers . . . still attached to the error that the utilization of electronic computing systems is restricted to numbers." For information theorists, on the contrary, "the concept 'compute' has . . . an essentially more general meaning. For the user of such a system, it is not critical what the machine does; im-

portant is only how one interprets the function of the machine."[101]
Just as Kentridge's Drawings for Projection—insofar as they move—
are produced, in part, through the automatic operations of the stop-
motion camera, Coetzee's poems—which, one might say, are writing
writing—are generated without intervention by the programmer once
the punch cards are read into the machine. Work shades into play, technology into art. The author is profoundly displaced—as the rerun of
"Line Generator," more than fifty years later, without Coetzee having
to press a button, shows. Somewhat paradoxically perhaps, given that
the computer's random selection is programmed, it achieves what
Coetzee, taking up Barthes, conceives as writing in the middle voice—
intransitively, as opposed to "a particular kind of writing, writing in
stereotyped forms and genres and characterological systems and narrative orderings, where the machine runs the operator."[102] Although
the random selection done by the computer results in a different set
of 120 lines each time the program is run, the repetition is, in a purely
technical sense, scarcely different from the first time that Coetzee ran
it at IBM's Newman Street office. It is, nevertheless, in nearly all other
respects, utterly removed from its context of production. It is toward
thinking ideas about art and automation in relation to that context
that I now turn.

Art, Authorship, and the Automation of Work

Only a handful of accounts have been published about how poetry
was produced on mainframe computers.[103] The scholars contributing
to one of them view computer poetry as a subset of early computer
art,[104] and depend on a received opposition between artist and computer programmer. Such an opposition appears to have emerged in the
1960s, as the mainstream art world came to terms with—and largely
rejected—computer art. They thus obscure a time when, although of
course a distinction was made between artists and programmers and
what they did, it had not hardened into an opposition, and questions
of work were thus more clearly at stake. Although the volume does not
ignore work, labor is marginal to its concern with art and the artist—
which, in its recounting of the era in question, come to be opposed to
the writing of programs and the tasks of the engineer. In other words,
a certain division of labor is already a given, anachronistically, with

artists driven to vindicate their occupation; they write, as it were, as members of a guild: computer art *is* art.

According to the editors, like other art making in the 1960s, computer art—drawing, music, poetry, film—challenged traditional notions of authorship and artistic expression: "There appeared to be some artistic rationale, especially in the 1960s, in the way the computer provided a means to distance the maker from artistic authorship and thus from the perceived excesses of expressionism. . . . Many of the artists . . . worked with methods and systems that generated unforeseeable results and distanced the subject from authorship."[105] This applied not only in the New York art scene, which is where the book starts, but also to the experiments of the Stuttgart school, which was informed by philosopher Max Bense's "information aesthetics," and the Zagreb New Tendencies group. The artist as author was displaced by the computer and its programmer, and the status of the artwork changed. In Stuttgart, "the concept of chance substituted for aesthetic intuition."[106] Bense's theories contemplated a "generative aesthetics," whereby a computer, having been programmed to analyze actual works of literature, could then be programmed to produce new works on the model of what its analysis had found.[107] Artists in Zagreb pursued similar experiments: "By emphasizing notions of planning and programming, New Tendencies introduced concepts that shifted the emphasis from the traditional artwork to ideas and procedures, but without abandoning the artwork completely."[108]

An interesting turn is given to the question of authorship in the late 1960s by Howard Nemerov in the essay I referred to previously. Although not himself using a computer to write poetry, Nemerov provides a careful and at times ironic theorization of the implications of doing so. In an essay evidently overlooked by theorists of new media, Nemerov contemplates a "hypothetical instance" of a computer randomly producing combinations of words from a list, having been programmed to do so according to "certain rules of combination." Nemerov allows that "within this range it is the machine, and not I, that has produced a statement that, let us suppose, I do not think I could have made up myself, a thought that I had not thought before and which overtook me with that sense of recognition that for Keats characterized the highest poetry."[109] If poetry is thought in terms of the "self, suddenly invaded by the Other, the Outside," then "it is tempting to be-

lieve that the computer has acted here as the true agent of poetry however named: inspiration, the Muse, trance, ecstasy, the Holy Spirit."[110]
Nemerov reaches the "somewhat surprising conclusion" that, viewed
in terms of the old contest between Plato and Aristotle, the computer
is "on . . . the side of Plato, where the poet is regarded as oracular, vatic,
not speaking so much as spoken through by something other than
himself."[111] Turning from poetry to music, Nemerov points to the pri-
macy of the machine, challenging those subscribing to an "unexam-
ined romanticism" to say "which came first, pianos or piano music."[112]
Citing formalization in classical music and the apprenticeship of the
hand of the painter, which aims to make certain gestures automatic,
Nemerov proposes a generalization of the concept of the machine beyond machines.[113] Poetry, he recalls, is distinguished from prose by
the "addition of mechanisms and mechanical requirements."[114] There
is thus, in the arts, mechanization and automation beyond, or before,
that which is performed by machines. Humans were, in effect, adapting
themselves to the technological support—paper, canvas, piano—in
order to draw, write poetry, and make music. Their interaction with
machines, actual and imagined, leads them to adapt to the latter. They
would thus, in all consistency, have to think of themselves as necessarily functioning automatically in certain respects. The adaptation to
computers may, as Hannah Arendt predicted would happen after the
application of theories of behaviorism, bring about a simplification
of the mind.[115] The philosophical questions, raised for Nemerov by
computer art, go beyond polemics of artist versus scientist, poet versus
programmer. That there is automation, or automatism, in the work of
the hand—which means also in the workings of the mind that guides
it—is something that will become apparent more and more when we
turn, in chapter 4, to the puppet theater. In that context, the idea of human automatism—a becoming-unconscious of regular learned manual and mental action—is a counterpart to the idea, suggested earlier
by my comparison of computer programming languages from different
eras, that a machine may only be automatic, relatively speaking, if to be
"automatic" means to be perfectly self-moving.

Because computer art of Nemerov's era was being produced on
mainframe computers, it meant that artists needed to form ties with
the institutions that used them. These were the major research universities and scientific institutes, certain arms of the military and gov-

ernment, and larger corporate entities. Ties of this kind could be politically compromising for artists, who produced their work "as the exigencies of the military, bureaucratic, and corporate entities that controlled computer access ran up against the grassroots and collective concerns of the bohemian, countercultural, antistate, and antiwar constituencies of the 1960s."[116] The composer James Tenney, for example, who informally taught FORTRAN to fellow New York artists in 1967, had a few years before that been an artist in residence at Bell Laboratories.[117] The political climate of the time is now regarded as having led to the elision, in art history, of the military provenance of early computer graphic art.[118] Along with the questions that computer art raised about the status of the artist and artwork, this implication contributed to a defensiveness, even a rejection, from the art world.[119]

This resonates with what Coetzee tells us in *Youth*. Without perhaps knowing it to begin with, John discovers that he has been involved in developing the software for the Atlas 2 computer used at the Aldermaston atomic weapons research station, which he then helps to install: "The hands of the people at Cambridge are not a great deal cleaner than his own hands. Nevertheless, by passing through these gates, by breathing the air here, he has aided the arms race, become an accomplice in the Cold War, and on the wrong side too."[120] And, if computer art was being rejected, for political or other reasons, it would have meant that the artist or writer, dependent on public recognition in order to *be* an artist or writer, would have a tenuous existence. A "distancing" of the author would have made it tenuous enough. That was the risk for the artistic avant-garde, especially for conceptualists — although, of course, Andy Warhol, whose fame came from exploiting mechanical reproducibility, and Sol Le Witt, whose best-known artworks are sets of instructions for installation, succeeded in spite of the risk. The brief notoriety achieved by *Youth*'s John after publishing a computer poem was not something Coetzee himself attempted to sustain. It was not how he chose to be the *Dichter*. Yet, for another seventeen years, Coetzee quietly pursued this path of writing alongside the novels that made him an author. "Why did I do it?" Coetzee asks, without really giving an answer. "It didn't lead anywhere interesting."[121] The dream of a synthesis between statistical and generative stylistics of the sort contemplated by Max Bense remained alive, one might imagine, at least until Coetzee the writer — and programmer — was eventually subsumed entirely into Coetzee the author.

As I have shown, in addition to asking us to reflect on the nature of authorship, *Youth* is occupied with questions of labor that, although prompted by John's computer programming, which he imagines replacing writers, may also be related to a peculiarly South African imperative that the "occupier" must work.[122] In the recounting of early digital art that I am discussing, however, work is, surprisingly, only a minor theme. The composer John Cage is quoted as saying in 1966 that "what we need is a computer that isn't labor-saving but which increases the work for us to do."[123] What Cage seems to have meant is that computers would challenge artists to extend their sense of what their practice was. In a more obvious sense, in those days, programming a computer was a laborious and time-consuming process—especially if the artist was a novice programmer. In yet another sense, however, what Cage was saying echoes, and responds to, the terms of a debate going on between labor and capital since at least the 1950s. Although conceding that millions will be put out of work in the long term by computerization, the dominant corporate voices claim that in the short term, more jobs will be created. This claim alternates with another assertion, mistrusted by organized labor: Because computers will contribute to economic growth, they will, ipso facto, lead to increased employment, albeit not in those occupations displaced by mechanization and computerization.[124]

Although recent accounts of 1960s computer art tend to ignore work, a decade before, in its earliest known beginnings, computer literature emerged amid a serious occupation with questions of labor. It is unlikely that its creator then viewed it as what is now called digital art.[125] I refer to the love letters published by Christopher Strachey in 1954, of which the following is an example:

Honey Dear

My sympathetic affection beautifully attracts your affectionate enthusiasm. You are my loving adoration: my breathless adoration. My fellow feeling breathlessly hopes for your dear eagerness. My lovesick adoration cherishes your avid ardour.

Yours wistfully
M.U.C.[126]

Strachey's love letters were generated by a Manchester Mark 1 computer, hence "M.U.C.," or Manchester University Computer.[127] This was a forerunner of the Atlas computer, also developed at Manchester, that John programs in *Youth*. In his essay in *Encounter* in which the love letters were published, Strachey introduces the texts by entertaining two questions that thinking people ask: Will they be out of a job? Can computers think? The love letters (and the draughts program that Strachey also wrote for the Manchester Mark 1) answer the second question: No, they can't, as they do only what they are programmed to do.[128] Addressing the first question, at the end of the essay, Strachey makes a then-standard observation about the effect of computerization on employment. Although many workers will be replaced by machines, and this will be felt keenly in the field of clerical work, "the introduction of a computer will probably not throw many people out of work." This is, in part, Strachey argues, because there is high turnover among office workers. They tend to be young women, "who leave after a few years to get married."[129] As I showed in chapter 1, South African observers note this tendency too in the case of white women.

As I argued in the same chapter, the meaning of automation depends, in any given context, on the meaning of work. There, my emphasis was on how work was racialized and how that influenced appeals to women. In the context I am analyzing now, gender is perhaps more salient in determining how the meaning of work depends on whether or not it is done with a machine, what kind of machine is being used, what it is being used to do, and who is using it. Analyzed in these terms, the meaning of work in the early days of computerization is highly overdetermined. It presupposes a division of labor between men and women, linked to a less than convincing distinction between what is work and what is not. Added to these determinants is an uncertainty about how producing literature and art on a machine originally designed for clerical work or scientific problem-solving fits into these divisions—which are, in any case, feeble when asked to account for the vocation of author or artist.

Although the love letters from "M.U.C." are literary in the minimal sense of being idiosyncratic in style—what Strachey calls "rather Victorian Babu"[130]—their production is never presented as having negative implications for human authorship or for the profession of writer. Programmer and writer coexist (that is, assuming that for them the latter was even a relevant category). The love letters suggest that computer poems are, for the programmer, not work but play. Parodies of conventional love letters, and of the process of writing them, they may have been a joke shared between Strachey and mathematician Alan Turing in an increasingly homophobic English society.[131] Whatever the case, "those doing real men's jobs on the computer, concerned with optics or aerodynamics, thought [the love letters] silly, but ... it greatly amused Alan and Christopher."[132]

What is remarkable, if this sentence is to be relied on as accurate, is that the gendering of the division of labor is not binary. In a queering of the machine room, computer literature is coded as being not exactly masculine—but it is not exactly not masculine either, as "real" qualifies the man and the work but does not negate them. Strachey, writing in *Encounter*, however, appears to accept a clear division between those who program and use computers—be they men or women—and those who perform clerical work, who are young, unmarried women. These clerical workers would include, one imagines, the women who work as punch operators. Not exactly not work, by men who are not exactly not men, the love letters thus fall outside the usual oppositions. J. M. Coetzee's computer poems may elude categorization in a similar way

That the computer poems shade into the category of play is implied in *Youth*, as John, still working at IBM, finds himself in the computer room in the evenings playing games and running programs on the 1401 computer.[133] What the printouts in Coetzee's papers in Texas show is that such "games" would have involved his programming a computer at IBM to print out poetry. The narrative in *Youth* that leaves it to the end of John's work at ICT makes the experiments seem like a last desperate bid to become a poet, as if the IBM years had been entirely barren. This is although Coetzee had already published his "Computer Poem" in *The Lion and the Impala*, which he tells his readers that he had written on the 1401. This divergence between John and Coetzee also raises the question of just when the reflections on authorship in *Youth* emerge. Do they date from when the poems were produced? Or, just as the recent scholarship that I have been discussing begins with the figure of the artist as a fait accompli, do they date, as it were, from a time when the author is speaking as a fully enrolled member of his guild—nay, as a guild master, a stature never to be attained by Jude Fawley?

On the second-to-last page of *Youth*, mutually exclusive vocations are presented in the form of an opposition that, although, rhetorically speaking, an epiphany for John, is historically determinate: "At eighteen he might have been a poet. Now he is not a poet, not a writer, not an artist. He is a computer programmer, a twenty-four-year-old computer programmer in a world in which there are no thirty-year-old computer programmers."[134] But the IBM years may, for Coetzee, at least, have been a time before the opposition hardened and before to be an artist meant to not be a programmer. In Coetzee's own trajectory—not John's—this might have been a time before work and play become mutually exclusive, before the one who writes becomes, for better or worse, the author, and work and play are reunited. For every hour spent reading after work, there is an hour spent staying after hours writing and running code of his own. Without access to Coetzee's diaries from that time, we cannot know how he understood these things as they were happening. The traits in the relevant paragraph in *Youth* seem so mixed that, by 2002, they are not being clearly distinguished. My sense, however, is that it is worth trying to separate them so that Coetzee the author is, in the early days, visible as Coetzee the worker—who plays. It is in so doing that the specifically South African resonances of his thoughts on work emerge, allowing us to read the computer poetry in a different way. The not-work of the writer, magnified through the automation of that not-work by programming an IBM 1401 or Atlas 2 computer to produce poetry, is an ethico-political problem for a young man from a country where the bulk of manual work is performed by black Africans. This is the implication one draws from the beginning of *Summertime*,[135] the sequel to *Youth*. Within this immovable frame—what Kentridge once called the "rock"—strange and interesting nuances are to be found relating to the meaning of work and automation.

The threads connecting Coetzee with Miriam Tlali seem tenuous until they have been woven together as I am doing. Office workers both, in the 1960s, they embrace the machine. By sheer sport of history, they appear together in the first issue of *Staffrider* magazine. She, with Mrs. Koae, the dressmaker, who contributes a paean to the machine. He, with a bizarre poem. The thread between her and him, involving work and its automation, remains hidden until years later, when "Hero and Bad Mother" is revealed to be a text that Coetzee programmed a computer to print. These two threads ramify until they become inextricably enmeshed in the system of racial capitalism known to history as apartheid and its division of labor. The system places its stamp on everything in some way. But there is another filament: What, exactly, is an author? In *Youth*, we witness John's agonizing over authorship. Tlali struggled abidingly for the recognition that would command her a living from the books that she wrote.

Yet, oddly enough, both betray something else: a mistrust of the occupation of writing. We witness this in *Youth*, as John, unemployed, pretends to go to work. He realizes that, at some level, to be a poet is to not work. The same mistrust emerges in the voices in Soweto Speaking, as Mrs. Konopi, a fruit and vegetable seller, complains about her fellow seller's husband, who is "educated but lazy."[136] He is the one who "sits and types the whole day on a typing machine," tapping out love letters that he passes on to the women. She adds, "He's lazy. Doesn't want to go and work like other men." Ultimately, though, what else does a writer do but write—be it at a typewriter or at a computer? And what does a writer ever write if not love letters?

Was this idea of the ostensible idleness of the writer an obstacle for Tlali, as it was for John in *Youth*? We do not know. But what we can see, in the words of the women who speak to her as America's workers spoke to Studs Terkel, is how, whereas "the woman *works*,"[137] the male who writes is styled as indolent. Almost all else is different, but this is what connects Miriam Tlali with Christopher Strachey: The man who uses a machine, designed for scientific or office work, to compose love letters, which others may consider to be "rubbish," risks having his manliness brought into question. If this is how Tlali antipathetically formulated things, it would probably have made no difference to Strachey, who had no pretensions as an author. But it does mean that Tlali displaces as significant figures in her writings both the woman who does "clerical work," like Muriel at her typewriter at Metropolitan or Mrs. Koae before she bought her sewing machine, and the woman—Tlali herself—who writes at her typewriter at home in Soweto. Protest writing after 1976, as practiced by Tlali, appears to afford little space for white-collar workers. I do not want to say that those women are simply "hidden figures," like the African American women who worked for NASA. But the meaning given to work, which, in turn, informs the meaning of mechanization or automation and thus what meaning is attached to the use of machines, leads, in this instance, to a bias. Because the division of labor is gendered—women work, men are lazy—certain types of work done by *women* are also rendered less visible. That includes work done with machines. The trajectory of John in *Youth* also looks like an elision of the machine: The Atlas 2 provides no way of making him a poet.

The irony that the machine generates endless lines of poetry for John but does not make him a poet is doubled by the fact that, by distancing the artist from authorship—which is what the artistic avant-garde sought from the computer—the machine deprives John of exactly what he wants. These ironies are still framed by ideas about work and how machines replace workers or alleviate work—ideas that connect Coetzee and Tlali. In the next two chapters, we turn from these writers toward artists working in the media of film and puppetry—from word to moving image and performing object. Although, like Goldblatt and Gordimer in *On the Mines*, these artists continue to be interested in workers and their machines, they turn from within that scene toward how the similarly constituted workings of human and machine make possible their interaction. A critical relation to the racial division of labor in South Africa is a necessary precondition for both William Kentridge and Handspring Puppet Company. The historical sedimentation is, as I show in the next chapter, particularly profound in Kentridge. Yet in the work of each, there is also an awareness of how the technical means through which animated film and puppet theater are realized relate to changes in technology dating back to the nineteenth century and extending into the age of computerization.

3

Race and Labor, Women and Machines

Stereoscopy is a powerful metaphor. In order to see normally, you need images from both eyes. The brain automatically converts the two flat images into a single image with depth. Objects appear as if in three dimensions. If film simulates movement by recording and projecting images at twenty-four frames per second, the stereoscope is an optical device that simulates the process of seeing by using lenses, positioned at specific focal lengths, to convert two nearly adjacent pictures or photographs of the same thing into a single image.[1] The effect of stereoscopic imaging can be quite striking—as anybody who has viewed, say, Eadweard Muybridge's large-scale stereographs of the Yosemite Valley will attest. There is an unreal quality to the artificial stereoscopic image, however, as if each object stands out all too distinctly, occupying a far too discrete place in the visual field.[2] Stereoscopic viewers were once popular as toys. William Kentridge had one as a child.[3]

As an improvisation on the metaphor of stereoscopy, Kentridge's *Stereoscope* (1999) is a film about isolation and the impossibility of insulation from one's surroundings.[4] One depends on two, the single is a function of the dual. *Stereoscope* is the eighth in a series of short films centered on the business magnate Soho Eckstein, some of which dramatize a love triangle involving him, Mrs. Eckstein, and Felix Teitlebaum, an artist.[5] In *Stereoscope*, Soho has long ago been abandoned by his wife, and we see him alone, except for his cat, and downcast. Who could possibly forget the image of him, in pinstripe suit, knee-deep in the tears he has shed? Although by himself, Soho Eckstein cannot separate himself from events taking place in the world around him—and they continue to impinge upon him. The theme of impossible separa-

Figure 3.1. William Kentridge, charcoal drawing for Stereoscope, *1999. Courtesy William Kentridge Studio.*

tion is a familiar, and critical, one from the country of apartheid. *Stereoscope*, however, is not in 3D, and, with Soho at the center, it symbolizes connection and complementarity by means of blue pastel lines joining him with different spaces in what looks like Johannesburg of the 1930s or 1940s and with scenes of violence from elsewhere and from other times. The lines, which are drawn in the same blue that Kentridge uses for Soho's tears, are an abstraction from what, in the context of the film, are telephone lines. The opening frames of *Stereoscope* show a telephone exchange of the old type, with its switchboards waiting for the men and women who operate it (figure. 3.1). To connect a call, an operator plugs a line into the switchboard, and the operator unplugs it to end the call. A similar visual vocabulary is employed in Kentridge's film *Ubu Tells the Truth* (1997), where electrical current, used in police torture, connects people in disparate spaces.

Stereoscope is thus a film that, by representing related technologies for speaking, listening, and viewing—telephones and telephone exchange, an eight-track tape machine, a stereoscopic viewer that appears briefly—also comments on its own technology.[6] Those familiar with the series of which *Stereoscope* is a part will know that they are short stop-motion animated films. The images on which they are based are a small number of charcoal drawings that are incrementally modified, with the resultant signs of erasure typically remaining visible on the paper. Like all film before the advent of video, where one speaks more precisely of refresh rates, animated film depends on being turned at twenty-four frames per second. Stop-motion animation is different because what is being photographed is not moving. The illusion of movement is created by changes made to what is before the camera—be it to actors or physical objects, including their location, or to images. In the celluloid animation perfected by Disney, and dominant in the twentieth century, a slightly different image takes the place of the one before it. In Kentridge's films, a relatively small set of drawings are altered, with each alteration being a new frame.[7]

Understood in the most general terms, the process mechanized in film or in stereoscopy depends on an underlying automaticity in how we see. Just as the stereoscope relies on how the human brain makes one image out of two, film as a technology depends on the persistence of vision. The automaticity of seeing is one of Kentridge's central concerns as an artist theorizing about his work. As he tells Angela Breidbach, "The drawings . . . are really an excuse for the pleasure of reminding ourselves, what it is that we do when we see."[8] An automaticity also enters into his artistic practice. As Rosalind Krauss argues, Kentridge's repeated walking across his studio between his camera and the drawing on the wall, altering the drawing slightly each time, makes for a "quasi-automatism" in which, although not given over to randomness, improvisation occurs within a preprogrammed routine.[9]

Moving from the automatically generated word to the image, in this chapter, I address the means used to make the films, their automaticity, and its relation to the automaticity of seeing. Elaborating on the framework that I introduced in my analysis of Miriam Tlali's fiction and oral histories and Coetzee's computer poetry, I address these topics in the context of the politics of labor in South Africa, at that juncture where racialized organizing and legislating converge with the use of machines. This is also, as we might expect, the point at which the labor of women becomes decisive. In the case of William Kentridge, there is yet another dimension. Because of his grandfather's political commitments, these elements assume a significance that is genealogical in ways that are not at first apparent.

What makes the automatic system depicted in *Stereoscope* stand out in Kentridge's oeuvre, which frequently represents machines of various kinds, is how it depicts human labor as being at the leading edge of the incipient mechanization and automation characteristic of technological modernity. What can easily be overlooked, in the depiction in *Stereoscope* of the telephone exchange as a quasi-automatic system—animated images of the underlying mechanical and electrical switching equipment punctuate the film—is the human labor complementing the workings of the machine. As he tells Matthew Kentridge, "In *Stereoscope*, one of the women in the telephone exchange was originally going to be a principal player but ended up only as a fleeting image."[10] The metaphor of stereoscopy as complementary duality is thus realized in another way: The machine requires the operator. In *Stereoscope*, a question of technology becomes a question of labor. Not as far from the mechanized or automated production process as one might think, the automaticity of perception and cognition that enables stereoscopic and film viewing is the same automaticity that makes it possible for anybody to use a machine. Historically, telecommunication converges with computerization to give us the internet.[11] The latter is Kentridge's stated reason for depicting older telecommunications technology,[12] which, although the result of several earlier technological advances, required human operators.

That labor should be so prominent in *Stereoscope* is not so surprising. Films earlier in the series, such as *Monument* (1990) and *Mine* (1991), bring to the screen labor writ large. The former features a monument to the worker, whereas the latter, to which I referred briefly in the introduction, features scenes of African men working in a mine. In one sequence, miners operate a rock drill. Kentridge's interest in labor, however, predates these films. At the beginning of his career, it took the form of artistic collaborations with trade unions representing black workers. These took place through the Junction Avenue Theatre Company, of which he was one of the original members.[13] The screen-printed posters that Kentridge created for Junction Avenue are sometimes included in retrospective exhibitions of his work. Developing its plays through workshopping,[14] the company staged its initial productions in 1975, one of them being an adaptation of Alfred Jarry's *Ubu Roi*,[15] which Kentridge revisited in several works in the late 1990s in response to the Truth and Reconciliation Commission.

The company's first success came in 1976 with *The Fantastical His-*

tory of a Useless Man. The play is a burlesque series of vignettes from South African history presented to a young man, who describes himself thus: "I'm a white English-speaking South African and I'm beginning to understand my situation."[16] His words that end the play— "I am a coward and a useless man—the most I can do is be the least obstruction"[17]—echo the conclusions of young white people of the liberal left during that time. They took guidance from Steve Biko and Rick Turner, who argued that the role of white people was not to be involved in the political struggle of Africans but to organize in their own communities.[18] Placing an emphasis on Marxist analysis, the play reads history in terms of an exploitation of workers by capital.[19] A student in politics and African studies at the University of the Witwatersrand,[20] Kentridge was twenty-one when the play was performed. It proved a success with white middle-class theatergoers at the Nunnery Theatre in Johannesburg.[21]

Junction Avenue's *Sophiatown* (1986), a play about life in the Johannesburg freehold township destroyed in the name of apartheid in the late 1950s,[22] was a notable commercial success for the company and was revived several times. Kentridge's role in the company included writing, directing, and acting, as well as set design.[23]

Some later Junction Avenue plays were aimed specifically at unionized industrial workers.[24] Speaking about these plays many years later, Kentridge emphasizes their limitations for him: "It became increasingly impossible and difficult for me to work within that paradigm. Not so much because I found it fundamentally false, but because I felt that I couldn't do it. I couldn't say: What did a trade union need to do? What would a worker in a factory understand or not? It became an extraordinarily paternalistic way of thinking on behalf of someone else."[25] Those plays may have been Kentridge's final attempt to engage with workers and trade unions directly. But they were not his only, or his last, attempt to represent workers, or the masses generally, in his work.[26]

Concentrating on *Stereoscope*, and how it depicts the telephone exchange, its operators, and the connections that depend on them, brings to light Kentridge's investment in labor as rooted in a matrix of ethical and political choices that stem from his paternal line. Given Kentridge's homage to Dziga Vertov elsewhere,[27] the visual allusion of this scene to Vertov's *Man with a Movie Camera* is important to note.[28] But it is this inherited matrix of choices that makes it possible to read the image by lending it words; this is a classic theory of the picture in Western art in which the picture is supposed to coalesce as *historia*.[29] In this case, the *historia* is not obvious and requires some investigation to come clear. In pursuing this inquiry, I am not proposing a strictly genealogical or ancestral determination but rather a logic that is historically determinate. My principal interest is in William Kentridge's paternal grandfather, Morris Kentridge (1881–1964). I have less to say about Kentridge's father and mother, Sydney Kentridge (b. 1922) and Felicia Kentridge (1930–2015), attorneys whose stature in the anti-apartheid struggle makes them and their commitments better known—and perhaps less interesting for being less problematic. I have little to say about his maternal grandfather and grandmother, who, like all the others, were also attorneys. The political inscription of William Kentridge's art is, in other words, not reducible to his own commitments of the 1970s and 1980s.

Going back two generations, one discovers that Sydney Kentridge's father, Morris Kentridge, who was a member of parliament for the Labour Party in South Africa, spoke up, on at least one occasion that has been recorded, for the country's telephonists—or telephone operators. *The Live Wire*, the monthly paper published by the South African Telephone and Telegraph Association, one of the organizations for public employees in the Union of South Africa, reported in its April 1926 issue that Morris Kentridge had asked a question in parliament of relevance to its members. Morris Kentridge asked the minister—Walter Madeley, also a member of the Labour Party and one of three Labour leaders given cabinet appointments in the Pact government[30]—to provide figures for how many telephonists were employed in the Union. He also asked Madeley how many of them were employed on a "fixed establishment" or contractual basis and whether the government was doing anything to "place . . . more of the unestablished upon the establishment." This would have entitled them to benefits such as a state pension.[31] In 1926, telephonists employed by the Department of Posts and Telegraphs numbered 839.[32] The vast majority were women.[33] With the first automatic telephone exchanges in South Africa having come into operation two years before,[34] Madeley was forced to defend the jobs of the telephone operators against questions from opposition members who called for the replacement of manual exchanges with automatic ones.[35]

Morris Kentridge, who looms large in the background of an early linocut by Kentridge entitled "Muizenberg 1933" (1976),[36] which I analyze in detail in the following, has also been identified as one of the origins for the George Grosz–like caricatures of the heavy-jowled capitalist that evolved into the figure of Soho Eckstein. The image of Morris Kentridge also lies behind Soho's appearance at Muizenberg beach in Kentridge's film *Tide Table* (2003). His transformation into Soho was an "ironic posthumous reversal for our grandfather," Matthew Kentridge writes, "a lifelong champion of the rights of workers."[37] Morris Kentridge's championing of workers did not start with his question for Madeley, however, but included a central role in the 1922 strike and rebellion by white miners on the Witwatersrand. This uprising was violently suppressed by Prime Minister Jan Smuts, who ordered in the army and air force, which, notoriously, bombed strikers' positions in Fordsburg in Johannesburg.[38] As a direct consequence, the Labour Party entered into an electoral pact with the Nationalist Party, which represented the interests of Afrikaners, to defeat Smuts's South African Party in the 1924 election. Morris Kentridge was duly elected to parliament as the Labour Party's representative for Troyeville in Johannesburg. He and his party represented the interests of the white workers who were its principal constituency, demanding a color bar in unskilled and semiskilled occupations. It is within this political framework that Morris Kentridge raised his voice on behalf of the women who worked as telephonists and, in earlier years, came out against mechanization in mining because it meant that fewer jobs would be created for white people.

The 1920s were years in which, in South Africa, the color bar operated differently than it did in the late 1960s, when Minister Haak saw the introduction of automation as a way of keeping certain occupations white. With unemployment high in the years in which Morris Kentridge and the Labour Party defended the telephonists against the automation of the exchanges, their central goal was to keep white workers in jobs and ensure that employment conditions were favorable to white workers. In order to do this, they saw two things as necessary. First, prevent competition by black workers. Second, oppose mechanization (in mining) and automation (in telephony). Morris Kentridge's advocacy of the telephonists in the context of growing calls for automation makes the second of these actions clear. But in order to understand more fully his and his party's position on mechanization and automation, one also has to understand how it justified the color bar ideologically. In the 1920s, the ideological struggle for the color bar was waged in terms of what its proponents termed "civilized labor." I analyze this unusual and tortured justification for a racialization of labor in the next section. As I argue in the final section of this chapter, the lengths to which the Pact government went to justify the color bar help, in turn, to explain why politicians began to be interested in how working with machines affects women physically, mentally, and psychologically. That interest in the effects on women workers is, of course, not limited to contexts in which it matters to the politician that the worker is white. But the continuities between the nervous system of the operator and the electromechanical machine posited by Mackenzie King in Canada, where race is not a central political concern, are taken up in South Africa, where race is central. These relays also suggest that, although also explicable in psychoanalytic terms as fantasy, the interest in women in William Kentridge's art making is an afterimage of an older struggle in which semiskilled women workers count as *white* workers. To the extent that it brings to the fore human-machine interaction and continuities between the workings of the machine and its user, *Stereoscope's* questions about the automaticity of perception and cognition also allude to a scene of labor that is highly contested. Before moving into the office, this labor struggle begins on the mines.

"Civilized Labor"

One of the key reasons for the 1922 strike was the decision by the Chamber of Mines to increase the employment of Africans in semiskilled positions that had, by agreement between owners and white mine workers, been reserved for white people. Africans were paid lower wages, and the argument, made by organized white labor, was that employing them in greater numbers would push wages down to a level unacceptable to white people. This is how Morris Kentridge tells the story in his memoirs, *I Recall* (1959):

> An effect of the depression [of 1920] was that large numbers of poor farmers were moving to the cities, and thousands of Natives were leaving the reserves to work on the gold mines on the Rand. As the un-

skilled Natives were urbanised, they began to compete with the better paid semi-skilled Whites. The trade unions on the Rand had been mainly developed by British immigrant workers, and aimed at protecting White workers from the Natives as well as protecting workers from the employers. Afrikaners who had come to the Rand were afraid that the mines might attempt to exploit unskilled Black labour, to reduce working costs, and many had joined the trade unions in their fight for maintaining White standards. It is clear, therefore, that the strike grew out of the depression and the colour bar. . . . The case of the Chamber of Mines was, that if it were not to close down some of the less profitable mines, it would have to cut the cost of production. It proposed to replace some 4,000 European workers with Native labour. The fight put up by the miners on the Witwatersrand and their supporters was to retain the ratio of 8.2 Natives for every White employee on the mines. This was also the policy of the Labour Party at the time. I naturally supported the miners, and from the beginning of February [1922], the greater part of my time was occupied in the legal defence of many of the strikers. This, of course, I did *pro deo*. I also addressed many meetings on behalf of the strikers.[39]

Playing a leading role in the strike, Morris Kentridge was selected as a member of the Council of Action, set up "to facilitate the conduct of the strike" after a general strike was declared.[40] This included the organization of Commandos, or armed militia, "to keep the men fit and to picket 'scab' labour."[41] Members of the Commandos were, however, also involved in arbitrary attacks against Africans.[42] During the uprising, Morris Kentridge was fired upon by the police, arrested and assaulted, and imprisoned at the Johannesburg Fort.[43]

The ratio, to which Morris Kentridge alludes, of 8.2 Africans for every white miner was an item of the 1918 Status Quo Agreement, following a strike in 1917.[44] Morris Kentridge states his view of the situation in more detail in *Unemployment in South Africa* (1922), a collation of minority reports he wrote as a member of the Unemployment Commission before the events of 1922.[45] Introducing his pamphlet, he views the victory of the Chamber of Mines over the strikers as having confirmed his fears: "The fear which I expressed in March, 1921, that for the purposes of securing cheaper labour, the mining industry, not content with importing further cheap native labour into the Union,

would seek to replace many of its white employees by cheap native labour, has proved to be the case. The ratio of 8.2 natives for every white
employee on the mines has been increased to a ratio of 10.5 natives for
every white employee on the mines, resulting in the displacement of
something like 5,000 European labourers."[46] Underlining how white
workers were being displaced by African workers, who were paid lower
wages,[47] *Unemployment in South Africa* also opposes the recruitment of
mine workers under indenture contracts from Mozambique. This took
place under the Mozambique Convention of 1909 concluded with the
Portuguese colonial government. In return for South Africa directing
50–55 percent of commercial rail traffic to the Witwatersrand through
the port of Lourenço Marques, the Chamber of Mines was allowed to
recruit workers from the Sul do Save region of Mozambique.[48] These
miners went to work in the collieries of the Eastern Transvaal and in
the gold mines of the Witwatersrand. The white unions had, a few years
earlier, successfully organized against the employment of indentured
Chinese miners.[49]

Behind the political positions in *Unemployment in South Africa* is
a theory, which is also a theory of history: There are in South Africa
two populations, a white and a black, a European and an African, one
"civilized" and the other comparatively "uncivilized." In this theory,
"civilization" is to be understood as an index for basic needs relative to
basic resources. Because the needs of Africans are comparatively few
compared to those of Europeans, and Africans have access to "tribal"
land,[50] Africans can accept work at a lower wage than Europeans. And
because their needs and resources diverge in this way, competition in
the sphere of labor between members of the two populations is unfair.
The recruitment of Africans from Mozambique by the mines exploited
this unfairness. The recruitment system was, furthermore, unfair to
Africans from within South Africa, who, in the process of being pro-
letarianized and urbanized like the white Afrikaners displaced from
farms,[51] were comparatively more "civilized" than they were.[52] The
theory is also a theory of historical progress. When *Unemployment in
South Africa* is not simply defending the color bar and opposing the
exploitation of indentured African migrant labor from Mozambique, it
advocates raising "the standard of the natives generally" to reduce the
interracial competition threatening the "white standard" and stands
for "equal pay for equal work" with "the minimum wage being based
on the white standard of living."[53]

Soon the term *civilized* became dominant in discussions of living standards, cost of living, and pay. But in the immediate aftermath of the 1922 strike and revolt, it alternated with *white*.[54] The received narrative—the one that even we learned in high school history in the 1980s—was that the strike was an unholy alliance between trade unionism and white supremacy. The infamous slogan "Workers of the World, Fight and Unite for a White South Africa" appeared on banners during the strike.[55]

The politics of the 1922 strike continued to resonate for the grandson and his generation. This is not necessarily to say that it was William Kentridge himself who introduced the issue in what was, like all of Junction Avenue's plays, a workshopped production; as Stephen Clingman relates, the 1922 strike was a focal point for National Union of South African Students consciousness-raising among white undergraduates at the University of the Witwatersrand in the mid-1970s.[56] In Junction Avenue Theatre Company's 1976 play, *The Fantastical History of a Useless Man*, two separate placards with the words "Workers of the World Unite" and "For a White South Africa" are joined to complete the slogan.[57] The moment follows a scene in which three characters speak, representing the Socialists, the Chamber of Mines, and the Afrikaner Nationalists.[58] Although there were deadly attacks on Africans during the uprising—which Jeremy Krikler describes as pogroms because of their partially popular nature[59]—and white workers defined their identity as distinct from black Africans, it has been argued that the white miners understood their class enemy to be the mine owners and, subsequently, the state, which sided with the owners.[60] It appears, then, that it was possible for the protagonists to hold that the strike was *for* white miners and not *against* Africans.[61] Politically, this position—in reality, a fairy tale—was tenable as long as a consensus held, and could be defended by force, that the South African state ought to favor the interests of white people over those of Africans. That consensus, unfortunately, lasted a long time.

Although the mine owners had won in 1922, the government reached a settlement with organized white labor. Before the defeat of the South African Party in the 1924 election, Smuts passed the first Industrial Conciliation Act.[62] This law provided for industrial councils in various industries, which were dominated by white workers, to set wage levels for African workers. By setting them higher than the market rate, the councils made employers less willing to employ Africans.

The Wages Act of 1925 reinforced these measures.[63] Shortly after the Pact government came to power, in October 1924, the office of Prime Minister J. B. M. Hertzog issued a circular mandating that the government employ "civilized labour" and encouraging all employers to do the same.[64] "Civilized labour," the circular declared, "is to be considered as the labour rendered by persons, whose standard of living conforms to the standard of living generally recognised as tolerable from the usual European standpoint. Uncivilized labour is to be regarded as the labour rendered by persons whose aim is restricted to the bare requirements of the necessities of life as understood among barbarous and undeveloped peoples."[65] The greatest change, in accordance with Hertzog's circular, took place at the Railways and Harbours Service, which employed large numbers of "poor whites" displaced from farms during the 1920 depression.[66] Over a decade later, the Commission of Inquiry Regarding Cape Coloured Population of the Union (1937) scrutinized the 1924 circular, subsequent minutes and notices from the Department of Labour, and the findings of earlier commissions of inquiry on wages and industrial legislation. It also solicited testimony from employers and workers' associations. In so doing, it brought into view a clearer picture of how the "civilized labour policy" was put into practice—although, "according to the evidence there was a *bona fide* doubt as to the significance of the term."[67] It is its attention to the ambiguity of the term that makes the commission's report a more informative source than the standard histories.

The government and its apologists denied that the "civilized labour" policy discriminated against Coloureds or Africans—because, in theory, an African or Coloured person could qualify as "civilized."[68] However, the commission, which included Dr. Abdullah Abdurahman, cited testimony to the effect that the 1924 circular and later directives were widely understood by employers as urging the employment of white people,[69] as well as the reduced employment of African workers.[70] Beyond Railways and Harbours, which, after 1924, employed significantly fewer Africans, with the proportion of Coloured workers not increasing,[71] this translated into general conditions of the possibility for racial discrimination by all employers. Such an outcome could easily have been predicted. It remains informative, nevertheless, to unravel the underlying logic of what was perpetrated in those years—even if it is not a simple matter to identify that logic's beginning or end, as things seem to go around in circles.[72] Seeking to secure a fixed point from which to begin its analysis, the commission decided that when reference is made to "civilized labour," this can be taken to refer to wage levels—a "civilized wage"—and not to the race of the worker: "The fact which emerges from the confusion of thought on this subject, and upon which there is agreement, is that the determination of whether a person is civilized or not is governed by the wages earned."[73] From this point, a peculiar logic unfolds. A "civilized wage" was the wage generally paid to white workers (although, after the 1920 depression and the exodus from the farms, white workers were often paid less to do unskilled work). Thus, the directive to employ "civilized labour" meant that employers had to pay a "civilized wage." And because a "civilized wage" was what was paid to white people—and not to Coloureds or Africans—employing "civilized labour" meant, generally speaking, employing white people (in the Cape, wage levels for Coloured workers sometimes matched those of white workers doing similar work, although Coloureds were usually subject to wage discrimination).[74]

In other words, although the government denied that it was mandating racial discrimination, by harassing employers in the private sector by not granting firms tariff exemptions and denying them state tenders,[75] for example, it had given them an incentive, or at least a robust pretext, to employ only white people. Yet although the reach of the Industrial Conciliation Act and the industrial councils was extended, leading to the artificially reduced employment of Africans and Coloureds in certain branches of semiskilled work, the government could never use the law to entirely prevent employers from continuing to employ Coloureds and Africans to perform semiskilled work. This was the case, for example, when white workers were not available or not prepared to do the work. In practice, it also did little to stop businesses from paying those workers less than they would pay white people. Charles Feinstein rightly states that "the creation of a 'colour bar' that rigorously excluded all Africans from any skilled or semi-skilled work," with "similar but less stringent restrictions" on Coloured and Asian workers, "is one of the most distinctive aspects of South Africa's economic history. Other countries have similar histories of conquest and dispossession, even if not on the same scale, but no other country has used its political and legal system to create and maintain such a comprehensive and formal colour bar."[76] It should nevertheless be observed that the ways racial discrimination took place in the South African labor market were more variegated—and more saturated by bad faith—than the term "color bar" would suggest, if it is taken to mean a finite set of statutory restrictions like those instituted on the mines between the 1890s and the 1920s, even as the Group Areas Act, the Separate Amenities Act, and other laws made it harder for an African to work in a white area or at a concern where white people were also employed. The bad faith inherent in the settlements made by successive governments with white labor and white capital became apparent in the later years of apartheid as the demand for labor rose rapidly with the long postwar economic boom. Then, as I detailed in chapter 1, most semiskilled jobs, and some skilled jobs, could not be filled from the ranks of white applicants. Without laws *against* employment discrimination and wage discrimination, private employers could either employ white workers, if they could find them, or employ Africans—or employ both white and African workers, at the same time, under unequal conditions. This is what Tlali's *Muriel at Metropolitan* shows us. Although Muriel works in the same office, and does the same work as, the two white women who are her coworkers, Metropolitan Radio pays them more than it pays her.

After 1922, Morris Kentridge's political positions shifted with those of the Labour Party until he left Labour to join Smuts's South African Party because of rising anti-Semitism in the National Party.[77] He and the others who switched parties saw the South African Party as safeguarding "White civilization."[78] By the 1950s, postwar industrial expansion saw rising black employment in the manufacturing industry "due to the impossibility of supplying the demand for European labour." It was in this context that Morris Kentridge spoke up for African workers: "Sir . . . that is contrary to the general policy of apartheid, but the Department [of Labour] shows that that is taking place day by day. A greater number of non-Europeans are being employed in industry, and it seems to me reasonable that opportunities should be given to them, to a much greater extent than is the case at present, to see that they are represented on the Wage Board and to give them an opportunity of arranging their terms of employment, so as to have greater industrial peace in this country."[79] Morris Kentridge's reference to the Wage Board does not, however, address a more fundamental fact of racial discrimination. The Industrial Conciliation Act, first passed in

1924, banned black Africans, but not Coloureds or Indians, from form-ing or belonging to trade unions.[80] In 1956, the act was amended to "al-low . . . the Government to reserve certain trades or sections of trades exclusively for White employees."[81] The relevant clause was Section 77, for which white trade unions agitated,[82] and which is typically cited to show that job reservation originated in apartheid lawmaking. The notion may stem from how terminology was employed. If "color bar" was associated with laws and regulations dating back to the 1920s and earlier, "job reservation" was be taken to be synonymous with the 1956 statute and its mandates.[83] But Section 77, applied at the discretion of the minister of labor, was, in fact, sparingly used and over time came to have a mainly symbolic significance for the National Party's shrinking constituency of white workers.[84] The spider's web of other laws and regulations that preceded it remained in force,[85] however, and contin-ued to have a significant effect, even as those measures failed to arrest a trend that was clear, not only to Morris Kentridge but to anybody pay-ing attention. By 1954, as the minister of labor acknowledged, a scarcity of white industrial workers meant that "industries that had been based on White workers were slowly 'changing colour.'"[86] At the same time, because apartheid labor laws and regulations were a result of gener-ations of compromise and bad faith, they were not comprehensive. This meant, among other things, that officials and police applied and enforced them arbitrarily. Historically, as is detailed in the following, it took skilled lawyers to locate the unlawfulness of their application and to challenge it in court. In the 1980s, a leading role in these challenges was played by the Legal Resources Centre. Directed by Arthur Chas-kalson, who later became the president of the Constitutional Court of South Africa, the center was founded in 1978 by Felicia Kentridge.

How did mechanization figure into Morris Kentridge's commit-ments? Can his views on mechanization be separated from his advo-cacy of the color bar? And can those views be related to his advocacy on behalf of the women who worked as telephonists? Some clues ex-ist in his published writings. In the struggles that brought about the 1922 revolt and helped shape Morris Kentridge's politics, the machine features as a factor in the calculations of both labor and capital. As he shows in *Unemployment in South Africa*, the mine owners, who did not employ more white mine workers when African labor was relatively scarce, viewed mechanization as a cost saver: "'A moderate shortage of native labour,'" the Low Grade Mines Commission of 1920 found, "'is not detrimental to the industry. It stimulates the endeavour to econo- mise in, and find substitutes for, native labour, such as mechanical de- vices like machine drilling, which enable one native to do the work of several when drilling by hand,' and this also appears to be the view of Sir Evelyn Wallers who, in the course of his evidence before the Select Committee of the House of Assembly on the Gold Mining In- dustry, appointed in January, 1918, stated, inter alia: 'When labour is short we employ more machines in order to break an equal quantity of rock.'"[87] Hand drilling was thus replaced by machine drilling when there was a shortage of African labor and not because it was preferred for technical reasons.[88] Machine drilling continued for the next one hundred years to be the dominant means for extracting ore in South African gold mines.[89] Although, in coal and platinum mines, greater mechanization has been possible, the geology of the gold-bearing reefs, combined with labor practices resistant to change, allowed this early form of mechanization to survive.[90]

Perhaps as significant as Morris Kentridge's conception of mech- anization as leading to a reduction in jobs for white miners—which evaluates the machine according to a racialized employment index, even against a racial quota—is that, in certain contexts, where race is factored out because the color bar is a given, a conceptual generaliza- tion becomes possible. Giving readers of *Unemployment in South Af- rica* a lesson in the labor theory of value, Morris Kentridge insists on the necessity of the labor of the worker, without whom the machine would, like any material, be "dead material."[91] "Who creates the sur- plus value?" he asks. "It is the application of human energy, that is the labour power, to the dead material which converts it into something else and creates the surplus value."[92] In other words, the artist's grand- father insists upon the fact of human-machine interaction and draws from that fact important ethical and political consequences. More than a century later, rock drillers remain indispensable in the gold and plati- num mines, where more intensive mechanization and automation have stalled because the machine is dependent on its operator.[93]

Although Communists played only a small role in the 1922 strike and uprising,[94] the strikers and rebels shared a vocabulary with the Communists. Strikers sang "The Red Flag" at their meetings, and Taffy Long, a striker sentenced to death and hanged, "went to his execution singing 'The Red Flag,' and the crowds who were outside, hearing him sing, sang with him."[95] The events having taken place shortly after the Russian Revolution, the strikers were, inevitably, branded as Bolsheviks.[96] It is perhaps this memory of revolutionary fervor, associated with his grandfather, that, in its partial accuracy, influences William Kentridge's image repertoire—including the red flag—and his long preoccupation with the unrealized potential, and mixed consequences, of the Russian and Chinese Revolutions (in *The Nose, This Is Not a Horse, The Horse Is Not Mine, O Sentimental Machine,* and *Notes Towards a Model Opera*).[97] This memory had been given additional force by William Kentridge's own political formation as an undergraduate at the University of the Witwatersrand in the 1970s, where Marxist theories of labor were pervasive. As is evident in his theatrical work with Junction Avenue Theatre Company from the same period, the memory of the Rand Revolt and its contradictions remained a live one, even if his grandfather was not brought on stage in propria persona. The political choices that William Kentridge made can thus be situated within the ideological matrix that informed those of his grandfather and as a significant departure from it. "For the workers, for the whites" and "For the workers, for all the workers" became, by the time Junction Avenue was staging plays for the trade unions in the 1970s and 1980s, "For the workers, for the Africans."

Influence thus appears to have skipped a generation. The artist's father, the eminent jurist Sydney Kentridge, although famous as an opponent of apartheid, did not pursue a political career,[98] and he was not a Socialist. The artist's mother, Felicia Kentridge, also directed her opposition to apartheid from within the sphere of law. After placing *Stereoscope* in the context of discussions about the working conditions of telephone operators in the years of the incipient automation of the exchanges, I venture an explanation as to why William Kentridge should, in his inclination toward politics, have taken after Morris Kentridge instead of either of his parents. My explanation, which is psychoanalytic, suggests how his challenge to his grandfather's commitments, patently informed by the changed politics of his time, was overdetermined by Oedipal fantasy. This may also explain why the figure of Morris Kentridge looms so large, and other figures, such as his uncles, who were engineers, one of whom studied automation at MIT, never feature in his art making or comments about it, although they might have contributed to his interest in technology.[99] The psycho-political overdetermination that I outline elucidates how, across generations, the emphasis shifts from the male worker at his machine to women and the inner workings of machines. As I have already explained, when viewed historically, the emphasis continues to stem from the fact that the woman who connects telephone calls at the exchange is a worker—as in Vertov's USSR—and that, in the South African context, she is a white worker. Her interaction with her machine becomes political to the extent that it can be factored into a racialization of labor.

Women and Machines

The Rand Revolt and the racial politics of "civilized labour" are the main contours of a history that, being emphasized in later years, informs a memory. Although the passing of a century has made that memory indistinct, the history is well documented and has been thoroughly analyzed. Although also documented, Morris Kentridge's advocacy of the telephonists has remained at the margins of historical memory. Like the rock drillers, they were also semiskilled machine operators. His advocacy was consistent with a time of rising awareness of the labor concerns of women—not only those women working in factories but also those in white-collar occupations. The trend in western Europe is well documented; when Siegfried Krakauer published *The Salaried Masses* in the 1920s, 40 percent of German salaried workers (*Angestellten*)—whose ranks included office workers as well as shop assistants—were female.[100] The plant was being displaced by the office.[101] Something similar would take place in South Africa in the 1950s, as white women moved "from industrial employment to clerical and other service occupations."[102] By the 1970s, as I observed in chapter 1, labor statistics show that the same became true for Coloured and, in turn, African women.

When we turn to William Kentridge, there is, to be sure, an investment in the office. Until he is struck by the image of how an actor playing a typist in the film installation *More Sweetly Play the Dance* (2015) adjusts her stockings as she sits down,[103] however, it is not the office of the average office worker, and it is coded as distinctly male. Discussing the sources for the depiction of Soho Eckstein's cluttered desk, at which he is depicted in a number of the films, including *Stereoscope*,

Matthew Kentridge remembers how he and his brother would visit the Rissik Street office of their maternal grandfather, the attorney Max Geffen. "Our grandfather's office equipment was scattered when his practice was wound up more than thirty years ago," he recalls. "Items such as the crescent-shaped blotting roller would occasionally resurface in a box of assorted objects or at the back of a drawer, reminding us of the world of our early childhoods, of a world that existed long before we were born."[104] When William Kentridge's concern with the office surfaces in comments made by fellow Junction Avenue member Pippa Stein in an interview with the writer Lionel Abrahams about the workshopping of *The Fantastical History of a Useless Man*, it is at a higher level of abstraction and impersonality and unconnected with ordinary office work: "For the opening scene I remember, Malcolm wanted Van Riebeeck and Van der Stel to be all camped up; and one night, William said, 'But this is bullshit, they're petty bureaucrats, and you've got to convey that idea.' That's where we got all the stamping from."[105] In the play, the two seventeenth-century Dutch East India Company governors "have rubber stamps, which they use liberally."[106] The stamp could also be associated with Morris Kentridge, who, in 1922, successfully concealed the Council of Action's stamp from the police.[107] It is facile to see the connection between the actual office and the stage office, with its boyish quasi-Oedipal aggression against the grandfathers. At the margins, however, almost as an afterthought, the mother appears, smaller, in synecdoche, compared to her own father, when it comes to their respective office equipment: "The typewriter brings back my grandfather's office in town, he did everything on this huge typewriter. I think there was a small typewriter on which my mother would write letters."[108] But what is more interesting is how, as I show, the inner workings of the machine are strongly associated, symbolically, with the maternal body and what is hidden within it: "There's a sense of those fingers, those keys—like a hand that would grab you and pull you back down in. Remember when you first typed as a child—you hit too many keys, they all interlocked, and you would have to unpick them from where they'd shrink back down into the belly of the typewriter and be hidden. That sense of grabbing and letting go is one of its attributes."[109]

But what operates at an unconscious level, or as fantasy, does not always directly guide a relation to social reality or an artist's response to it. Recall how the comedian Trevor Noah confidently declares, "Under apartheid, if you were a black man you worked on a farm or in a factory or in a mine. If you were a black woman, you worked in a factory or as a maid. Those were pretty much your only options. . . . Black people didn't work in offices."[110] As limited as these options were, the South African cultural imagination has tended to narrow them even further, privileging the worker from the mine. From the songs of migrants from Mozambique and Lesotho, to the fiction of Peter Abrahams and Wilbur Smith, to the music of Johnny Clegg and Sipho Mchunu, the male mine worker is the dominant figure. Factory workers are far less frequently represented.[111] Farmworkers, to be sure, often feature in Afrikaans fiction of the 1920s and 1930s. As we have seen, ordinary office work is rarely represented, making Miriam Tlali virtually unique in South African literature. And the only representation of telephone operators that I am aware of, in any kind of South African cultural production, is the 1979 television comedy series *Nommer asseblief!* (Number please!) and the spinoff film made a couple of years later. They center around Grieta, an operator at a rural exchange in the Western Cape. By the time the series was screened, the "party line" was largely a thing of the past, with the tone of the series being one of lighthearted nostalgia for an age of crossed lines and eavesdropped calls.

In the 1920s, however, when cities like Johannesburg, Cape Town, and Durban still had manually operated telephone exchanges, only getting their first automatic exchanges in the early 1930s,[112] over eight hundred people worked as telephonists. Like other white-collar workers during this period, and women in, say, the garment industry, telephonists were becoming a priority for labor organization. Whereas labor organizing in the garment industry included white and Coloured women, the South African Telephone and Telegraph Association was explicit in its insistence on the application of the "civilized labor" policy by the post office after 1924. In the December 1925 issue of *The Live Wire*, we read of an objection made to the alleged employment of an African man as a "brush hand" to a painter, evidently a semiskilled occupation that members believed ought to be reserved for a white person.[113] In the same issue, the policy of employing white men as casual unskilled and semiskilled manual workers by the post office is rated an "economic success." Between August 1924 and March 1925, this policy resulted in an increase in white employment of about 150 percent and a corresponding drop in African employment of around 70 percent.[114] The organizing among women working as telephonists thus took place against the background of a racial division of labor that, with the force of the government at its back, organized white labor sought to make mandatory and effective.

It is nevertheless because of this organizing that we have a record, albeit fragmentary, of the effects of mechanization and automation on their occupations. Several historical studies of mechanization in South African mining exist, although comparatively little has been written about the effects of mechanization in agriculture.[115] But the implications of mechanization and automation in the South African office and telephone exchange have been completely overlooked by scholars.[116] For organized labor, the implications of automation are relatively straightforward: jobs will be lost, operators will need to be reassigned. But what are more interesting are the effects, from the period before the automation of the exchanges, on the women who operated machines that, being both mechanical and electrical, were at the forefront of late nineteenth- and early twentieth-century technological modernity and a harbinger of the future that is our present, in which computers and telecommunications networks have converged technologically to give us the internet.[117] Programming early computers such as ENIAC, in the late 1940s, actually required lines to be plugged in by hand to complete the circuits that effected the machine's functions—a task that was often performed by women, much as women had connected telephone calls between human beings.[118]

As with computerization in South Africa, when it came to telephony, little critical discourse originated locally. It is therefore not surprising that when *The Live Wire*, the association paper for telephone and telegraph workers, looked for a description, it sought it abroad. The fact that it endorsed that description assures us that, if we read comparatively, we can infer broad similarities between the situation of South African telephonists and those elsewhere. *The Live Wire*, in which Morris Kentridge is mentioned for his parliamentary advocacy of the telephonists, refers in two separate issues to Mackenzie King and to the Canadian royal commission that investigated the historic Toronto Bell telephone operators' strike of 1907—which, although broken by the company, gained the sympathy of the public for the strikers.[119] King, who would become Canada's longest-serving prime minister, was minister of labor when he was appointed to chair the commission while the strike was in progress. The relay is indirect, with *The Live Wire* quoting from an Australian labor case in which the telephonists' advocate quotes from King's book *Industry and Humanity* (1918), in which the physical and mental toll on the women who worked with the machines is described:

> There seems little about the occupation of telephone operating to make it a matter of special concern on the part of the State. It is commonly thought that any girl with intelligence may quickly acquire the skill necessary to become a successful operator. To the onlooker, except at the switchboard of some large exchange, when the wires are carrying "the peak of the load," telephone operating seems to afford plenty of opportunities of rest, and even, at times, of recreation. How considerably telephone operating differs from other occupations in which women are commonly employed, is not observed until attention is drawn to the strain upon the nervous system which the work under most conditions involves. Contrary to general belief, the work is not automatic or mechanical, but requires considerable mental effort, and real mental capacity.
>
> In most occupations in which female labor is employed, strain is mainly physical. In telephone operating, there is physical strain through the reaching required to make connections at switchboards, through inability to relax, and the fatigue of long continued sitting in one position. In addition, the special senses of sight, hearing, and touch, the faculties of speech, memory, and perception, are called into operation not only continuously, but in a concerted manner; when not actually employed, they are not resting, because necessarily upon the alert. The brain is in constant use, the mind on the *qui vive*. Not only are the special senses active, but there is a high tension on the special senses, and a certain amount of mental worry. The strain is in proportion to the nervous force exhausted, and the exhaustion of nervous energy is a matter only of degree. The liability to occasional injury from shocks, the irritation caused by the intermittent glowing of lights reflecting the impatience of users, the occasional buzzing and snapping of instruments in the ear, the sense of crowding where work accumulates, the consciousness of supervision, the sense of responsibility in responding to calls, and the inevitable anxiety occasioned by

seeking to make necessary connections whenever a rush takes place, all combine to accentuate the strain upon the nervous energies of an operator. These factors are present in lesser degree in other callings in which women are engaged. A woman's nature, moreover, is peculiarly sensitive to reproaches; to be liable to harsh words without means of redress tends to intensify the nervousness of operating an exchange.[120]

The rhetoric of these two paragraphs works through elision and a naming of parts. Almost entirely absent is the machine. Instead, King describes a human being conformed to — and deformed by — the machine that she operates. That this machine is electrical as well as mechanical is given less emphasis in *Industry and Humanity* than in the royal commission's report of 1907.[121] Summarizing the findings of the commission, King begins by addressing a common misconception regarding telephone operation — that, for the women working the exchanges, it is not a particularly demanding occupation. This is where King introduces a decisive bifurcation — between physical and mental effort. Physical strain, he tells us, can be considerable, but what is really taxing about operating an exchange is how mentally demanding it is. It requires both mental effort and mental capacity. King's rhetoric is classical, moving from the general to the specific, as he names the "special senses" and faculties affected: "The special senses of sight, hearing, and touch, the faculties of speech, memory, and perception, are called into operation not only continuously, but in a concerted manner; when not actually employed, they are not resting, because necessarily upon the alert."[122] "The brain is in constant use," King continues, "the mind on the *qui vive*. Not only are the special senses active, but there is a high tension on the special senses, and a certain amount of mental worry."[123] It is because the labor being performed recruits multiple senses and faculties, and does so in a way that allows none of them to rest, that there is excessive strain on the brain and the nervous system. Strain is increased as a result of the subjective feelings of the operator in response to the pressures of her job. The theory introduced by King is *dynamic* in the sense that, as in a key part of Freud's neuropsychology, it analyzes mental processes as an interplay of quantitatively measurable forces: "The strain is in proportion to the nervous force exhausted, and the exhaustion of nervous energy is a matter only of degree."[124] Asked by the royal commission to comment on the effects of operating on the optic and auditory nerves, as well as on the nervous system generally,[125] the testimony of physicians before the commission dwelt upon "the high state of nervous tension . . . as well as its inevitable effects in depletion of nervous energy, culminating sooner or later in debility, breakdown, and prostration."[126] What King wishes to show is that, with this new technology, new and unanticipated strains are introduced. If labor has always involved physical effort and strain, this new kind of labor adds mental effort and strain that are unprecedented.[127] It should come as no surprise to us—whose everyday activities, and thus our senses and faculties, are conscripted by an "attention economy" that keeps us at screens and keyboards—that the continual state of alert is described by King as the hallmark of the modernity inaugurated by the emergence of electromechanical machines such as the telephone. If operators were "human switches,"[128] so are we—in the vast computerized switching system to which we nowadays give names such as "the internet" and "social media." The mental and nervous strain, King emphasizes, is as consequential as that to the spine and the shoulders. It may be for this reason that King emphasizes the effects of this new kind of work on women and generalizes, in a way that seems outmoded now, about "a woman's nature."[129] Supposedly light work, and thus suitable for young women of the middle class, he seems to be instructing his readers, it is in fact much harder than you would imagine—because it has profound but unseen consequences beneath the surface of the body. Most of the women who struck at Bell in 1907 were between seventeen and twenty-three years old. These young women were sending Canadians this message—which would be relayed, thanks to King's book, across the Dominions and around the world via Australia to South Africa.[130]

What King says about "a woman's nature" and its susceptibility to "nervousness" will trigger every feminist critique of early psychiatry. But the words that King uses tell us a great deal about the social expectations to which women of a certain class were subject—which, according to these assumptions, fitted them for work as telephone operators. King never plays on words for rhetorical effect. But when he writes of "the sense of responsibility in responding to calls" and of "callings in which women are engaged," we can see the makings of a theory of femininity as responsiveness—which in, say, Carol Gilligan's "ethics of care" and Kelly Oliver's "response-ability" has assumed a critical feminist form. The point to be made here is that because certain work is routinely done by women, the skills needed to do it become gendered as feminine. Affective work, to be sure, the labor of telephone operating was viewed, in the relatively short epoch of the manual exchanges, as continuous with work that women had been doing for a long time. This is what we see in the list of qualifications thought to be important for the telephonist. Articles in *The Live Wire* laud the "devoted and patient" telephonist, emphasizing that she is "well educated and highly intelligent." It reprints a mock-heroic paean from *The Baltimore Sun* to a young woman operator who took "an unfailing delight in performing the miracle of establishing communication between remote souls."[131]

Notions of femininity thus inform assumptions and observations about the effects of telephony on operators and about who is best fitted for the occupation. It could be argued that an idea about femininity as responsiveness provides a structure, in King, to a crucial point that he makes about human-machine interaction. By the frequency with which they address the matter in their answers,[132] it appears that the physicians who were prompted by the 1907 royal commission to comment on the effects on the operators' nerves must also have been asked to voice an opinion about whether the work was automatic or mechanical. "Contrary to general belief," King summarizes their testimony, "the work is not automatic or mechanical, but requires considerable mental effort, and real mental capacity."[133] That effort, and that capacity, as we have observed, relate to an alertness, a being "on the *qui vive*," a readiness to "respond . . . to calls." If these traits are coded as being feminine, then the female operator is being figured as exemplary of the human element required despite the technological advances that made many parts of the telephone switching system automatic and continued to do so. The fact that, in *Working*, when Studs Terkel interviews a switchboard operator in the early 1970s, she says that she feels like a "servo-mechanism,"[134] confirms rather than contradicts the idea that, in order for certain kinds of machines to function, a human operator has to be responding to feedback from it continually. Many machines cannot fully self-regulate. This remains true of the rock drills still in use in South African gold and platinum mines. Machines that make it possible for humans to communicate with one another across distances also cannot self-regulate completely. This does not mean, of course, whether it is a telephone exchange of the 1907 pattern, a smartphone, or audiovisual conferencing software from 2020, that the nature of the machine does not determine, or at least shape, the type of response required of the user. This is why the young women at the Toronto exchange were prone to "nervous breakdown."[135]

Requiring the presence of a human operator, the telephone exchange of the early twentieth century is a quasi-automatic system that artificially produces continuous communication, across a distance, between human mouths and ears. In that respect, it parallels technologies, dating from the same time or somewhat earlier, that artificially produce still and moving images—the ones that William Kentridge uses to make his stereoscopic images and animated films.[136] When the machine requires an operator, as I have asserted, the question of technology becomes a question of labor.

My brief account of the career and commitments of the artist's grandfather shows that, in South Africa, the question of technology was also thereby racialized. A question of labor, in those days, was a question of white or African labor. Espousing the politics of the Labour Party, Morris Kentridge favored the employment of white mine workers over the efficiency of mechanical rock drills, introduced by mining companies when trained African workers were in short supply. When he advocates in parliament for the telephonists, he is advocating for women workers, who, being semiskilled workers, are probably mostly, if not exclusively, white (some, in the Western Cape, may have been Coloured). And, by trying to preserve white workers' jobs, their association is also, in effect, making their workplace whiter. That this became the subject of a demand would have consequences forty years later, as I detail in chapter 1. Although technology is not explicitly mentioned as a factor when Morris Kentridge spoke up on the telephonists' behalf, *The Live Wire*, their association's paper, gives it strong emphasis. The physical and mental strain of working an exchange, as operator conforms to machine, are a key reason why working hours should be strictly regulated. Historically, arguments in South Africa for or against mechanization and automation were implicated in positions for or against the color bar. This is plainly the case on the mines in the years before and after the 1922 strike. With the telephonists, the implication is less obvious. This is because the bar is not being contested by the employees or their employer—the Union government, which, after 1924, was providing sheltered employment to white people through the post office as much as through the railways and harbors and other state enterprises and parastatals. This is why Morris Kentridge's general concept of the machine would seem to apply without much qualification.

Thus, when we turn to *Stereoscope*, if William Kentridge is emphasizing a quasi-automatism of the telephone that parallels, technologically, the stereoscope and moving pictures, and finds itself realized recursively in Kentridge's artistic practice, then he is emphasizing three things of relevance to my argument. Two of these are implied or elided. First, he is drawing attention to the use of machines. Second, he gives us a brief glimpse of the women who operated those machines. Third, by elision, he makes it possible for us to think the implication of those women in a racialized labor politics, in which his grandfather was once involved. In the years before and after the 1922 revolt, white labor politicians opposed mechanization because they thought it would weaken the color bar. By the late 1960s, however, apartheid ideologues considered mechanization and automation as ways of *sustaining* the color bar. They also saw it as sustaining segregation in the workplace and contributing, indirectly, to grand apartheid. As Tlali's *Muriel at Metropolitan* registers, changes in racial employment patterns of the 1960s and 1970s overtook their ideas and schemes. That supersession does not mean that traces of those ideas as well as their antecedents do not make themselves felt in the way in which labor figures in the work of writers and artists.

At another level, I am making an argument about how to read an image—which can be a still or moving image, manually and/or mechanically produced and reproduced. For William Kentridge, the 1930s are the past of his future in the 1990s and early 2000s. Elided are the years in between—roughly coinciding with what Dan O'Meara calls the "forty lost years" of apartheid and National Party rule (1948–1994). Elided also is the *discourse* that circulated then, which gave a raison d'être to certain forms of mechanization and automation or came up in opposition to them. This not to say that this elision—or the supplementation that I am venturing—is what Kentridge intended. I think, however, that there is enough in his family history and in his early commitments for us to posit an *unconscious*, of which the images and smudges are traces. One may not even have to posit an unconscious but just a preconscious, in which a certain political syntax will have been deposited, through a dialogue with father, mother, and paternal grand-father. This would also have been, with the attendant negations, the dialogue of a generation of radicalized white university students. The maternal grandfather, too, may have contributed more than he knew in the realm of images: the box of obsolete office equipment, the book on landscape painting he gave to his grandson as a Hanukkah gift, the landscape by Dutch-born South African artist Tinus de Jongh on the wall in the dining room.[137] We see the verbal preconscious given ex-pression in *The Fantastical History of a Useless Man*. There words—we could say, the words of the paternal grandfather, although his name is not spoken in the play—are fractured in a syntax that, on the Nunnery Theatre stage, is completed graphically as well as dramatically: "Work-ers of the World Unite—for a White South Africa."

Speaking broadly, I am arguing for ekphrasis: history speaks from out of the picture. William Kentridge places great store in how, despite the deformations of line and outline, when we see an image, we see the image of *something*. Torn-up pieces of paper, arranged in a certain way, suggest a horse—this is one of his favorite examples. There is a moment of recognition. The film theorists who applied Lacan's dis-tinctions between the imaginary and the symbolic, and his theory of their relationship, call this "suture." What I wish to say is that, when I watch Kentridge's films, I recognize something—*what* that some-thing is, though, is not as easy to name as a horse. And even to begin to put my finger on it has required a great deal of research—reading texts that I never imagined existed, or if I had, that I would ever dream of reading them (Morris Kentridge's memoirs; various official reports on labor matters from South Africa, Canada, and Australia; *The Live Wire* magazine). You yourself recognize something, you *know*, but to start to make intelligible the unconscious text that you share with both novel and report, you have to locate and decipher the intertext—like the Freudian "switch word" that allows everything—or enough of everything—to resolve itself into intelligibility.

The title of the film, *Stereoscope*, may be unique in William Ken-tridge's oeuvre—in that it both titles the film and names a device for producing images mechanically and automatically. Since film is also such a technology, there is an element of recursion, as the title refers not only to the theme of the film but also alludes to its technics.[138] The frames with which *Stereoscope* closes are the nearest that the film comes to realizing the metaphor of stereoscopy with the technology of animated film. It does so by representing words in order to bring into relief the syntax of the moving image. Coming just before and after the unforgettable image of Soho Eckstein knee-deep in his own tears, we see the word *GIVE* becoming the word *FORGIVE*. The relevance of the words to the film is not explained, although we can guess that Soho has, at one level, to give—to those whom he exploits—whereas, at another level, he has to forgive—Mrs. Eckstein, perhaps.[139] Is it that it is not enough to give and that it is also necessary to forgive? It is not clear that the sequence, which is like one of those old flashing neon signs completing an advertising slogan or image, can be interpreted as encouraging a moral. Formally, however, the frames suggest the reliance of any meaning on mechanism, since that is what combines the material of words (and images) into a syntax (or a picture). The fact that two different words—*for* and *give*—combine to form a single word obviously alludes to stereoscopy, although the effects of mechanical combination, when it comes to language, are not always of this form.

The sequence also alludes to the workings of the unconscious. Although we may think that *FORGIVE* is the full and final imperative, the unconscious does not have that hierarchy, and the words are just words, and no imperatives at all: *FOR*, *GIVE*, and *FORGIVE*. But something is struggling to come to the surface and needs the combination of two parts. This parallels when, in the Junction Avenue play, the banner with the 1922 miners' slogan was split before being completed so that imperative and preference could be made visible in their distinctness before coalescing into what was declared historically. The *for* in "for a white South Africa" does not mean the same as the *FOR* in *FORGIVE*, but it is morphologically identical. It can therefore be treated, at the human mechanism's most primitive level, as the same word. The word *for* marks a return—of the repressed, to be sure, but, in more elemental terms, of an irreducible materiality. We see a parallel in early computer poetry such as Coetzee's. His "Line Generator" produces unusual combinations because the computer is programmed not to recognize words but to convert verbal input into numbers. These numbers it then manipulates—for example, through a random number generator—and outputs as words in set combinations, but it remains indifferent to their meaning. As Beatriz in Coetzee's *The Pole* realizes, at some level, "the computer . . . is stupid."[140] When the labor of verbal manipulation—one hesitates to call it "writing"—is automated, that automation reveals an unconscious and technics as the unconscious. Although the word *FOR* is not in Coetzee's word list for "Line Generator," the same would be true for the prepositions that are in the database: *INTO, IN, BY, AMONG, WITH, ON*, and *THRUGH*.

The frames to which *Stereoscope* most frequently returns are those that, coming just after the opening ones showing the empty telephone exchange, show Soho standing alone in his living room (this is also where the film ends, with his tears flooding the room).[141] At first, it appears that this is a complete image. But later in the film, it looks as if this was the right side of a dual image, divided by a blue line, with the image on the left showing another Soho beset by thoughts of columns of figures, with sporadic flashes of his wife, always pictured as a reclining nude. The left-hand side always has a frenetic Soho, suggesting business, and an imperviousness to what is happening elsewhere. The Soho on the right-hand side, alone except for his cat, seems more vulnerable to emotion and is affected by events outside his living room. The most dramatic sequence of the film is when the right-hand Soho puts his ear to the wall—which is also the blue line splitting the diptych—and we see a series of images of civic protest; police assault and firing on demonstrators; an abandoned corpse; an execution by revolver to the head; the slinging of people over the edge of what could be a bridge, followed by shooting over that edge. The first image could easily be from the 1922 miners' strike. The last of the images recalled to me a photograph or video from the 1994 genocide in Rwanda. No doubt the other images could also be traced back to documentary sources.[142] That Soho begins to block his ears could be a sign both that he does not want to hear/see/imagine more of this violence and that he, previously oblivious and uncaring, is now traumatically affected by what he hears/sees. The images are also shown to reach him through the blue lines that run through the telephone exchange. He is pictured using a telephone in an earlier sequence, but the blue lines are what convey, throughout the film, the abstract ideas of communication and interconnection.[143] Periodically, these blue lines begin to form their own images, as blue-on-black animation suggests another space of formation or metamorphosis. This is also where the image of the stereoscopic viewer appears momentarily, as telephone lines become lines of optical perspective.[144] The sequences connote an autonomy of the medium and an automaticity of the line—independent of the idea. Technics, or the unconscious, returns. Toward the end of *Stereoscope*, this nexus is suggested in two aspects, which work together. A globular bomb of the old-fashioned type with a burning fuse, part of the standard iconography of animated cartoons, appears and then explodes. We then see two things. An image of a white background with gray smudging—as if the medium of charcoal and paper has devolved into an elemental nonsignifying state. Then we see the blue lines erased—their gray paths remain—as they recede into the depths of the mechanism of the telephone exchange. "The connections are broken," as Matthew Kentridge astutely writes, drawing a parallel between body and machine, "reduced to a few pinpricks of blue light against the darkness—the last few synapses firing after a beheading."[145] We know, from the royal commission report on the Bell telephone operators' strike, that the neuropsychology of the early 1900s assumed a continuity, through the medium of electricity, of telephone cable and nerve. In *Stereoscope*, then, blankness or indefinition of media—paper, charcoal—connote technical and neural shutdown. It is then that the blue of the lines masses and liquefies as Soho's tears.

When I wrote that technics, or the unconscious, returns, I was also suggesting that we can close the circle, or at least complete the Möbius strip, by connecting technology and genealogy. In an interview with Dan Cameron, published in 2001, Kentridge explains why he depicts certain technologies in his films. Having said how the Bakelite telephone is relatively unchanging, over decades, compared to contemporary telephones, and thus has greater stability as an image, Kentridge continues:

But a further reason, I think, for using drawings of old technologies is wanting to do things that convey a more visible explanation of how they work. It's a mechanical rather than an electrical modus operandi, something in which you can see the cause and effect of switches, levers, wheels, visible mechanics.

The same holds true even if I'm referring to a contemporary phenomenon, such as the proliferation of points of contact through increased use of telephones, Internet, all these other things. It's still easier to show all that in a mechanical way, using a technology that might have predated the phenomenon I'm interested in. So an old mechanical telephone exchange, for me, is an easy way of drawing the points of exchange and of communication that we are all locked into now.

But I think even more than that, there is a sense of trusting childhood more than adulthood, that provides a reason for a lot of the objects that I draw. These come from images of those objects that I saw in childhood—not necessarily 1950s objects, but maybe 1930s objects that would have been illustrated in books I was looking at in the 1950s.

There is a sense of the clarity of impulse we get as a child, seeing something new; for example the first time one sees extraordinary adult violence. The first shock one gets when seeing photographs either horrific or pornographic. The strength of the response is something that gets dulled and lessened as the experience gets repeated and as the thing being seen gets more and more familiar.

So part of going back to images from my childhood is not so much an interest necessarily in those objects, but trying to use them as a talisman, to get back to the clarity of sensation that one would have had as a child.[146]

Two themes are interconnected: the desire to show the inner workings of technology and the way in which doing so activates what Kentridge calls the "clarity of impulse" or "clarity of sensation that one would have had as a child."[147] It is interesting to know that Kentridge views his use of images of old technologies as referring to the "contemporary phenomenon" of the "proliferation of points of contact through increased use of telephones, Internet, all these other things."[148] It is also important that he emphasizes the fact that doing so makes visible, through allusion, the processes underlying these things. Even if electricity was a key part of the telephone, there is enough of a mechanism to make its moving parts directly visible to the eye, whereas with electrical circuitry, this is not the case.[149] Visual artists like Nam June Paik and Bill Viola have found ways of bringing the electrical directly before the eye of the viewer. But Kentridge's solution is to allude to it via mechanism. This making visible is a constant impulse in Kentridge's work, whether in the films or his puppetry. When he employs anamorphosis, as he does in several works, including the film *What Will Come (Has Already Come)* (2007) (figure 3.2), this is because it brings the process of transformation of an unrecognizably distorted image into a regular image directly before the eye in a way that is not possible with the processes of digital media.

Figure 3.2. William Kentridge, What Will Come (Has Already Come), *2007. Courtesy William Kentridge Studio.*

The passage I have quoted from the interview with Cameron begins with a *but*. What follows the next *but* connects all this artistic strategizing to what psychoanalysis calls the *Wißtrieb*, or the drive for knowledge, which is linked, in Freud and Klein, to the primal scene.[150] This is what Kentridge gives as a "reason for a lot of the objects I draw." It is the source of the "impulse" and "sensation" that have a clarity in childhood that is dulled in later life. The temporality of the account given by Kentridge is complicated. In one respect, the old technologies allow the new ones to emerge before the eye—and, presumably, for them to do so with greater clarity than would be achieved if he were to have drawn a cellular phone. A way of understanding this is to argue, as does Krauss,[151] that reference to the old technology inevitably reads contemporary technology as the realization—with its paths taken and not taken—of a future of that past. A complex visual nostalgia, in other words.

But, in the context of the argument I am making, which situates William Kentridge in a symbolic matrix of political choices that come down genealogically from his grandfather, one can go further. The dates that he tosses out for Cameron are unexpectedly revealing. What he saw was mediated by the illustration and, at another level, by the book. Kentridge, who was born in 1955, remembers looking not at 1950s objects, or even at images of them, but at images of 1930s objects. Is there a displacement? Let us say that his "1950s objects" include him, as well as the father and mother. In that case, we have a primal scene, with him doing the looking. But this primal scene is partially negated—"not necessarily"—and another one tentatively affirmed: "but maybe 1930s objects that would have been illustrated in books." His father, Sydney, was born in 1922 (the same year as my late adoptive father and the same year as the miners' strike), but his mother, Felicia, was born in 1930. If the "1930s objects" are the father and mother, then it is their conception that is either alluded to directly, in a scene therefore involving two sets of grandparents, or, if it is a displacement, it is William's own conception, as a "1950s object." We know that after somebody points it out to him twelve years after he made the film *Johannesburg, 2nd Greatest City After Paris* (1989), William Kentridge perceives that the name of his mother resides in that of the character Felix Teitlebaum. His dream from which the characters in his films' names come thus refers to his mother: "Who is the Felix? . . . Of course, it is so obvious that I must have been repressing it for all those years."[152] Family lore attests to the name being a negation of sorrow in the wake of tragedy and maternal "nervous breakdown."[153]

Perhaps it is not either the parental or the grandparental scene but both. The powerful investment in the paternal grandfather—in visual and verbal terms—suggests that the latter overdetermines the former. We know Morris Kentridge's looming familial presence from the young Kentridge's 1976 linocut "Muizenberg 1933."[154] The work's heavily invested date of 1933, with its two 3's written backward in the work itself, alludes to the medium of printing that reverses the artist's gouging and scoring of the linoleum. It also alludes to Freud's insight that things said or described from dreams might need to be reversed in order to make sense.[155] An argument could be made that Morris Kentridge— thanks to his own apparent narcissism—was available to his grandson primarily through a proliferation of images, the most memorable of which were caricatures.[156] The linocut itself is fully a primal scene, composed of the father (Sydney Kentridge) and his brother and their father and mother.[157]

Kentridge's description fits almost exactly the standard description that comes down to us, from Freud and Klein, of how the primal scene of parental sexual intercourse looks, or registers affectively, to the young child: "There is a sense of the clarity of impulse we get as a child, seeing something new; for example the first time one sees extraordinary adult violence. The first shock one gets when seeing photographs either horrific or pornographic." In other statements, the photographs in question—which he recalls after making the film *Felix in Exile*—are of victims of Sharpeville that he furtively peruses in his father's study.[158] They thus, of course, connect to Sydney Kentridge's work as an attorney, suggesting that the shock is inseparable from Oedipal rivalry, and, of course, from his fear of castration—the horrific and the pornographic are two sides of the same coin.[159]

The libidinal is connected with violence, which, in due course, becomes Oedipal. The boy, following his *Wißtrieb*, which is why he is poring over encyclopedias, wants to see the inner workings (of the mother). But he thereby risks repeating the violence done to her, in the boy's fantasy, by the father.[160] All of this is before words, before image becomes overlaid with word, before "historial" ekphrasis. A "talisman," although it can be an image or contain one, is not exactly a picture. But here it is mediating visually, a violence that is repeated—and has already been repeated, in different forms: in the 1950s, as parental intercourse; in the 1930s, as an (unspoken) legacy of race politics for which 1933 is a synecdoche, as is 1922 in South Africa. The Muizenberg linocut was done in the same year as *The Fantastical History of a Useless Man*, 1976, when apartheid reached its terminal crisis with the Soweto uprising. The following year, Steve Biko was beaten to death by his police interrogators, and Sydney Kentridge, who, as junior counsel, represented Mandela and others in the Treason Trial of 1958–61,[161] represented the Biko family at the inquest.[162]

I cannot stop wondering, with the example of a father and mother who were as actively involved as attorneys in the anti-apartheid struggle, and the political connections that would have been available through them, how William Kentridge could have signed on to a play that proclaimed the "uselessness" of somebody of his background. The implicit contrast is with my own background: my adoptive father voted for the United Party until it was defunct, and the family home was largely disconnected from left-liberal politics. Perhaps I am underestimating the extent to which progressive white people felt pushed aside, by the early 1970s, by the politics of Black Consciousness. You certainly see this in Gordimer, who was a Kentridge family friend. But then Sydney Kentridge represents the Biko family; he finds a way to remain "useful."[163] Or perhaps there is a psychological explanation for the plea of uselessness, with William Kentridge needing to emerge from the shadow of his father (and mother), who presented him with a tough act to follow.[164] There is the one that Kentridge gives in various interviews, especially when he refers to his father: "I come from a very logical and rational family. My father is a lawyer. I had to establish myself in the world as not just being his son, his child. I had to find a way of arriving at knowledge that was not subject to cross-examination, not subject to legal reasoning. When I was in the field of ordinary reasoning I found I was always under his opinions."[165] Felicia Kentridge, also a "lawyer,"[166] and a notable one, is never figured in this way.[167] In the classic Oedipal scenario, she would be unlikely to be, for she is the one toward whom the path is barred by the father. His opinions prevent the son from "arriving at knowledge" in his pursuit of the *Wißtrieb*, which is in relation to the mother. She, again classically, is the one whom the boy artist wants to make happy with his landscape drawings.[168] Or, if this looks all too neat, maybe the Oedipal violence that could not be openly directed at the father (and mother) because they are too "good" is displaced toward the paternal grandfather, whom Kentridge scholars hardly notice,[169] and toward the ambiguity of his politics: the workerist slogan only complete with the subtext of white supremacy. Impossible to *know*, of course. But possible to investigate, and to *read* the images, moving or still—in this instance, *Stereoscope*, the Muizenberg linocut, *Tide Table*, and so forth—as implicated in this fierce genealogical drama, mediated by successive primal scenes, from the 1950s, the 1930s, and the 1920s. In this nexus, wherever there is a machine, there is also a woman: Where there is a telephone exchange, there is a telephone operator. For Mackenzie King, to describe the machine is to describe the woman—and, in fact, in his description of the effects of the machine, the rhetoric he uses practically elides the machine and concentrates on what it did to the bodies and psyches of the women who operated it. If, in Canada, the woman was described thus because she was a worker, in South Africa, it was because she was a *white* worker.

Another way of formulating the nexus of technology, gender, race, and labor is to observe that, historically, in the tradition of writing and image making of which Goldblatt and Gordimer's *On the Mines* is a classic, white-collar workers are in the background. And so are women. In Kentridge, women who work, and work in offices, are brought to the fore indirectly—when the machines they use are represented (which itself can be indirectly). The working of machines, as imagined by Kentridge, is inseparable from the work that *those* workers do with machines. This is another way of stating the case that the meaning of the machine, mechanization, and automation depends on the division of labor. In South African offices, until things begin to change in the 1960s, the division of labor was racial. In ways that attracted the attention of apartheid ideologues, it was also gendered. As the meaning of the machine is, in turn, elaborated in South African artistic production, the scene of the worker at her machine gives way, first, to ideas, familiar to readers of Marx, about how she conforms to her machine. Then the scene gives way to ideas of how, because the human body functions both mechanically and electrically, her physical and mental adaptation to the machine rests on how its workings utilize the same physical pathways. In my final chapter, I show how, over against a longer tradition of these ideas and critical reactions to them, the puppet theater stages and challenges these notions but also suggests another way of thinking the relation between human and machine that has much in common with how, at a phenomenal level, human-machine interaction looks in an age of computerization.

4

The Puppet Theater

Handspring Puppet Company is probably best known outside of South Africa for its London National Theatre adaptation of *War Horse* (2007), a novel by Michael Morpurgo about cavalry horses in the Great War, and *Tall Horse* (2004), produced with the Sogolon Puppet Troupe of Mali. Founded by Basil Jones, Adrian Kohler, Jill Joubert, and Jon Weinberg in 1981,[1] Handspring soon became known for its variety of techniques and the types of puppets corresponding to them. These ranged from the giant Bamana puppets of Mali to the smaller-than-life-size figures that feature in its version of Bunraku. To them one can add shadow or silhouette puppetry. They inspired William Kentridge, who collaborated with Handspring in several productions between 1992 and 2000, to create a series of films, installations, and sculptures using silhouettes, including *Shadow Procession*.[2]

In 1992, Handspring Puppet Company first staged *Woyzeck on the Highveld*, an adaptation of Georg Büchner's 1836 play. Under Kentridge's direction, Handspring transposed the action from Germany to Johannesburg in the 1950s, turning its protagonist, a soldier, into an African migrant worker.[3] The production combined Handspring's puppetry, live actors, and Kentridge's animated film. Projected as a backdrop, what is on the screen sometimes complements the motions of the puppets and voices of the puppeteers by suggesting Woyzeck's unvoiced thoughts and imaginings.

As I showed in the previous chapter, these films, like any film, depend on a technics that functions automatically. In this chapter, I extend my argument by showing how an automaticity is simulated by the puppet theater. This simulation can be interpreted as a commentary on how human beings interact with machines, including whether they are, in certain respects, machinelike, or in any respect not. I also show, however, that the puppet theater, as it has been the subject of commentary historically, invites those who observe it closely to discern something else—which relates, specifically, to how human beings interact with computers. That is anamorphosis. The name for how a distorted image is transformed into a regular image, the term has migrated from Renaissance European painting and the early modern science of optics to being a metaphor for the experience of using a computer. In each case, some technical means is required for something unintelligible to become intelligible. As with *Stereoscope*, in *Woyzeck on the Highveld* the automaticity of perception and cognition required for this transformation to take place is represented as profoundly related to the labor process in its automated form.

Diceromaton

Büchner never finished *Woyzeck*. Among the manuscripts he left behind when he died of typhus at the age of twenty-three were four sets of brief scenes. Only some of these were written down in sequence. Evidently a story of love and jealousy and murder, of a poor man and his struggle for existence, and against the loss of his reason, the remnants had no title. Contemporaries may have recognized, in the main character's name, that of a former soldier and wigmaker's apprentice publicly beheaded in Leipzig in 1824 for stabbing to death the woman who had been his lover and landlady. In 1879, a version of the play was published for the first time by Karl Emil Franzos, who, erring in deciphering Büchner's difficult hand, gave it the title *Wozzeck*. Since then, successive editors have established different orderings for a "reading text."[4] The fragmentary nature of the text that survived its author has always invited avant-garde dramatic experiment. The earliest productions nevertheless relied on Franzos, and into the repertory came a script that remained unchallenged as late as 1925. The title of Alban Berg's opera with its immortal opening words—"Langsam, Wozzeck, langsam"—bore Franzos's imprint. This was in spite of two revised scholarly editions, published between 1920 and 1922, that had corrected the title and altered Franzos's sequence to better match the manuscript. For its part, Handspring Puppet Company's production

Figure 4.1. *The puppet rhinoceros in* Woyzeck on the Highveld, *2008. Courtesy William Kentridge Studio.*

largely follows the order established by Werner Lehmann and published in 1968.[5]

In its most significant deviation from that sequence, in which the corresponding scene is early in the play, about halfway into *Woyzeck on the Highveld*, there is a scene in which the fairground barker, played by Mncedisi Shabangu in the 2008 revival,[6] and doing his best to translate his heteroglossia into something sounding South African,[7] invites the audience in the house to behold what sounds like the "astronomical diceromaton"—in other words, the *Diceros bicornis*, or black rhinoceros, in the form of an automaton. That would figure: The marvelous beast is a puppet miniature rhinoceros placed on a table, and Basil Jones and Adrian Kohler, its two manipulators, are in plain view (figure 4.1). A puppet, as much as a bicycle, say, is a near automaton. Although there is no way that it could be started up and left to run on its own, as the automata of Büchner's time did by means of wind-up clockwork mechanisms that produced the same effects every time, it also cannot move by itself. It thus offers an occasion to reflect on what we mean by *automatic*.

What do the members of Handspring say about the puppet's automatism? Their commitment to humanist—and animist—ideas about puppetry remains firm. Basil Jones tells us, for example, that the puppet seeks life.[8] The puppeteers are nevertheless rigorous in never eliding the careful artifice involved in making puppets. This artifice makes it possible for the puppeteer, by following a regular and predictable series of movements, to produce an acceptable illusion of life. Achieving such predictability is the greater part of the preparation for any production. As much is clear from the descriptions of the modifications the company needed to make to the puppets in *War Horse* so it would be possible for the puppeteers to work with them without developing repetitive-strain injuries.[9] The puppet may thus be viewed as primary. As Basil Jones, speaking on a different occasion, explained to an interviewer, "You're always serving the puppet, and when serving the puppet is painful you can easily start thinking of it as an enslavement. I've just come from an operating theater where I had surgery, because the last play I did was so painful that I did some damage to the tendons in my arm."[10]

In the conditions of possibility for the illusion, the human conforms to what is made possible by a machine or tool constructed in a certain way, just as other things are not made possible, or made not-possible. Although the puppet depends on its puppeteer as its "animator" in performance, as artist and Handspring collaborator Gerhard Marx rightly observes, one discerns, as one of its conditions of possibility, a system of automation that should make us hesitate to *oppose* it to the automaton or machine.[11] Animation, whether in film or puppetry, depends on automation. Even if Basil Jones is correct to call the puppetry "very old-fashioned technology," it may not be inaccurate to view puppets and their puppeteers in performance as *cyborgs*, the term used by theorists of less old-fashioned modern media to describe entities reducible neither to human nor machine but operating through their interdependence.[12] This is an insight developed in different ways by contemporary theorists of puppetry.[13] Most examples of the cyborg, historically, involve a high degree of programming. Applying the term in a general way, this means that the human user has to learn to conform to the device or software platform—like the regularity and predictability of motion sought after during the design phase of the horse puppets in *War Horse*. If tradition tells us that the nonhuman puppet depends on the human puppeteer for life, the reverse may be equally true—that the "life" of the human entity depends on whatever the nonhuman entity allows by virtue of its design. If true, it is true not only for puppeteers but for any user of a machine or tool.

It is nevertheless the case that, in an age of programmable machines, whether of the nineteenth or the twenty-first century, the puppet will be a *but*. In that epoch, the puppet is a reminder and trace of the irreducible excess or remainder of skilled work by the human hand. At a more allegorical level, it issues a claim on behalf of the life abiding within the human being who, through training and mindless labor, has come to function—or work—like a machine.[14] In a persona alternately menacing and desperate to draw laughter or applause, the Barker in *Woyzeck on the Highveld* demonstrates what the performing "diceromaton" can do. It is no accident that, contrasting it to what is "natural," he harps on "education" with an insistence that is not in the source text:

Ladies and gentlemen, the astronomical diceromaton! He is the favorite in all of the capitals and all the boardrooms. He is a trustee of all charitable institutions. *Come on, show your talent! Show your beastly intelligence. Up!* (Rhino rises on hind legs.) Everything can be taught. Observe his powers. He can add but he can't count on his fingers. Whahahahaha! Whahahahaha! Whahahahaha! Ladies and gentlemen, education. E-du-cation. *Spell!* (Rhino paws with right front foot, and the letter "R" appears on blackboard in a small empty room drawn on the screen in animation.) Tomorrow he learns punctuation. He will put human society to shame yet. He is a professor at all our universities. *How many children has that man?* (Rhino paws with right front leg, and vertical lines appear in several rows crossed out on animated blackboard on screen.) That was simple arithmetic. Now, use your double reason. *What is the cause of that man's toothache?* (Rhino paws with front foot, and a dental diagram appears on the blackboard on the screen, with a tooth falling out.) *What is the cause of that lady's heartbreak?* (Paws with front foot, and a penis with spots on it appears on blackboard on the screen.) Is there anyone more beastly than him? Is there anyone less beastly than him? No dumb animals anywhere here. But all beasts nonetheless! Put society to shame. Observe the progress of civilization. Everything progresses. A beast, a diceronatos.[15] (Shoots out stream of urine. Barker wipes forehead with handkerchief.) It's all dust, sand. Fools! Ekskuus! [Excuse me!] (Throws handkerchief to audience.) No matter—he has other skills. He can sing, in three languages. He can ride a bicycle. He can fire a gun. (Barker uses cord to connect horn of rhino with trigger of revolver in his hand. Rhino lifts head to fire several shots, as targets and various animals appear and disappear on animated screen. Barker aims gun at rhino's head. Rhino moves backwards, pulls trigger, rises up on hind legs, then collapses in a heap. Rhino shows signs of motion.) *Out!* (Rhino exits, with puppeteers.) It's not natural. It's all educaaation! Ladies and gentlemen, thank you very much. I am finished. Sengiqedile! [I am now finished!] (Barker exits.)[16]

Those familiar with the scene in Büchner's play notice immediately that, although Handspring preserves several elements, including the detail that the beast can fire a gun,[17] the performed pseudo-suicide of the beast is an audacious addition. Being a performance—a "räpräsentation," in Büchner's Barker's borrowed French[18]—it figures, making the act of self-killing into a metaphor that can be interpreted in different ways: as an allegory about colonial violence,[19] or, the rhinoceros being today an endangered species, as a plea against environmental destruction, which is, ultimately, a slow act of human suicide. Any such interpretation, however, needs to be placed within an analysis of the conventions and technics involved in *Woyzeck on the Highveld*. The conventions are those of the theater, whereas the technics are specifically those of puppetry. Each gives rise to its own set of metaphors and allegories. The *sui* in *suicide* is Latin for the Greek *autos*, or self. With a puppet performing self-murder, not only with the intervention of the Barker, which is theatrical, but with that of the puppeteers, on which everything depends technologically, the self as *autos* is placed in question. Is what is "automatic" self-moving—the ancient Greek meaning of *automatos*—or is it that which carries out predictable or programmable actions like a machine? In ages of mechanization and automation of labor, physical and mental, puppetry will inevitably raise this question. Just as inevitably, it will complicate the distinction on which the question is based. Let us therefore conduct a closer examination.

Although a few other turns of phrase survive from Büchner in Handspring's adaptation, relating to "beastly intelligence," "civilization," and "double reason," by making education the central theme, it condenses and simplifies the Barker's speech as well as the mise-en-scène. The delayed placement of the scene, the introduction of a rhinoceros, and the beast's act of suicide are not the only changes made to it. In Büchner, the scene is a play within a play, as Woyzeck, Marie, the Drum Major, and the Sergeant all go to see the sideshow attraction. Marie voices her expectations, which double as a commentary for the audience, after having seen the dressed-up monkeys that are its prelude: "Must be real lovely. Just look at his tassles [*sic*], and the woman's in trousers."[20] In *Woyzeck on the Highveld*, none of the characters sees the show. Handspring thus relinquishes, in favor of a montage played solely for the house, the doubling of audience—on stage and in the house—entailed by any play within a play. Whether it is *The Mousetrap* or this fairground sideshow, whether it is for the King and Queen or for Woyzeck and Marie, it is an old form of Verfremdung, breaking the fourth wall between players and audience. It is curious how this was left out, since the scene, in Handspring's production, effects another doubling: of puppetry. If the play within the play leads one to think about the artifice of theater generally, then the recursion of puppet in the form of trained performing animal ought to draw forth a reflection on the art and technics of puppetry.

As is typical in productions by Handspring, who frequently work in the Bunraku style, in which the puppeteers appear on stage with the puppets, artifice is visible. However lifelike it appears to be, the puppet cannot move on its own. With this scene, there is, however, another dimension, in which the difference between a living being and a machine is put into question. It is here that the relationship between the source text and its adaptation for the puppet theater is especially complex. When Handspring simplifies Büchner's text in order to have the Barker emphasize education, and thereby bring into question the difference between civilized humans and trained animals, it passes over an important detail of the Barker's provocation—namely the question of whether humans, like intelligent animals, are to be thought as machines. Unlikely to have been a view to which Büchner himself subscribed, the idea is there for the audience—in the house and in the play—to consider, and to consider its relevance for their own situation. But because Handspring adapts Büchner for puppets, the question returns, implicitly but inevitably, at the level of theatrical mise-en-scène and technical mise-en-oeuvre, and the montage becomes ambiguous and even unreadable: The Barker is not simply *telling* the audience what is so, but the puppetry is *demonstrating*, or at least suggesting, that it is so. The puppet play can distance itself from the Barker's words, but it cannot evade the implications of its own technics, which tend to verify them.

In Büchner, the animal is a performing horse, and there is also a canary: "Roll up, ladies and gentlemen, roll up and see the astronomical horse and the dwarf canary; favorites of the entire crowned 'eads of Europe and members of all the known learned societies."[21] Its supposed intelligence is, presumably, the carrying out of certain movements on command: "Any asses out there amongst our learned assembly? [*The horse shakes its head*]."[22] But there is an ambiguity, in which the ability to *rechnen* (reckon, calculate) could be viewed as more essential than the ability to count on one's fingers—which the Barker in *Woyzeck on the Highveld* makes into a joke about hooved animals that he laughs at himself—or the ability to express oneself in words. It depends on how you hear the "kann doch nit" (still can't) and the "kann sich nur nit" (just can't) in the Barker's final lines: "Sehn Sie, was Vernunft, es kann rechnen und kann doch nit an de Finger herzählen, warum? Kann sich nur nit ausdrücke, nur nit expliziern, ist ein verwandlter Mensch!"[23] Do these privatives, which make the horse like one of the earliest mechanical calculators or the first electronic computers, which had neither printer nor screen, necessarily count in humans' favor? If calculation is the sign of reason (Vernunft), and reason is the leading criterion, the Barker seems to ask, how is the horse any less a beast of reason, when, after all, it "has a beastly reason, or rather an entirely reasonable beastliness" (*haben eine viehische Vernunft, oder vielmehr eine ganze vernünftige Viehigkeit*)?[24] And, in that case, the satire appears to run, on what grounds could any human object to being *verwandelt* (transformed) into such a beast? "A 'uman he is," the Barker declares, "a 'uman being in animal form, but a beast, an animal all the same.... There's reason [Vernunft] for yer: he can add up all right [*rechnen*] but he still can't count on 'is fingers. And why? Just can't express 'isself, just can't explain things, he's a 'uman bein' in all but shape [*verwandlter Mensch*]! Tell the good people what time it is. Any of you ladies and gentlemen got a watch? A watch?"[25] The relevant parallel suggested by the Barker's presentation of the horse is not between the human being and just any machine. Rather, it is between them and those prototypes of twentieth- and twenty-first-century machines that were already in evidence in the form of mechanical calculators, devised as early as the seventeenth century by Pascal and Leibniz, among others, and clock-work automata. Just over a century before *Woyzeck*, Jonathan Swift had the parallel come from a horse's mouth.[26]

The Barker's provocation is of its time. We know, for example, from E. T. A. Hoffmann's "Die Automate" (1814), that, in Büchner's life-time, automata of various kinds were sometimes sideshow attractions to be marveled at in the fairground booths, as one imagines, down from the performing horses and monkeys.[27] In a century in which even human beings doubled as automata to be exhibited,[28] it is thus no stretch of historical verisimilitude for Handspring's rhinoceros to be both a performing animal and an automaton. In *Woyzeck on the High-veld*, although the Barker's reductio on *rechnen*—isn't a human being machinelike, and why wouldn't it want to be?—is passed over in the *text*, along with its implications, the idea of a living being *operated* as a machine is set in bold. The satire against mechanization receives its exclamation point when, in a detail true to Büchner's stage direction, which could also be interpreted as calling for defecation,[29] the rhino spontaneously lifts its leg and squirts out a stream of urine. It reverts, as does Woyzeck in a different scene, to what comes naturally. It will not be a machine for entertaining the audience—although, of course, this satire can be missed, given how the urinating animal is played for laughs and how the characters in the adaptation are absent from the scene as viewers and commentators.

What was it about Büchner and his play—other than the fact that *Woyzeck* was in the repertory—that drew Handspring and William Kentridge to his work? In both the source play and the adaptation, Woyzeck is a poor man who works more than one job so as to scrape together enough for himself, Marie, and their child—although dis-agreement exists among scholars about whether Büchner's Woyzeck is quite as destitute as was the historical Johann Christian Woyzeck, the murderer on whom he is based.[30] Well into the 1980s, as I noted in chapter 3, Kentridge acted in and directed plays aimed at members of African trade unions. It does not require taking a position on whether Büchner's *Woyzeck* is a "social drama," or entertains more philosoph-ical themes,[31] or does something of both, to observe that, as Hand-spring frames its adaptation, *Woyzeck* is, in certain respects, workers' theater. The company refers to Woyzeck as a migrant worker, and Adrian Kohler tells us that he is a mine worker, "living from hand-to-

mouth in the industrialised landscape of twentieth-century Johannesburg."[32] This characterization is confusing, inexplicably at odds with
who *their* Woyzeck is. The only work that he does is to lay the table for
the Captain—who is an effete burgher, not a military man. This scenario would fit with the 1950s, the decade in which Handspring says
their adaptation is set, a time when African men in the city still found
work as "houseboys."[33]

There is, of course, a mine worker in *Woyzeck on the Highveld*. The
Drum Major in the source play, he is Woyzeck's sexual rival. Just as he
is of higher rank in Büchner, and thus of superior means to Woyzeck, in
the adaptation, he is the more formidable figure of the two and clearly
better off. In both versions, he has the money to buy Marie a pair of
earrings. How to make sense of the discrepancy?

What may be happening is that the adapters are having trouble sep-
arating the status of the mine worker of the 1950s from that of the mine
worker of the early 1990s.[34] We can tell from *Cry, the Beloved Country*, *Mine Boy*, *Come Back Africa!*, and other works from the late 1940s
into the 1960s that the African migrant come to work on the mines of
the Rand is, for South African (and American) high-cultural production, the worker who is quintessentially exploited under South African
capitalist modernity. Mine workers maintain this status although, in
actuality, African and Coloured farmworkers probably suffered more
severe exploitation, as *Drum* magazine's Bethal exposé revealed.[35] The
Afrikaans *plaasroman* (farm novel) of the era, although representing
them as poor people, still portrayed farmworkers in more sentimental
terms. And perhaps because Johannesburg remained the imaginative
center of cultural production, a shining lure to writers and filmmakers,
as much as it was for capitalists and workers, such investigative forays
into the rural hinterland appear to have had a less than lasting impact.
Even the houseboy, who features in the film *Jim Comes to Joburg* (1949),
makes only a fleeting appearance.

By the early 1990s, when *Woyzeck on the Highveld* was first produced,
the mine worker should have been relieved of the dubious distinction
of being the worst exploited. Black miners' wages rose dramatically in
the 1970s, albeit from a low base, and continued to rise in smaller increments during the 1980s.[36] More than a decade of unionization, following the legalization of black trade unions in 1979, meant that, by the late
1980s, although not paid as much as black factory workers, and paid a

fraction of what their white counterparts earned, African mine workers were still less exploited than farmworkers.[37] In 1987, the National Union of Mineworkers, led by Cyril Ramaphosa (who became president of South Africa in 2018), called a strike in which three hundred thousand workers struck for three weeks.[38] Although not achieving the union's wage demands, the strike was a sign of the growing power and militancy of organized African labor that had led to the formation of the Congress of South African Trade Unions (COSATU) in 1985. As in Goldblatt and Gordimer's *On the Mines* in an earlier era, it continued to be mine workers who commanded the attention of artists and writers, despite the fact that, by 1994, South African clerical workers numbered more than 750,000.[39]

At the same time, the loosening of apartheid influx control, repealed in 1986, meant that more Africans came to the cities to eke out a living, even as unemployment among black South Africans was rising dramatically. A new, more marginal figure emerges in, and perhaps moves toward the center of, the elite cultural imagination. Athol Fugard's *Boesman and Lena* (1969) is an important precursor. Then we have Coetzee's Vercueil in *Age of Iron* (1990) and K. Sello Duiker's Azure in *Thirteen Cents* (2000). Both are homeless, and the latter is also a child. It thus comes as little surprise to learn from Handspring that Kentridge wanted to make "Harry, a homeless person living in the neighbourhood, who had acted in a live-action film made some time before by William, . . . the central character" in their "experiment with puppet figures and animated film."[40] In the absence of a script, the pressure of a deadline made them rely more heavily on Büchner's play, which was to have been a "reference, a kicking-off point for this experiment with puppet figures and animated film."[41] Harry, however, remains as a trace, with their play featuring Johann Harry Woyzeck, who appears to have no home of his own and whose economic status is clearly below that of the Drum Major as mine worker.

There is more. In order to perceive it, we turn from the figure of the worker to an intimation of inner workings. As is clear from authors I referred to in chapter 3, by the early twentieth century, it had for some time been accepted that nerves function by conducting electricity. Walt Whitman's "I Sing the Body Electric" (1855) was probably only partly metaphorical. With that scientific consensus, electrical impulses could become part of the theoretical framework of neurology and its offshoots, including neuropsychology, of which Freud's uncollected early writings are a well-known testament. Electricity thus also became an element in explaining the occurrence of mental and physical stress, as well as injury, in work requiring human interaction with electromechanical machines. This we observed in Mackenzie King's account of the effects of telephony on young women. If human and machine were still held to be distinct in advocacy for the worker, there could have been no doubt, when their respective inner workings were considered and compared, that electricity was an irreducible point of convergence.

In the early nineteenth century in Germany, however, the polemic against the machine, as it touched on the nervous system, was waged on different ground. As Freud did nearly fifty years later, Büchner, as a medical student, was dissecting fish to study their nerves.[42] Presenting the results of his experiments in his November 1836 Zürich examination lecture, "On Cranial Nerves," Büchner stands as the proponent of a Goethian holism and a follower of the comparative anatomists of whom Cuvier remains the best known and whose theories were superseded shortly thereafter by Darwin's theory of evolution.[43] As a prelude to stating his theory of cranial nerve morphology, Büchner mounts a brief critique of teleology. He makes a telling distinction between two opposing basic views (*Grundansichten*) in physiology and anatomy, "which even bear a national stamp in that one is dominant in England and France, the other in Germany."[44] As Reddick points out, the English trends were in step with the Industrial Revolution, in which machines were precisely what was revolutionary.[45] "The one [view]," Büchner declares, "considers all phenomena of organic life from a *teleological* standpoint . . . every organism is a complex machine provided with functional devices enabling it to survive over a certain span of time."[46]

In *Woyzeck*, Büchner joins his polemic against the machine with an advocacy of the poor man and woman, of those who have to work—and even sell their bodies—in order to live. In Büchner's play, Woyzeck has his soldier's wage, earning something extra from the Captain, whom he shaves in the famous scene that lends itself so memorably to operatic adaptation: "Steady, Woyzeck, steady" (*Langsam, Woyzeck, langsam*).[47] He also earns some money participating in an experiment for the Doctor in which he is to eat only peas. There is no evidence that the historical Woyzeck was ever paid to take part in medical experiments. In the years before committing his crime, however, Johann Christian Woyzeck had no regular employment, getting what work he could as a cardboard maker and gilder. Often homeless, he relied on the charity of people in Leipzig and nearby towns, who gave him a roof over his head, although sometimes he found himself turned out of doors during the warmer months. He tended to get into conflict with those who helped him, and he harassed and assaulted his lover, Johanna Christiane Woost, who had once been his landlady, in the months leading up to her murder. What strikes most later commentators is that, for years, he, like Büchner's character, had visions and heard voices—one of which told him to stab Woost.[48] These facts were, however, discounted by Clarus, the doctor appointed by the court to determine whether, at the time of the killing, Woyzeck was *zurechnungsfähig*, or legally responsible for his actions. According to Clarus, it was a crime of jealous rage. Büchner's play does not decide. It does, however, contain a trace of the psychological theory that might perhaps have spared Woyzeck's life when the Doctor diagnoses an "aberratio mentalis partialis,"[49] which would allow for the possibility of temporary lapses of reason.[50] The object of forensic psychology, the figure of the worker and his acts, gives way to a theory of the mind and its workings—and that is when the question of automatism arises.[51] As a theory of the mind, psychic automatism would have made sense to Clarus and Büchner's contemporaries because they were familiar with machines. The general public knew that automata were not self-moving and, once set in motion, were powerless to move in any way other than how they were designed to move.

Georg Büchner's interest in Woyzeck was consistent with his political radicalism. The son and grandson of physicians, and recently qualified as one himself, having already fled to Strasbourg, Büchner left France in 1836 for exile in Switzerland.[52] He was a wanted man. A founder of the Gesellschaft der Menschenrechte, he had written an anonymous pamphlet entitled *Der Hessische Landbote* (The Hessian messenger). This pamphlet called, in an apocalyptic style, for a popular uprising by Hessian peasants against the princes who ruled over them and the landowners who exploited them. Although his political sympathies are not apparent in his lecture on cranial nerves, they come through with clarity in *Woyzeck*, which Büchner was drafting in the months prior to his lecture.[53] Among the most memorable lines in the play are Woyzeck's words to his sleeping child, which, like the Hessian pamphlet, activate a metonymy of poverty, work, and sweat: "His forehead's all shiny with sweat; nothing in the world but work, even in your sleep you sweats. That's us, that is: the bloody poor!"[54] Equally well known are the lines spoken in the shaving scene in response to the Captain's "you've got no morals" (*Er hat keine Moral*): "Us lot just don't have a chance in this world or the next; if we ever got to heaven I reckon we'd have to help with the thunder."[55]

Connecting Büchner and Plato many years after the debut of *Woyzeck on the Highveld*, Kentridge seems to discern in these words an allusion to the artifice of theater and the human labor that brings that artifice about.[56] He thereby brings into relief how Handspring Puppet Company's style of puppetry exposes the necessity of mechanism, even as its rewriting of Büchner's text muffles the Barker's provocation, hesitating, in effect, to have humans—and animals—declared to be machinelike. At the same time, Handspring allows for a critical view of mechanization by sustaining a technique that, although undeniably dependent on mechanism, on a machine, ultimately cannot dispense with the power and skill of the human hand—which imparts "life" to the puppet. Yet, inevitably, as I am arguing, that technique also demonstrates an idea about the mechanicity that human being and performing object have in common. This idea is suppressed textually when Büchner's fragment is taken up in the adaptation but cannot be prevented from emerging technically.

It is necessary to be clear that the Barker's view is probably not Büchner's. Although a great deal of the wonder—and seduction—of the automata in Hoffmann is due to the skill of their makers and operators—the talking Turk is referred to as a "work of art," its operator as an "artist"[57]—things are different in Büchner. One could say that, although he advocates for the worker, because he is also against the machine, Büchner stops short of approving the exposure of the inner workings of a human being as machinelike. Given the philosophical commitments of "On Cranial Nerves," that would mean subscribing to teleology. If the age in which he lived was ambivalent about automata, his disposition appears to have been negative. In *Leonce und Lena*, the farce that Büchner wrote in same year that he drafted the scenes that posthumously became *Woyzeck*, when the betrothed are described by the cynic Valerio in a long speech as "two world-famous automata," he is commenting on the conventionality of love and marriage and the roles of men and women.[58] As with his sideshow performing horse in *Woyzeck*, which may as well have been an automaton, Büchner appears to have found little to redeem puppetry as an art form. His references to puppets, as a metaphor, are uniformly negative. "Puppets, that's all we are," Danton declares in *Danton's Death* (1835), "made to dance on strings by unknown forces; ourselves we are nothing, nothing."[59] And, almost predictably, in *Der Hessische Landbote*, the powerlessness of honorable men who become ministers in the existing dispensation is described as puppetry *en abyme*: "The way things are in Germany [an honest man] could only be a puppet [*Drahtpuppe*] manipulated by the princely puppet [*Puppe*], himself a ridiculous puppet [*Popanz*] manipulated in his turn by a valet or coachman or the coachman's wife and her lover or the coachman's stepbrother or all of them together."[60] It appears that the sole instance in the oeuvre that eludes this indictment of the puppet—perhaps because it eludes metaphor—is Marie's shadow puppetry for her son, when she uses the mirror in which she admires herself wearing the earrings given to her by the Drum Major: "Quiet, child, shut your eyes, the sandman's coming! See him run along the wall?"[61]

Anamorphosis

Not all of Büchner's contemporaries viewed puppetry in the same light as he did. Dating from 1810, Heinrich von Kleist's "Über das Marionettentheater" ("The Puppet Theatre"), a text favorably noted by E. T. A. Hoffmann,[62] is perhaps the most famous puppet text after Carlo Collodi's *The Adventures of Pinocchio*, published in 1883, the same year as Olive Schreiner's *The Story of an African Farm*. Memorable for its claim that greater grace of movement is accomplished when the "soul" is disengaged and when the performer is not self-conscious, Kleist's text has a special place for scholars of puppetry as well as puppeteers. Like Edward Gordon Craig's "The Actor and the Über-Marionette" (1908),[63] it challenges the hierarchy of human and nonhuman—of spirit and matter, of performer and performing object.

But there is a different way of conceptualizing the relationship between performer and object—as that between human and machine—which settles neither for a reversal of this hierarchy nor on the insight that human beings are machinelike. This other view is that something of a different order emerges from interaction between human beings and machines. Although surely not unavailable in the early nineteenth century, this view is strongly urged in an age of programmed machines and computerization. It is to that urgency that Paul de Man's interpretation of "Über das Marionettentheater" speaks, drawing our attention to a "transformational system" that "spins itself between" puppeteer and puppet.

As part of a longer disquisition on an increased formalization in literary theory and criticism in the 1960s and 1970s, de Man discusses the section of Kleist's tale in which a dancer, whom the narrator has seen attending the town puppet theater, explains his fascination with puppets. "He added that this movement was a very simple one," the narrator relates, "that whenever the centre of gravity was moved *in a straight line* the limbs described a *curve*; and that often, if shaken by accident, the whole thing was brought into a kind of rhythmical activity similar to dancing."[64] This is when, commenting on this passage, Paul de Man introduces the concept of anamorphosis:

> The puppets have no motion by themselves but only in relation to the motions of the puppeteer, to whom they are connected by a system of lines and threads. All their aesthetic charm stems from the transformations undergone by the linear motion of the puppeteer as it becomes a dazzling display of curves and arabesques. By itself, the motion is devoid of any aesthetic interest or effect. The aesthetic power is located neither in the puppet nor in the puppeteer but in the text that spins itself between them. This text is the transformational system, the anamorphosis of the line as it twists and turns into the tropes of ellipses, parabola, and hyperbole. Tropes are quantified systems of motion. The indeterminations of imitation and of hermeneutics have at last been formalized into a mathematics that no longer depends on role models or on semantic intentions.[65]

What makes de Man's use of the concept of anamorphosis so interesting is that the concept is typically encountered in descriptions not of puppetry but of perspective in painting and drawing. An anamorphosis is a distorted image so devised that, when viewed from a particular angle, it resolves itself into a regular image. Hans Holbein the Younger's painting *The Ambassadors* (1533) is the most famous example in the genealogy of anamorphic painting, drawing, and systems of optics richly detailed by Jurgis Baltrušaitis.[66] Instead of images and optics, what de Man emphasizes from Kleist is a "transformational system" between one order of movement and another: from line to curve. This "system" is neither the motion of the puppet nor of the puppeteer. Perhaps it is not even motion at all, strictly speaking, because naming it a "system" involves a greater cognitive abstraction. If meaning arises from this process, de Man explains, it is not a result of intention, even if "the puppets have no motion by themselves, but only in relation to the motions of the puppeteer," and no "role model" provides any thing to be imitated.[67] If the puppet is given a "soul" by the puppeteer, as puppeteers sometimes say, this animation takes place through a process that is automatic for being predictable. By asking us to turn our attention to this system of automatic regulated transformation, de Man prompts us to reframe what the members of Handspring Puppet Company say about their practice, to extract something else that is implicit in it.

Having read how the dancer in Kleist's tale describes the conversion of the shape of movement, nobody watches a puppeteer at work in quite the same way again. And having read de Man on Kleist, one is ready to see how the puppet theater, beyond the ideas of the human being *conforming to* the machine and of the human *as* machine, suggests a commentary on the automation and computerization that had become pervasive in the United States and elsewhere by the time de Man wrote his essay. De Man could be saying something like the following: If, in an era of mechanization, it remains interesting to attend to how the machine moves as a result of what its operator does—and, in a feedback loop, *must* do because the machine is designed in a certain way—then, in an era of computerization, although such aspects remain relevant, what is most interesting is that the motion imparted by the operator translates into another phenomenon entirely. This is the system of transformation that de Man terms anamorphosis. De Man's extension of the concept of anamorphosis beyond image making and optics into something more abstract prompts us say that, with computers, something comparable is true. Anamorphosis is the phenomenal counterpart of the digital.

This can be so in any number of ways. For example, what I see on the screen of my computer—using, say, the word-processing program in which I am now composing—although it somewhat resembles a typed page, in no way resembles the code that is activated by input from my keystrokes and that gives the machine its instructions to output what I am viewing on the screen. Referring to the use of typewriters, in the 1940s, Heidegger perceived an "increasing destruction of the word" (*zunehmende Zerstörung des Wortes*) when writing is done with a machine, as the unity of handwriting disintegrates into keystroke and printed letter.[68] In contemporary word processing, a word begins as a series of keystrokes and ends as a pattern of light on a screen.[69] Stored at an address in memory, the numerical designation of which it assumes for the purposes of retrieval and output, the word I see on the screen is no longer a word but an electromagnetic inscription. The process of the instantaneous conversion of keystrokes into recognizable patterns of light may thus be understood as anamorphic—as, perhaps, is any process of representation involving the use of a machine.

A disintegration of the word is even more palpable with older computers. With the old mainframe system that J. M. Coetzee used to run his "Line Generator" program, discussed in chapter 2, a word begins as a series of holes in a punch card and ends as a set of marks printed on paper. When "Line Generator" is run, the locative phrases *IN THE ROCKS* or *AMONG THE TREES* start out as separate words before becoming numbers denoting a place in computer memory. Output, they turn into printed phrases readable as naming a natural location. When the narrator in Coetzee's second novel, the metafictional *In the Heart of the Country* (1977), declares "I exist intermittently,"[70] her statement can be related to the programming experiments that Coetzee was still pursuing when he wrote the novel. In Coetzee's program, *I* is one of four words in the first of five "types." The appearance of *I* in the output is "intermittent" in the sense that its place is sometimes taken by *YOU, WE,* or *THEY.* Just as the meaning of the locative phrase *IN THE ROCKS* and its alternatives depends on their being selected at random after words are chosen from the first two types, it is only when *I* is selected from the first of the four types, and also appears at the beginning of a line, that it will be read as being the subject of a sentence with the syntax that the narrator of Coetzee's novel utters. For example, "Line Generator" outputs:

I   STAND   /   AMONG   ROCKS   /   SAD

What is stored in the computer memory location, and printed out as spatial position, becomes grammar. A *machine* is designed to bring about, automatically, a regulated and regular conversion. It is on this fact that Coetzee's early experiments rely. Although, in the realm of writing, this is also true of typewriters (and perhaps also pens and pencils and brushes, as Nemerov suggests),[71] the essential role of the machine is particularly obvious with computers, which are programmed to effect such conversion. What looks like a word or a sentence is something that is produced by processes in no way resembling handwriting—although printing is simulated both on computer screens of the PC era and in the programming command PRINT that remains from the mainframe era—as keystrokes are converted into electrical impulses, patterns of light, printed letters, and so forth.[72] If one does not view what one sees on the screen as one types as being ontologically distinct from what one types on the keyboard, perhaps one ought to. The machine is what shows us that, because of the irreducibility of physical inscription, what we call writing is never continuous with thought or imagination and that the conversion of the two discontinuous orders must always be automatic. It is true, of course, that we will have had to pick apart the automatic process in order to perceive the absence of continuity and the "anamorphic" conversion of orders. The critical interpreter finds interest not only—and perhaps not principally—in the two images or entities but, as de Man suggests, in the system necessary for one order to be converted into the other. With computers, as indeed with puppets in Kleist, the system of conversion itself is not visible. It is, however, intelligible.

It is perhaps computerization or digitization that prompts artists, generally, to recognize how their work is anamorphic. Their appeal to anamorphosis might thus offer a commentary on computerization as a system of regulated conversion of representationally inert marks into meaningful syntagms and recognizable images.[73] If, in the computer poetry that Coetzee created in the 1960s, this is literally what he and others did, adapting a number machine into a word machine, in other art making, the realization takes forms that are more oblique.

Recall how Kentridge talks about how he uses images of older telecommunication technologies to comment on the internet, where the visible workings of the former figure the invisible workings of the latter.[74] The maker of images of new technologies faces the challenge of bringing into visibility workings that are merely, or even barely, intelligible to the human observer. In order to make sense of how image making relates to computer use, Kentridge finds a fruitful explanatory analogy in anamorphosis. Having made several anamorphic works, including a short animated film (see figure 3.2), anamorphosis has significant power for him theoretically and resonance autobiographically.[75] When he relates anamorphosis to the use of a computer keyboard and mouse, he seems to allude directly to Kleist:

> Within half an hour . . . it was possible to find out the grammar of what it is to draw an anamorphic drawing. We discovered a lot of things. The first principle of it was that it is a contemporary activity in the sense that until recently there was the assumption that if you are drawing or writing, doing and looking fall into one place. You control the activity under the pencil, as if the hand is seeing what it does. The image on a computer screen has become a common way of working now and it creates a displacement between doing with the mouse in one hand and the keyboard underneath it and the place on the screen where your eyes focus. There is a kind of a shifting space, which your arm muscles need to know to move in relation to the image on the screen. You get used to it in a few minutes. The displacement in the anamorphic drawing was one of looking at the screen, the cylindrical mirror, and not at this drawing hand. When you think, "I need to draw a circle," you cannot follow your arm muscles' experience of making this round form; to get a shape which will look like a circle in the cylindrical mirror, in fact you have to do a long kidney bean. All the marks that one does to create something on a mirror are anticipations of a translated form. A straight line on the paper becomes a perfect parabola on the mirror, whereas to get a straight line in the reflection, you have to draw a particular curve on the sheet. One of the images of all these beautifully looped hanging lines was made by ruler lines drawn across the circle. You get beautiful curves: parabolas.[76]

For those familiar with his filmmaking technique, Kentridge's remarks suggest parallels between the films I discussed in chapter 3 and puppetry—which his description of drawing and using a mouse evokes.[77] But it is when puppetry itself is conceived in terms of anamorphosis—beyond the making of images—that the art form suggests a unique commentary on computerization and automation. When we turn toward Handspring's *Woyzeck*, we see represented the figure of the worker. But in its mise-en-scène, as in its mise-en-oeuvre, we witness an essay on the becoming-machine of the human being by virtue of the workings they share. This is doubled in the way in which the puppeteer has to adapt to the puppet—which is not always a painless process for the puppeteer. That adaptation takes place in order to bring about the regulated transformation that de Man describes as anamorphic. With a marionette, it is easy to see what Kleist's dancer saw, especially if the puppeteer's hands are not visible. Because the puppet has articulated joints, the straight lines of the strings bring about movements that are varied and often include motion that is curved.

With Handspring's version of Bunraku, however, the puppeteer's hand is in direct contact with the puppet. This sometimes means that the movement of the puppet appears to be isomorphic with that of the puppeteer. When we turn to the scene in *Woyzeck* when Harry sets the table for the Captain, because both puppet and puppeteers are visible, members of the audience witness how the motion of the puppeteer's hand, which holds and guides the puppet's, is mirrored by Woyzeck's. Because both have articulated joints and are almost of the same dimensions, the mechanics of their arms are similar. But then we also observe that this isomorphism of motion is not always in evidence— that, although the direction of movement might be the same, the shape is not. The eye is easily fooled and may not notice when the curve of Woyzeck's arm is the reflex of Jones's.[78] Thus, out of the corner of one's eye—or in the ability to watch a video replay—one notices how South African arts, so regular in its alternation between workers and workings, opens into a different logic. The computer poetry of J. M. Coetzee, in biographical terms a stalled experiment for the author, sees its anamorphic logic continued in puppetry, which, viewed in terms of this continuity, still looks unchanged to its practitioners.[79] Another way of putting this is to say that, although their mise-en-oeuvre suggests the operations of a computer, their *mode d'emploi* remains one drafted for an older type of machine.

Basil Jones, just out of surgery, speaks of being enslaved. But viewed as anamorphic, in the sense of the regulated system of transformation that de Man noted in Kleist's tale, the puppet and puppet theater put on stage the problem of the age: We use computers, but few of us have any idea how it is that when we type or swipe, we bring about certain effects. Perhaps this is why the tech-savvy street or club kid in a book by Namwali Serpell or Lauren Beukes (and in any number of other cyberpunk authors) is the new hero of our time rather than the computer scientist. Coding can be known, and it can be hacked—but you have to know how. For the average "user," this is not possible. For most of us, it is all we can do to ensure that we exert just the right pressure with our digits or cant our faces at just the right angle for recognition so that the image on the lock screen of our smartphone can resolve itself into a display of "usable" apps. We serve and adapt to the machine. But perhaps there is another way of seeing this "interactivity." Although neither organic nor strictly electromechanical, what de Man intuited as taking place "between" the user and the usable could be termed "life" in the sense of a code that, like DNA, generates more code. I do not attribute this view to any of the writers and artists that I am writing about. Handspring perhaps comes closest to demonstrating it in performance with their puppets, making Vilakazi's address to the machines prescient, although perhaps naive. Who would imagine today that humans could possibly enslave machines? But the will for the machine, as insistent as it is—whether for typewriter or sewing machine or bicycle or computer or smartphone—must, in the end, open and concede the possibility that the human in human life will survive only as a minor term, even if it does not and cannot imagine it.[80]

Trajectory

In a fascinating reading of three works by Handspring Puppet Company and its collaborators, Premesh Lalu observes that "the puppet keeps watch over the becoming technical of the human, resisting the slide into mechanized life that took shape as the racial logic of petty apartheid."[81] By petty apartheid, Lalu refers to the measures of "population control" that complemented grand apartheid by instituting a racialization that, as a result, dictated the futures of those racialized. Once instituted, this system operated like a machine. Setting out a complex genealogy in the history of science, Lalu views this racialization as a survival of the ending of slavery in the British Empire in 1834 and as surviving the end of apartheid 160 years later. The reason for its survival, Lalu explains, is that, under apartheid, media technologies were employed to tie perception to sensation in ways that were not simply causal but also automatic and predictable. An example is how apartheid "lock[ed] race strategically into a repertoire of images of racial and ethnic origins in machine relays. In this way, it foreclosed protension as a distinct possibility, prohibiting a process of relinking sense and perception by intermittently disturbing the relay between the two cognitive dimensions of the psychic structure."[82] Lalu's guiding question is how to break the hold of apartheid cognition on the future—how to "undo apartheid." His answer is that theater—specifically the puppet theater, or theater of objects more generally—can undertake an "aesthetic education" whereby perception, which is locked into an automatic relation with sensation, can be freed through the unshackled engagement of the senses that theater, ideally, allows.

Although Lalu takes into account how humans interact with machines and quotes Marx on how machines do not free workers,[83] he is not as interested in machines per se as in what he terms, employing the machine as a metaphor, the "mechanized life" instituted through the racializing of petty apartheid. One of the ways its "racial logic" worked was through a distribution of educational opportunities. Verwoerd, as Lalu notes, questioned teaching mathematics to black youths.[84] As minister of native affairs, Verwoerd also stated, in 1954, that "for [the Bantu] there is no place in the white community above the level of certain forms of labour,"[85] with the implication that the state would not provide certain forms of education for Africans. This earned Verwoerd a special infamy. Lalu rightly adduces continuities between this vision and slavery. But the key point, historically, is that something like slavery was, in certain respects, instituted through measures distinct from those that brought about and sustained slavery in the Atlantic world. In this case, it worked through a racialized distribution of education. The *school* becomes a vector in a system that works to render a specific racial division of labor automatic. Although not entering into the *longue durée* as Lalu does, this is what I register in chapter 1 when I summarize debates about automation in the late 1960s and early 1970s. There, the main thrust of my argument is that the apartheid state, having exercised control over the school, also began to view the *machine* as a vector for racialization—although it came too late for its purposes (and, in any case, would also have entailed a degree of control over *white* workers that had been impossible since after the 1922 uprising). In other words, for apartheid ideologues, it is not simply a question of whether the machine frees the worker or not but of what depriving the black African worker of access to the machine will accomplish. The corresponding question for workers is what ensuring such access will accomplish.

Although the mise-en-oeuvre in *Woyzeck on the Highveld* and Handspring's other productions allows us a glimpse of what de Man calls a "transformational system," my own reading has emphasized the presence of the human hand as puppeteer and puppet interact. I thus read Handspring as hesitating before a complete identification of human and machine, or a subsumption—as a function of their shared workings—of worker into machine. At a different level of analysis, I am therefore also showing that when black workers voiced and enacted a will for the machine, they were also, perhaps paradoxically, defying what Lalu calls the mechanization of life under apartheid— its making of race in order to make race into destiny. Despite all its measures, which included a repertoire of rhetorical images—"levels of labor" is one example—that operated on the *senses*, those workers, whose history in a minor key I narrate, did not *perceive* their futures to be foreclosed. The failure of apartheid ideologues to realize their vision was overdetermined by a boom-time expansion of the economy, which brought about a shortage of skilled white workers. Equally overdetermined, after 1973 and the oil crisis, was the failure of this history of what C. Wright Mills called the "white collar people" to unfold in ways that would give direction to the history of the society more generally. In this reading of history, Soweto 1976, in contrast to the 1973 Durban strikes, was less a proletarian uprising than an outcome of dashed hopes for upward mobility among a class with access to education—however inferior that education was compared to that provided for white people.[86] One should, of course, never discount the effects of news of the recent decolonization of Mozambique and Angola, which changed the sense of the possible.[87] But the white collars of the marching and fleeing and dying pupils' school shirts that show above their tunics and jerseys, in photographs from the uprising, are far more than an iconic sign.

What my analysis and Lalu's retain in common is the idea that technology—which I call the machine—is where human history moves. The history of technology is human history. Although Lalu hints that a rejoining of sense and perception in theater and film broke the hold of the factory—and factory work—as destiny for school students in Athlone in the Western Cape around 1985,[88] he appears less interested than I am in considering what the machines in use in the factories, and in offices too, might have meant for their operators. This is also where gender difference, which is not a factor for Lalu, discloses nuances in the meaning of the machine. In certain industries, such as the textile and clothing manufacturing that declined with trade liberalization after 1994,[89] factory workers in the Western Cape were mainly female. As I note in chapter 1, in better economic times, and assuming a certain level of education, it was possible for some among those workers to move into office work and other white-collar occupations.[90] In their daily lives, people were making choices that asserted their freedom in defiance of all the scripts that, still racialized, defined and restricted their futures.

A trajectory thus comes clear. In chapter 3, I showed how, in Kentridge, it was by exploring the inner workings of machines and telecommunications networks that the woman, and the woman as worker, comes to the fore. I attached some importance to this because of the emergence of women as semiskilled and skilled workers in the boom of the 1960s. More and more of these workers were African, and many of them used machines—especially in office work. On this reading, broadly speaking, William Kentridge takes up the advocacy of the worker—including woman workers—by his grandfather. But by then, the white supremacy that guided the latter's politics for most of his career had given way definitively, in the succeeding generation, to the left-liberal nonracialism that earned the artist's father and mother their places in history. As attorneys, Sydney and Felicia Kentridge sought to undo a web of policies and laws imposed on Africans in favor of which, for some years, Morris Kentridge had taken a direct role in advocating. But William Kentridge's interest in the inner workings of machines is not just a path toward bringing to the fore the labor of people whose work and worklessness, and their historical significance, have been eclipsed in dominant narratives and image making. If it were so, simply placing the telephonist or typist in a procession led by the mine worker, the houseboy, and the landless or homeless person would be sufficient.[91]

Although this sort of image making is one key facet of his work up to and including *The Head and the Load* (2018), Kentridge does not leave it at that. The image changes, just as the sculpture from *Waiting for the Sibyl* (2019) by Kentridge and Gerhard Marx turns in relation to the viewer, simultaneously casting the shadow of a thorn tree on one wall and a typewriter on the wall that shares a corner with it. Its facets alternating, what looked organic now looks mechanical.[92] In the same way, in works by Kentridge and in performances by Handspring, we see the human, as well as the similarly constituted inner workings of humans and machines. Unseen and unconscious, these workings make possible the interaction of human and machine. How else would such a thing be possible?

But there are also the exigencies of the epoch. As Kentridge notes, in the same interview in which he alludes to a primal scene, some of the images in *Stereoscope* evoke the internet and its effects. Although we do not necessarily *see* this taking place, the hierarchy of human and machine is reversed. The first Industrial Revolution, so ran the critique, made workers into machine minders. They had to adapt to the machines. With electromechanical machines, this adaptation was revealed more definitively than when Karl Marx wrote that operating a machine in a factory "exhausts the nervous system to the uttermost,"[93] as it modifies the nervous response—as telephonists experienced to their detriment. Having each had arms and legs and heads and feet, humans and machines were now understood to have something new in common— namely, electricity. And, unlike arms and legs, this was not metaphorical but actual. An early twentieth-century Woyzeck's "donnern helfen" (help with the thunder)[94] would be less the work of a servant to the Germanic god Donner, as might have been imaginable in an opera by Wagner, than the result of flipping an electrical switch. In the twenty-first century, with the computers and smartphones that have made us their extensions, and as we don our spectacles for filtering out their blue light, this "closed circuit" should be a given.

But it is not a given—either in historiography or in the politics guided by historical mythography. The former has, in the South African context, barely scratched the surface of computerization. The latter, as in most places, remains stuck on the idea—or dogma—that computers and computation are, like other machines, tools that humans can utilize for good or ill. But we ought to be beyond that. If computers are using us, then we are also machinelike. The conventional rhetoric of scholarly argument can hinder. If one says, following a familiar script, that Handspring's work responds to computerization and automation in South Africa, then one presupposes that "computerization and automation in South Africa" are, in some sense, a given. Or, at least, that they are things that are commonly understood and thought about. That is, unfortunately, far from being the case. Although the country has certainly had its science fiction aficionados, avid readers and imitators of Isaac Asimov, Philip K. Dick, and other American authors, South Africa never really had its "cybernetics moment."[95] It is only recently, in Willem Anker's *Skepsel* (2020), which I discuss in my conclusion, that a cyborg has been a central character in a novel. As I have demonstrated, there is not even a basic chronicle for ready reference of milestones in computer history in the country—let alone, with the exceptions noted, a critical body of work about that history. This presents a contrast to the history of technology in mining and its attendant labor system—where rock drills and railway networks have enjoyed exceptionally insightful study[96]—or, more recently, infrastructure.[97] A scholar of computerization—as of telephony[98]—has thus to modify their rhetoric. They need to say something like the following: In some of their works, Handspring Puppet Company, like William Kentridge, realizes just enough, in the form of images, objects, and sounds, and their members' comments about them, to suggest a starting point to anybody with the impulse and imagination to respond critically to the technological changes of the era in which we find ourselves. In the absence of a historiography that takes stock of these changes in their profundity, let alone puts its assessment into general circulation, the scholar might continue, this artistic oeuvre is an indispensable resource. Although the history that remains to be written lies largely beyond the scope of the present study, and I can only gesture toward it in the hope that others take up the task, the work of Handspring Puppet Company, like that of Tlali, Coetzee, and Kentridge, suggests a way to think the history that is unfolding.

What path of thinking does Handspring suggest? The following: For every figure, there are logical conditions of possibility, just as for every worker there are inner workings. One way of making visible those conditions of possibility—shared by worker and machine—is by analogy—just as images of the mechanical in Kentridge evoke the electrical and digital in *Stereoscope* without representing them directly. Another expedient, which preserves the figure of the worker in its *Aufhebung*, is to make the puppet a concept-metaphor for the conditions of possibility for the animated image.[99] The latter stands, more generally, for the filmic image and its conditions of possibility in the filmic "apparatus," which combines the electromechanical with the human cognitive. Neither the literature on Handspring nor that on William

Kentridge, however, ever refers to the history of computing in South Africa. This is surprising because of how the apartheid government used, or hoped to use, computers. Systems supplied by IBM, ICL, and other companies were introduced to modernize the racial population registry and other apartheid measures. It is important to emphasize that many of these measures related to the racially discriminatory regulation of African labor in "grand apartheid." Examples include the pass laws and influx control. In the light of the meaning that apartheid ideologues attached to the automation of labor, this history is, as I have shown, a crucial context for understanding the work of these artists who are so deeply occupied with labor—and for showing how it suggests a critical vocabulary for engaging computerization.

In theory as well as artistic practice, Handspring sustains an idea that, at another level, connects a critique of labor exploitation with a critique of computation and digitization. As I have suggested in my discussion of de Man on Kleist's "The Puppet Theater," the term that performs this connection is *anamorphosis*. Anamorphosis leads us to reflect on the "transformational system" it involves by making visible each of the things between which transformation occurs. It provides us with a rough and ready explanation of how a computer works from the point of view of its user, just as it helps explain how a puppet performance or animated film is realized. It also leads us to reflect on how, because of inner workings that are constituted alike and even compatible—which does not mean that they are visible or even knowable—human beings can use machines. This similitude, in turn, explains, more generally, how work can be automated. Such a path of thinking is not negated by the fact that, for a long time, machines, automatic and not, have carried out tasks that no human being or group of human beings would ever be able to perform. Handspring's—and Kentridge's—participation in this larger ensemble of ideas places them, perhaps unexpectedly, beside J. M. Coetzee. His experiments in computer poetry in the early 1960s took place at a time when computers were not yet ubiquitous and debates in the United States and the United Kingdom about the automation of routine mental work were perhaps only a decade old. Yet they now make Coetzee more clearly legible as an example of how South African writers and artists have engaged with the machine. His computer poetry reflects little-noted parallels with the European and American artistic avant-garde in its response to automation and computerization. Coetzee's experiments look anamorphic now that what has since time immemorial been produced by poets through unknowable mental processes is now produced through one that is perfectly describable from "input" to "output." The fact that it is bad poetry is no contradiction, since if better verse can be produced in the same way, as has been done since, the process would be no less fully describable.

It is really only when these experiments, like those of Kentridge and Handspring, are viewed in relation to the works of Miriam Tlali, in a historical context informed by a knowledge of apartheid policies and the discourse of its ideologues, as well as of the labor statistics of the relevant years, that the force of these artistic projects comes clear in relation to a set of choices facing an actual worker within a racialized labor market. In the world portrayed by Tlali—and by others in less detail—the alternative is between work and work, between working with or without the aid of a machine. And the choice that she and the women she talked to in 1970s Soweto make is clear—*for* the machine. What this means is that, when the humanist asks, "What of the machine?" and expects to hear a story of dehumanization, which relieves them of the task of thinking the machine, which is to say thinking the human in an age of machines, the writer or artist or scholar needs to be ready to demonstrate, for all the reasons I have given in this book, that the task in question cannot be eschewed.

It is possible, then, that the South African instance, by virtue of its unexpected turns, stands out, not because of its *uniqueness* but because it is in that instance that a humanist framework is most firmly entrenched in the formulation of a historiographical donnée. That donnée raises the agon of oppressed and oppressor, colonizer and colonized, black and white, and so forth to a mythic level. As a result, any phenomenon can be coded as boon or bane depending on whether it is of the oppressed or of the oppressor.[100] The move that I make, to show how African women workers were, at a certain time, *for* the machine, obviously participates in this tautological historiographical game. But the protagonists themselves, who did not always judge it in those terms, decided on the benefit of technology to them according to other criteria. There appears, for example, to be room in their stories for the machine, or the one who provides them with access to it, to be what Vladímir Propp, introducing categories distinct from the antagonist, calls the "helper" and "donor."[101] My hope is thus that my move will be viewed as provisional—as an invitation to explore the differing valuations given to the machine, to mechanization and automation of work, and, ultimately, to the idea of an automaticity that humans and machines share, even if the automatic processes are in each instance distinct. It seems like a long time ago that the machine could be viewed as a work of art, as it evidently was in Emerson and in the mind of his namesake, Waldo Farber, in Olive Schreiner's *The Story of an African Farm*—a view that, as E. T. A. Hoffmann attests, certainly applied to automata of the early nineteenth century. By the time that Heidegger wrote "The Question Concerning Technology" in the 1950s, however, a bifurcation of *tékhnē* and *poíēsis* had long since taken place,[102] and only a trace of their once closer relation remained. The world we live in now is one constituted through this bifurcation: The inventor of a machine is no longer an artist, and works of art are viewed as the very opposite of machines. It is our good fortune that not all artists accept this epochal determination and that, in making their art, they also construct or program machines or, if they do not do those things, lead us to question what we know of the machine.

Conclusion

One in three South Africans uses a smartphone, and that proportion is growing.[1] Despite the ubiquity of what are in fact powerful miniature computers, and the resultant everyday dependence of their users on digital networks, the history of computers in South Africa has only been sparsely documented. My study has endeavored to remedy that by concentrating on a historical time when computers were still understood, like other machines before them, to be potential substitutes for workers—or, if not, as a means for alleviating the tasks of workers. What I have found is that automation and mechanization are not one thing, and neither is computerization. What they are depends on the meaning of a machine in historical context, which depends on how a machine is used. And that, in turn, depends on the division of labor. In the absence of critical discourse on technological change, as in South Africa, writers and artists tend to be the ones defining that meaning in relation to the dominant terms put forward by business, labor, and public policymakers. Although the rigid racial division of labor that typified apartheid makes its path of mechanization and automation different from other countries, my study suggests criteria for future studies of technological change in Africa and across the Global South. It does so by proposing the following questions when mechanization and automation take place: How is the labor process divided? How does that division of labor shape ideas and ideology concerning the machine? How do artistic works represent the division of labor and engage critically with these ideas and/or propose other ways of thinking technological change?

Instead of undertaking a full-scale comparison, across multiple countries and their literatures and art, in this conclusion, I briefly indicate a direction for future investigation. This I do by entertaining a counterexample that calls for an additional question. That question stems from the sense that there is perhaps a deeper reason, if not for the relative scholarly neglect of the history of computerization in South Africa exactly, then for why it might not occur to users of smartphones, in South Africa and elsewhere, to ask historical questions about mechanization, automation, and the division of labor. This deeper reason is that, although a smartphone is a computer, for the average user of a smartphone, a computer is no longer understood as a machine that takes the place of a worker. The meaning of *this* machine has changed. Smartphones are the result of a technological convergence of telecommunications and computation that began in the 1940s, accelerated from the 1960s, and assumed the familiar-to-us form of the internet in the 1990s.[2] In this history, one can observe different phases of the displacement of the worker. Here are two examples. In the 1920s, automated telephone exchanges were resisted by some because they put operators out of work.[3] In the 1950s and 1960s, and perhaps into the 1970s, computers were seen in a similar light.[4] Nowadays, although automation is still challenged because of its effects on employment, such challenges are almost never directed at computers. The fact that their being directed at cellular telephones is practically inconceivable suggests that the labor that both automated exchanges and computers once displaced no longer factors into what they mean for their users. That labor has effectively been forgotten. Where advanced technology is pervasive, the machine, so to say, runs in the background. This is what prompts the additional question: What are the implications of representing automation and computerization when the labor process—for instance, in factories and mines, on farms, and in the office—is not the main sphere in which humans and machines interact?

I have already pointed out how, in recent South African literature, art, and theater, a shift has taken place from the figure of the worker to the inner workings common to humans and machines and how that shift calls for a rethinking of human-machine interaction. With the aid of two recent works of speculative fiction by southern African authors, the counterexample can be formulated in two additional respects. Both are relevant to the Global South, with its uneven economic development and implementation of technology. There are countries that have a history of industrialization and mechanization that informs the meaning given to machines in relation to labor and carries over into the meaning of automation and computerization. But there are also countries where industrialization was not throughgoing, was almost entirely absent, or has undergone decline. In those countries, the meaning of the machine will not have been restricted to its relation to labor.

Such is the difference, perhaps, as it is staged in Namwali Serpell's *The Old Drift* (2019), between Zambia and South Africa. In the near future projected by Serpell's novel, technology is almost entirely detached from how machines are used by workers. This may have something to do with genre—her turn toward speculative fiction in the third part of the novel—but it is also a function of social verisimilitude. Copper mining and the textile and clothing industries have both declined in Zambia in recent decades. The signal confrontation in *The Old Drift* is not between worker and capitalist who contest the meaning of mechanization and automation. Instead, it is between rival forms of computerized automation: corporate and state data extraction and surveillance and resistance to it by economically marginal yet tech-savvy individuals relatively marginal to the labor process. For the latter, worklessness, rather than being at work, is the rule. For the economically marginal, the machine can figure differently. Even if, for Miriam Tlali's Mrs. Koae,[5] for example, her sewing machine is directly linked to productive labor, there is, all over the world, an economic marginalization that means that the labor process is no longer the mediating term when humans and machines interact.[6]

In the Lusaka of *The Old Drift*, a young man named Jacob repairs and sells electronics from an e-waste dump. A self-taught inventor, he eventually designs and builds a tiny drone from the discarded components that he scavenges. In the speculative future of Serpell's genealogical novel, smartphones are superseded by "Digit-All Beads," implanted in people's hands, which transnational corporations use to extract biological data. In return for participating in this covert surveillance, the beaded gain access to the internet and its communications network.[7] Although his drones ultimately fall into the wrong hands, Jacob's techno-hacking looks like a people's response to technologies of control, a form of resistance from below. Although he has work helping make coffins for people who have died of AIDS, his interaction with machines is not part of his job. Jacob's marginality makes him dependent on powerful people in Zambia, who broker deals with Chinese and American investors.[8] Without a formal education, his "best bet was to hustle—scrape some profit by hawking goods to those Zambians with better luck or richer relatives."[9] Jacob's relation to the labor process is perhaps also a function of Zambia's position in the regional and world economy. As Serpell's novel pointedly tells us, although not so distant in miles from Johannesburg, Lusaka may as well be on another planet, economically speaking; its e-waste dumps "housed leftover gadgets . . . [from] America, South Africa, China, all of the countries that had run out of room to discard their obsolete and broken tech."[10] But that difference does not stop Zambians from shooting for the moon; Jacob's experiments are inspired by the Zambian Space Programme of the 1960s, the imaginative brainchild of Edward Mukuka Nkoloso.[11] If Jacob's microdrone is not simply a weapon, which is what it in a sense becomes, perhaps it is also a work of art—like Waldo Farber's shearing machine in *The Story of an African Farm*, had it been realized.

This is certainly the case in another recent work of speculative fiction from southern Africa, Willem Anker's *Skepsel* (Creature) (2020), in which a cyborg performance artist weds a supertanker and, absorbing the ship's sounds and vibrations from a computer-mediated and regulated system of sensors connected to its body, flirts with destruction when it bypasses the safety settings.[12] The cyborg's name is Sulla Čapek, recalling Karel Čapek, to whom we owe the word *robot*.[13] Giving us an even more dramatic instance of interconnected inner workings than in Kentridge and in Handspring, Anker's fiction suggests, when compared with Serpell's, that there is a deeper link than one would suspect between Sulla's avant-garde high art and the bricolage of the economic marginal as imagined in *The Old Drift*. The remoteness of his book's technological scenarios from the labor process is clearly on Anker's mind. A smart home near Cape Town features in the second of his book's plotlines. Before it is abandoned, is occupied by wayfarers, is ransacked, and eventually disintegrates, it figures as an island of advanced technology and privilege in a vast ocean of underdevelopment and privation. The South African contrast with itself obviates the contrast with Zambia. Staying in this house, the character Rebecca discovers a strand of human hair sewn under the label of a T-shirt she has bought at a clothing chain. This prompts her to invent the story of

Piku, a young Bangladeshi factory worker, who has sent the hair out into the world as a message.[14] The message is perhaps that at the machine sits a living human being despite her near-complete adaptation to it: "She knows the women who sit next to her at their sewing machines and stitch T-shirts better than her own family. Piku no longer needs to look down at her hands; for fourteen to sixteen hours a day she is an automaton that every day stitches the seams of the same Large T-shirts."[15] Rebecca learns from the internet that the garment industry is responsible for 80 percent of Bangladesh's export revenue and that 85 percent of garment workers in Bangladesh are women.[16]

There is thus a way in which the division of labor—and with it the racial and gender meaning of the machine—is imaginable even when the machine and its use are far away. There is still a labor process, of course, but, in the variegated Global South, and in a globalized division of labor, connection to it must be actively *imagined*. In the end, in *Skepsel*, it is the machines themselves that connect with Pris, the smart home's AI communicating with the supertanker via Sulla's computer.[17] The scenario in *The Old Drift* is, of course, not quite the same. Although computerization is distinctly detached from the labor process in Serpell's Lusaka, and although discarded computer parts from more "developed" economies, one of them relatively nearby, are cleverly repurposed—Turing's "universal machine" should, in principle, be able to function as a weapon or a toy, if we recall Coetzee programming the IBM 1401 or, as his technological precursor, Tlali's Sowetan writing love letters at his typewriter—the labor of manufacturing electronics on the other side of the world is not placed within the book's imaginative frame. And nor is it in Anker's. Yet both Serpell and Anker, in their respective ways, alert us to ways in which, although machines are separated from the labor process in ways they were not a hundred, or even fifty, years ago, a separation that is taken for granted when machines are "background," there is always an elsewhere in which a human being uses a machine to make things—including other machines.

The symbolic act of the Bangladeshi factory worker, as imagined by the character of Rebecca in Willem Anker's novel, is a sign of the global division of labor—or, better, a certain North-South division of labor in manufacturing.[18] A factory of the sort at which she works may be in an export processing zone, or EPZ, of the kind that emerged in different countries after trade liberalization in the 1980s and especially the 1990s (which, as has been noted, led to the decline of the textile and clothing industries in certain countries of the South). But the North-South, and South-South, division of labor is not everywhere the same. This is especially the case in information technology. Although US-based transnational corporations locate manufacturing in "low wage" countries, with the implication being that what is made there is designed in the North, for Northern needs, the situation may also be understood otherwise when viewed historically. In India, for example, where the state promoted scientific development after independence, computer science programs were established at the Indian Institutes of Technology beginning in the 1960s.[19] Adapting Soviet and American designs and components, in the early days, engineers at the Indian Statistical Institute and Tata Institute of Fundamental Research built their own computers.[20] This degree of innovation appears not to have taken place in South Africa, where technology transfer took a more predictable course at its principal state-sponsored node, the Council for Scientific and Industrial Research.[21] It is probably more correct to speak not of a transfer of technology but rather of products; even during the 1980s, when anti-apartheid trade sanctions were in force, local manufacturing hardly developed.[22]

In India, although for a short time in the late 1970s and early 1980s, after IBM left and before trade was liberalized, computer manufacturing grew,[23] the subsequent period saw India become a world leader in software development and related services through outsourcing by transnational companies. This was possible because of India's legacy of expertise and training in programming and system design but also because of how little skilled programmers earned there compared to programmers in the United States and Europe.[24] The "low wage" economy driving globalization in the 1990s thus spread, in India, as in certain other Asian countries, from manufacturing to services—some of them also concentrated in EPZs. The unique path of India in the history of computerization does not mean, however, that familiar concerns of organized labor were absent; Indian banking workers' unions resisted computerization into the 1980s.[25] Nevertheless, when cellular phone use spread in India after 2000,[26] as it did in South Africa and across the South, bringing computers into mass use, it was over against a history significantly different from many of the other countries.

Without having drawn full-scale technological and economic

comparisons between countries, I have suggested a method for reading technological change in dialogue with art and literature from the Global South. I have indicated a set of questions that could be asked when research turns toward other countries and their artistic production. I have shown that, for a long time, the meaning of the machine depended on the division of labor. In South Africa, this dependence of meaning stretched into the early days of computerization, when views of labor and its division were perversely racialized. I suggest thus that, in other countries, it would be instructive to ask: What is the division of labor? How does it influence the meaning of the machine? When I show that, after apartheid, with the country in a later stage of computerization, the meaning of the machine was no longer dominated by the meaning of automation and mechanization, this is because machines were increasingly used away from the production process. This prompts us to ask, with reference to other places: Where machines are no longer "tools" for work,[27] or not solely, and therefore not linked to the division of labor, what do machines mean? The extremes meet somewhere between Anker's smart-house and cyborg and Serpell's techno-hackers: machines but no labor. A work of art, a weapon, but no work in the narrow sense. I have proposed a method for writing a history of technology, along with one for interpreting literature and art in relation to that history. Pursuing this method also allows us to acknowledge that not all machine use tends toward the extremes. As Anker reminds us, although no longer reducible to its use in the labor process, there may still be contexts in which the meaning of the machine is to be thought in terms of the mine or the factory or the office — and the workers in it.

A different set of questions could be asked, and observations made, however, if the starting point is not the labor process and the division of labor in the narrow sense but what, in chapter 4, I described in terms of anamorphosis — the regulated transformation of one order of marks into another. As I explained, this can take a number of forms, the most instructive being from representationally inert marks into intelligible signs or images. With the Renaissance paintings to which the term was applied, the transformation conforms to a system of optics that makes it calculable and predictable. As de Man realized, a similar system is discernible in string puppetry as described in Kleist: straight lines become parabolas and hyperbolas. But it is with computing that such a system becomes paradigmatic. A computer is an electromechanical switching system that operates at high speed. How it operates depends on what a program tells it to do. For the user, the relation between input and output is a transformation. When the user thinks of that transformation as involving a conversion of orders—keystrokes into letters, words into numbers into words, and so forth—anamorphosis suits as a phenomenological shorthand for the process. In this sense, anamorphosis may capture what is epoch making about computer technology. One would not necessarily wish to contend that it is what answers Heidegger's "Question Concerning Technology"—that it delivers the "essence" of technology—which he famously said was "nothing technical."[28] Yet what is epoch making about computing, in this respect, is not simply the *use* of computers—although that is crucial, as always, since use is what guides adaptation and makes meaning.

This is what makes it so instructive, within the space of the South, to draw a comparison with computerization in China. As Thomas Mullaney explains in *The Chinese Computer: A Global History of the Information Age*, because of computer technology's inbuilt bias toward alphabetical scripts, Chinese engineers had significantly to alter aspects of the technology, especially those relating to how users interact with it.[29] Accordingly, Mullaney turns toward language, or the "technolinguistic"—those elements of language, not meaningful in themselves, required by a machine in order for it to function, from the perspective of its user, as if it had command of a human language.[30] Mullaney places his history within the context of modernization in China, where intellectuals of the stature of Lu Xun and leaders such as Mao Zedong viewed the Chinese writing system as an obstacle to modernization.[31] To begin with, China was at a technological disadvantage because computers—like the telegraph and typewriter before them—were designed to work with alphabetical scripts,[32] as well as for interaction with users who wrote using those scripts. Chinese writing, which is not alphabetical, has thousands of characters, making the QWERTY keyboard not easily adaptable.[33] Like the telegraph and typewriter, computers thus had to be modified for Chinese users. Lessons learned during the long course of reinventing the typewriter for Chinese and Japanese were applied to computers, from the late 1940s onward, by scientists and inventors from China, Taiwan, and the United States. Although not ignoring some of the changes to hardware and software that were necessary for output (printers and displays),[34] Mullaney concentrates mainly on input, or "inputting." With an alphabetical keyboard, ideally, "what-you-type-is-what-you-get."[35] If I depress the *A* key, *A* appears on my screen. With "inputting," however, there is another layer of mediation between what you type and what you get. A ubiquitous contemporary form of this mediation is the IME—or input method editor.[36] This software enables a Chinese user of a QWERTY keyboard to select characters or a series of characters from a pop-up menu. When an IME is in use, depressing the *A* key does not immediately produce an *A* on the screen. Instead, it retrieves from computer memory a set of options from which the user selects.[37] Mullaney calls this writing, which exists temporarily between input and output, "hypography."[38] As he observes, the use of IMEs explodes the identity of input and output that, phenomenologically speaking, informs Western computer use—itself a "mythology," concealing the mediation necessary to produce the effect, for the user, of immediacy.[39]

The terms in which Mullaney describes input and its mediated relation to output are very similar to the ones that, drawing on Kittler, Heim, and Kirschenbaum, I apply to the processes that I describe as anamorphic. Mullaney employs an explanatory analogy with MIDI, or musical instrument digital interface, that strongly suggests anamorphosis: "Just as one could use a MIDI piano to play the cello, or a MIDI woodwind to play a drum kit, within the context of input, one could use a QWERTY keyboard and the Latin alphabet to 'play' Chinese."[40] The phenomenon that Mullaney describes is, conceptually speaking, something happening "not only in China, but worldwide."[41] This relates not only to the use of IMEs—with which computer and smartphone users typing in Devangari or Arabic script are also familiar[42]—but to the sea change prompted by this in how humans experience interaction with computers. "It was not the Western-designed computer," Mullaney writes, "that saved China and the non-Western world. It was China and the non-Western world that saved the Western-designed computer—saved it, that is, from its foundational limitations, both conceptual and material."[43] In the process, I would add, they revealed something about the very nature—if not the "essence," as Heidegger put it—of that technology.

Previously, I showed how the productions of Handspring Puppet Company make visible and tangible nonidentity between input and output as anamorphosis. Their technique reveals a system of transformation, as de Man put it, between puppeteer and puppet. The technology inheres not simply in the puppet, as itself being a machine, but in the interaction of puppet and puppeteer. To the careful observer, output looks different from input. It would not be controversial, in the context of South African computer history, which is unashamedly duplicative or derivative even as it takes turns that are perverse, to introduce the word *cyborg* (just as *cyberpunk* is a valid genre term for, say, Lauren Beukes's *Moxyland* [2008]). But the cyborg denotes a merging. Stopping at the cyborg would thus perhaps underrate Handspring's achievement in urging questions about human-computer interaction and human-machine interaction more generally. In describing his experience of using a computer mouse, William Kentridge brings into relief an anamorphosis that, in the early days of computing, would have been evident to J. M. Coetzee and others as they adapted a machine for numbers into a machine for words. It is in the realization of what is required, of both human and machine, in order to "merge," that something else comes to light.

As is often the case, what is decisive comes into relief through comparison. The unique history of computerization in China, the rethinking and remaking of the computational given, may have found its imaginative counterpart in the work of internationally acclaimed Chinese science fiction author Liu Cixin, himself a computer engineer. As is likely familiar to readers, and lately also viewers,[44] Liu's vision is of a multiplicity of universes, someplace in which different levels of civilizational and scientific advance are achieved: computer, atomic, subatomic, and so forth. Trisolaris, the extraterrestrial civilization imagined by computer-game designers in *The Three-Body Problem* (2014), passes through the computer age. It does so not by building machines powered by electricity but rather by having Isaac Newton help John von Neumann "invent" the computer as a switching system involving up to thirty million human signalers who signal according to predetermined routines.[45] To add to the anachronism, the signalers are soldiers in the army of Qin Shi Huang, the first emperor of China (221–210 BC). The most basic function, carried out by a group of three soldiers, looks like this:

> Qin Shi Huang waved his hand and three soldiers came forward. They were all very young. Like other Qin soldiers, they moved like order-obeying machines.
>
> "I don't know your names," Von Neumann said, tapping the shoul-

ders of two of the soldiers. "The two of you will be responsible for signal input, so I'll call you 'Input 1' and 'Input 2.'" He pointed to the last soldier. "You will be responsible for signal output, so I'll call you 'Output.'" He shoved the soldiers to where he wanted them to stand. "Form a triangle. Like this. Output is the apex. Input 1 and Input 2 form the base." . . .

Newton took out six small flags: three white, three black. Von Neumann handed them out to the three soldiers so that each held a black flag and a white flag. "White represents 0; black represents 1. Good. Now, listen to me. Output, you turn around and look at Input 1 and Input 2. If they both raise black flags, you raise a black flag as well. Under all other circumstances, you raise the white flag. . . ."

He shouted orders at the three soldiers. "Begin operation! Input 1 and Input 2, you can raise whichever flag you want. Good. Raise! Good. Raise again! Raise!"

Input 1 and Input 2 raised their flags three times. The first time they were black-black, the second time white-black, and the third time black-white. Output reacted correctly each time, raising the black flag once and the white one twice.

"Very good. Your Imperial Majesty, your soldiers are very smart."

"Even an idiot would be capable of that. Tell me, what are they really doing?" Qin Shi Huang looked baffled.

"The three soldiers form a computing component. It's a type of gate, an AND gate." Von Neumann paused to let the emperor digest this information.[46]

Next, Von Neumann has the soldiers demonstrate an OR gate, then a NAND gate, a NOR gate, an XOR gate, an XNOR gate, a tristate gate, and a NOT gate.[47] After three months, thirty million soldiers are assembled to form a "system"—a "large machine, the most complex machine in the history of the world." Wang, the contemporary nano-materials scientist through whose eyes we experience the game, calls it a "computer." The soldiers form a motherboard, a CPU, and memory enough to run the "Qin 1.0 operating system." A unit of light cavalry are the "system bus, responsible for transmitting information between the components of the whole system."[48] Before being set in motion, the "phalanx remained still like a giant carpet made up of thirty million terra-cotta warriors"—an allusion to the famous terra-cotta army unearthed in the 1970s from the mausoleum of Emperor Qin.

In the context of Liu's novel, because the calculations the computer makes to determine the orbits of the three suns from which Trisolaris gets its name turn out to be in error, the civilization is obliterated "by the stacked gravitational attractions of a tri-solar syzygy."[49] Within the world of the *Three Body* game, the achievements of "Civilization Number 184" are summarized as follows: "This civilization had advanced to the Scientific Revolution and the Industrial Revolution. In this civilization, Newton invented nonrelativistic classical mechanics. At the same time, due to the invention of calculus and the Von Neumann architecture computer, the foundation was set for the quantitative mathematical analysis of the three bodies."[50] Dating from 1945, the Von Neumann architecture is one of the earliest, most widely adopted, and most durable designs for a computer system.[51] The other references to the history of science are well known. Toward the beginning of the episode, Wang asks Von Neumann, "Why did you have to come to the East to build a computer?"[52] Von Neumann does not provide an answer, suggesting that the reader is being asked to reflect on the question. For Chinese readers, Qin and his army are familiar coordinates. The violence entailed for technological progress—the "'repair...'" of "faulty component[s]" by beheading the relevant soldiers, the famine resulting from the concentration of imperial resources[53]—may be a historical composite. Aside from claims to antiquity, however, what the episode suggests is that, if the work of computation can be accomplished by an organized mass of human beings,[54] something that was a fact, albeit on a smaller scale, in the days of human "computers,"[55] then the workers not only inhabit and animate the machine's inner workings but *are* the machine. In China, this may be a figure that is ideologically overdetermined, given the investment in the "people"—and thus, in Liu's text, a target of satire or critique (from various imagined vantages, assuming that, like Qin, Von Neumann and the others are the gamers' avatars). "Disgusting philosophy!" is Von Neumann's judgment on Newton's view, as communicated to the Emperor Qin: "Each of these lowly individuals is just a zero. Only when someone like you is added to the front as a one can the whole have any meaning."[56]

But by prompting the reader to continue to ask the question "Why did you have to come to the East...?," the novel gestures beyond such markers of Chinese context. When Wang meets up in real life with a group of fellow gamers in the next chapter, the organizer, Pan Han, explains, "The computer did in fact make its first appearance in Trisolaris as formations of people, before becoming mechanical and then electronic." But the invention in Trisolaris—or in the East—of the electronic computer is not the point. As Pan goes on to stipulate, "As a game, Three Body only borrows the background of human society to simulate the development of Trisolaris. This is done to give players a familiar environment. The real Trisolaris is very different from the world of the game."[57]

We thus reach the limit of the question "Why did you have to come to the East to build a computer?" If this is a question not simply of imagining a world in which a computer is built from human materials and thus *could* perhaps be built—as in Liu's novel—or of describing how computers *actually* came to be built in China in a different way—as in Mullaney's history—it could also be a question about the conditions of possibility for the emergence of any technology. Liu's novel acknowledges that, at the limit, what will have been produced under given conditions of possibility is unimaginable and unknowable. But it nevertheless maintains, at another level of theoretical reflection, that what those conditions are will have been what determined the shape, and meaning, of any such technology. This, at its limit, is also the wager of my book. Be it the East, Africa, or in the Global South, wherever you happen to launch your inquiry, know the relevant conditions of possibility as well as you are able. Even if you do not succeed in predicting what is to come, you will know better why the technology will have taken the form that it ultimately did.

Acknowledgments

A Will for the Machine is my pandemic book. Although I began work on it before the coming of SARS-CoV-2 and continued thereafter, my most vivid memory is of drafting chapters in the comparative isolation of rural New York state where my partner and I worked remotely in 2020 and 2021. My first vote of gratitude therefore goes to the librarians at New York University Libraries, who, in the months after March 2020, when in-person operations were suspended, made provisions to mail books to us wherever we were when they could not be obtained online, access that they also helped to ensure by dramatically expanding the library's electronic collections.

Librarians elsewhere also continued to be at their posts. Having assisted me in my research projects over many years, and in the early stages of what became *A Will for the Machine*, Najwa Hendrickse and her staff at the National Library of South Africa in Cape Town extended their assistance at a time when the library was beset by repeated viral outbreaks that, on occasion, forced it to close. Likewise, Sadeck Casoojee at Cape Town's Library of Parliament was diligent in providing me with digital copies of Debates of the House of Assembly and Reports of the Postmaster-General.

The help of all these librarians reminded me that, although as researchers we now rely heavily on vast automated networked computer systems, a reliance the pandemic made feel almost total, those systems, in turn, rely on those of us who use them.

The shape taken by my book would probably have been different had it not been for the time taken by Paul N. Edwards and Nick Montfort to engage critically with my initial ideas. The same is true of Robert Garner and Michael Albaugh of the IBM 1401 restoration project at the Computer History Museum in Mountain View, California. I am particularly grateful to Michael, who brought both his programming skills and inspiration as he engaged with my project. Both he and Robert gave me a glimpse of an intellectual universe refreshingly different from the one I inhabit as a scholar in the humanities.

Within my usual intellectual universe, I had the opportunity to present part of what became *A Will for the Machine* at Stellenbosch University, for which I thank Sally-Ann Murray and Louise Green, who both provided invaluable feedback. Shortly before the pandemic, a fellowship at the Stellenbosch Institute for Advanced Study (STIAS) gave me the time to draft the second chapter.

Stephen Clingman, Snow Yunxue Fu, Loren Kruger, Jaqueline Mitchell, Thomas Mullaney, Claudia Orenstein, Eyal Peretz, Vanessa Place, Rebecca Roach, Benjamin Robinson, Adam Sitze, Jane Taylor, Andrew van der Vlies, Gretchen Van Lente, Andries Visagie, and Leif Weatherby all contributed in meaningful ways to the gestation and birth of *A Will for the Machine*. Although they would probably be surprised to hear it, through their lectures in the late 1980s at the University of Cape Town, David Kaplan and Ian Phimister sowed the seeds for my interest in economic history.

I thank Alan Thomas, my editor at the University of Chicago Press, for his confidence in my project and for his suggestions for shaping my manuscript. Likewise, I thank the two anonymous reviewers who provided valuable suggestions on how to improve it. My thanks also go to Randy Petilos, who shepherded my manuscript through the initial stages of production at the press, to Lindsy Rice for managing the remainder of the process, and to Carol McGillivray for presiding over the copy editing.

I am grateful to J. M. Coetzee and William Kentridge for allowing me to reproduce examples of their work. I would especially like to thank Anne McIlleron at the William Kentridge Studio for her kind assistance in providing copies of the relevant images. My thanks also go to Brenda Goldblatt and the David Goldblatt Legacy Trust for graciously giving me permission to reproduce photographs by David Goldblatt.

Although the book I was writing receded into the background as a topic of conversation at home, as the initial shock and fear and grief of the virus's spread gave way to an adapted routine of social distancing, masks, and, eventually, vaccinations, I know, as always, that, but for the loving support of Louise Kuhn, before, during, and after the pandemic, this book would never have been written.

Notes

Introduction

1. David Goldblatt and Nadine Gordimer, *On the Mines* (Cape Town: Struik, 1973), 12. Because *On the Mines* is unpaginated, for ease of reference, I have introduced pagination, with the title page as page 1. *On the Mines* was republished in 2012 in a different format, with many additional photographs and some new text. Although the latter is the more comprehensive book, these additions alter the vision of the 1973 edition, which so powerfully resonates in the historical era on which I concentrate.

2. Goldblatt and Gordimer, 9–10, 13–14.

3. See Stephen Clingman, *The Novels of Nadine Gordimer: History from the Inside* (Johannesburg: Ravan, 1986).

4. Goldblatt and Gordimer, *On the Mines*, 11.

5. Goldblatt and Gordimer, 12.

6. Goldblatt and Gordimer, 72.

7. Goldblatt and Gordimer, 73.

8. Goldblatt and Gordimer, 89.

9. Goldblatt and Gordimer, 72–74.

10. *Miners' Dictionary English—Fanakalo, Woordeboek vir Mynwerkers Afrikaans—Fanakalo*, rev. ed. (Johannesburg: Mine Safety Division of the Chamber of Mines, 1985), 38.

11. Goldblatt and Gordimer, *On the Mines*, 13–14. For a discussion of Fanagalo, see Mark Sanders, *Learning Zulu: A Secret History of Language in South Africa* (Princeton, NJ: Princeton University Press, 2016), 22–29.

12. Jeff Guy and Motlatsi Thabane, "Technology, Ethnicity and Ideology: Basotho Miners and Shaft-Sinking on the South African Gold Mines," *Journal of Southern African Studies* 14, no. 2 (1988): 261–62.

13. Guy and Thabane, 262–63.

14. Guy and Thabane, 270.

15. Guy and Thabane, 260–61.

16. Guy and Thabane, 270.

17. Guy and Thabane, 274–76.

18. When some of the photographs were published in *Optima*, they were preceded by a brief essay by Errol Fyfe, company PR man, whose description of the process includes mention of the lashing crew, but then he tells us, "All that remains [after

blasting] is the formality of removal—the giant cactus snorts as it grabs, lifts and drops the rock." Fyfe's essay also names the company involved in the project, "Shaft Sinkers, an international company which specialises in deep-level sinking based on South African techniques." David Goldblatt, "The Sinkers," *Optima* 19, no. 3 (1969): 130–31. Shaft Sinkers, which was controlled by Anglo American, is not named in Goldblatt's essay. In contrast to Fyfe, Goldblatt explains how the Basotho lashers work in coordination with the cactus grab: "After the large rocks have been lifted out [by the grab], the smaller stuff is hand-shovelled into a kibble." Goldblatt and Gordimer, *On the Mines*, 72.

19. B. W. Vilakazi, "In the Gold Mines," trans. A. C. Jordan, *Africa South* 1, no. 2 (1957): 115.

20. In her novel, *Kompoun* (Cape Town: Kwela, 2021), Ronelda S. Kamfer explores, in fascinating ways, the polysemy of the word *compound*, in its various senses and divergent etymological roots. The word *kompoun* of her title is meant to render the word in the speech of the farmworkers in her book who speak a colloquial Afrikaans suffused with English words. In standard Afrikaans, the word used for "compound," in the sense of workers' barracks or hostel, is *kampong*.

21. Vilakazi, "In the Gold Mines," 118.

22. For a different reading of the sound of the machines in Vilakazi's poem, see Rosalind Morris, "The Miner's Ear," *Transition* 98 (2008): 105–7.

23. Vilakazi, "In the Gold Mines," 117.

24. Vilakazi, 115.

25. Vilakazi, 118.

26. Vilakazi, 115.

27. Goldblatt and Gordimer, *On the Mines*, 10.

28. Goldblatt and Gordimer, 12.

29. Karl Marx and Friedrich Engels, *The German Ideology* (Amherst, NY: Prometheus, 1988), 42.

30. Nadine Gordimer, "The Witwatersrand: A Time and Tailings," *Optima* 18, no. 1 (1968): 21–27. When their essay was included in *On the Mines*, the number of photographs was far larger. *Optima* was edited at the time by the poet Charles Eglington (1918–71). Other photographs by Goldblatt suggest a pattern of artistic patronage by the mining houses. A sculpture by Moses Kottler at the headquarters of General Mining appears in a 1965 photograph in the 2012 edition of *On the Mines* (Göttingen, Germany: Steidl, 2012), 62–63, and an abstract sculpted figurine appears, visible only in that edition, in the background of the portrait of Harry Oppenheimer, 165. Goldblatt continued to publish in *Optima* until 1980. He also "worked for mining companies . . . commissioned to do annual reports" until 1987, when, during the miners' strike, he turned down a commission from Anglo American. Alexandra Dodd, *David Goldblatt: The Last Interview* (Göttingen, Germany: Steidl, 2019), 132, 53. The catalog to Goldblatt's photographs and papers in the Beinecke Library at Yale University, however, includes an annual report for Anglo from 1989—as well as numerous other examples of Goldblatt's corporate work.

31. By contrast, Anglo's annual reports from these years often depict Oppenheimer, at mines and other sites, in shirtsleeves and hard hat.

32. "The sooner the shaft is completed, the sooner can mining—and profits—begin." Goldblatt and Gordimer, *On the Mines*, 74.

33. A notable recent exception, in investigative journalism, is Greg Marinovich's *Murder at Small Koppie: The Real Story of South Africa's Marikana Massacre* (East Lansing: Michigan State University Press, 2017), which is at pains to delineate the network linking the mine office, the head office, and, in this case, the South African state.

34. Goldblatt and Gordimer, *On the Mines*, 12.

35. P. C. Pirow, "Use of a Computer for Clerical Procedures in the Rand Mines Group," in *Proceedings of the First Symposium on Automation and Computation* (Johannesburg: SACAC, 1965), i-8-28.

36. Pirow.

37. K. C. G. Heath, "Computers for Copperbelt Mining," *Optima* 14, no. 4 (1964): 231.

38. "Electronic Preparation of Dividend Warrants," *Optima* 12, no. 2 (1962): 84.

39. "Electronic Preparation of Dividend Warrants."

40. Heath, "Computers for Copperbelt Mining," 229, 235.

41. Nowadays, although derived from the Dutch *kantoor*, in Zulu, *inkantolo* usually refers to a law court or a police charge office. *Ihhovisi* is the word commonly used for "office."

42. See, for example, Charles van Onselen, *New Babylon, New Nineveh: Everyday Life on the Witwatersrand 1886–1914* (Johannesburg: Jonathan Ball, 1982), 1–46.

43. For informative discussions of advances in the field, see David Serlin, "Confronting African Histories of Technology: A Conversation with Keith Breckenridge and Gabrielle Hecht," *Radical History Review* 127 (2017): 87–102; Laura Ann Twagira, "Introduction: Africanizing the History of Technology," Supplement, *Technology and Culture* 61, no. 2 (2020): S1–S19. An insight guiding the newer work is that what is meant by *technology* is different in different societies. See Clapperton Chakanetsa Mavhunga, "Introduction: What Do Science, Technology, and Innovation Mean from Africa?," in *What Do Science, Technology, and Innovation Mean from Africa?* (Cambridge, MA: MIT Press, 2017), 1–27. Also see Clapperton Chakanetsa Mavhunga, *Transient Workspaces: Technologies of Everyday Innovation in Zimbabwe* (Cambridge, MA: MIT Press, 2014); Gabrielle Hecht, *Being Nuclear: Africans and the Global Uranium Trade* (Cambridge, MA: MIT Press, 2012), 15. Some of the more recent research contends that technology may not entail industrialization, as it unreflexively does in modern European and American history. In important case studies, these technologies adapt those from elsewhere for specifically African imperatives. See Robyn D'Avignon, *A Ritual Geology: Gold and Subterranean Knowledge in Savannah West Africa* (Durham, NC: Duke University Press, 2022), 6–7; Mavhunga, *Transient Workspaces*, 15–16.

44. Although not strictly a work of literary history, Premesh Lalu's *Undoing Apartheid* (Cambridge: Polity, 2023) is perhaps a first attempt at changing that.

45. See, for example, Guy and Thabane, "Technology, Ethnicity and Ideology"; T. Dunbar Moodie and Vivienne Ndatshe, *Going for Gold: Men, Mines, and Migration* (Berkeley: University of California Press, 1994), 50–53; Paul Stewart, "'Kings of

the Mine': Rock Drill Operators and the 2012 Strike Wave on South African Mines," *South African Review of Sociology* 44, no. 3 (2013): 42–63.

46. Keith Breckenridge, *Biometric State: The Global Politics of Identification and Surveillance in South Africa, 1850 to the Present* (Cambridge: Cambridge University Press, 2014), 171–75.

47. Faeeza Ballim, *Apartheid's Leviathan: Electricity and the Power of Technological Ambivalence* (Athens: Ohio University Press, 2023), 22–23. Also see Antina von Schnitzler, *Democracy's Infrastructure: Techno-Politics and Protest After Apartheid* (Princeton, NJ: Princeton University Press, 2016), 8–17, 105–31.

48. "The white-collar people slipped quietly into modern society. Whatever history they have had is a history without events; whatever common interests they have do not lead to unity; whatever future they have will not be of their own making." C. Wright Mills, *White Collar: The American Middle Classes* (New York: Oxford University Press, 1951), ix.

49. There is much to learn, in this regard, from Louis Chude-Sokei, who takes as his point of departure how, in certain works of nineteenth- and twentieth-century American and European literature, the automaton and robot are metaphors for the slave as machine: laboring entities putatively under the control of a master and supposedly unthinking in their performance of the work assigned to them by him. In other words, the robot may be read as a figure for a historically recognizable racial organization of labor. What my project shares with Chude-Sokei's is the assumption that a racialized labor system is identifiably a condition of possibility for specific literary and artistic phenomena. Although I also make a historically specific division of labor my starting point, the fact that automaticity figures quite differently in that context means that it would be impossible, without extensive qualification, to transfer Chude-Sokei's findings, so instructive in his context, to mine. Louis Chude-Sokei, *The Sound of Culture: Diaspora and Black Technopoetics* (Middletown, CT: Wesleyan University Press, 2016), esp. 1–127. Other recent studies of race and technology have drawn attention to how digital technologies perpetuate antiblack discrimination. See, for example, Ruha Benjamin, *Race After Technology: Abolitionist Tools for the New Jim Code* (Cambridge: Polity, 2019), 5. Also instructive is Seb Franklin, who, situating his argument at a different level, insightfully argues that capitalism, which institutes an "informatics of value," anticipates digital technology as understood by information theory. He carefully theorizes how the labor of members of certain populations, defined by race and gender, is either devalued, or does not "compute," because of the marginalization of their members from the circuits of information and capital. Seb Franklin, *The Digitally Disposed: Racial Capitalism and the Informatics of Value* (Minneapolis: University of Minnesota Press, 2021). Works by Charlton McIlwain and Clyde Ford describe in detail how, despite facing discrimination, black Americans have played a role in the computer industry and made an impact on how digital technologies have been developed and used. Charlton D. McIlwain, *Black Software: The Internet and Racial Justice, from the AfroNet to Black Lives Matter* (New York: Oxford University Press, 2020); Clyde W. Ford, *Think Black: A Memoir* (New York: Amistad, 2019).

50. Moodie and Ndatshe, *Going for Gold*, 48.

51. See, for example, N. Katherine Hayles, *How We Became Posthuman: Virtual*

Bodies in Cybernetics, Literature, and Informatics (Chicago: University of Chicago Press, 1999).

52. See Ballim, *Apartheid's Leviathan*, 127.

53. Schreiner's posthumously published first novel, *Undine*, includes a section set at the diamond diggings. Olive Schreiner, *Undine* (New York: Harper & Brothers, 1928), 280–374.

54. "Beauty must come back to the useful arts, and the distinction between the fine and the useful arts be forgotten." Ralph Waldo Emerson, "Art," originally published 1841, in *Essays and Representative Men* (London: Collins Clear-Type Press, n.d.), 217.

55. See Mark Sanders, "Schreiner and the Machine," in *Olive Schreiner: Writing Networks and Global Contexts*, ed. Jade Munslow Ong and Andrew van der Vlies (Edinburgh: University of Edinburgh Press, 2023), 23–38.

56. See, for example, Donald N. Michael, *Cybernation and Social Change* (Washington, DC: US Department of Labor, Manpower Administration, 1964).

57. David F. Noble, *Forces of Production: A Social History of Industrial Automation* (London: Routledge, 2017; originally published 1984), 66.

58. These terms, which assume a currency in the United States in the early 1950s, when they are used widely, from works of management theory to works of literature, come from the mathematician Norbert Wiener, who is best known for his part in the origins of cybernetics. Norbert Wiener, "The First and the Second Industrial Revolution," in *The Human Use of Human Beings: Cybernetics and Society* (New York: Da Capo, 1988; originally published 1954), 136–62. In this essay, Wiener himself uses the term *automatization*. See Wiener, 150. See also John Diebold, *Automation: The Advent of the Automatic Factory* (New York: Van Nostrand, 1952), 2; Kurt Vonnegut, *Player Piano* (New York: Dial Press, 2006; originally published 1952), 14. The term "second industrial revolution" had, however, been used since the 1920s to refer to electrification and the growth of the chemical industry. Ronald R. Kline, *The Cybernetics Moment; Or Why We Call Our Age the Information Age* (Baltimore: Johns Hopkins University Press, 2015), 273n51.

59. For the classical account of how this idea informed dynamics between these instances in the United States after World War II, see Noble, *Forces of Production*.

60. Trevor Noah, *Born a Crime: Stories from a South African Childhood*, paperback ed. (New York: Spiegel and Grau, 2019), 23.

61. Although their gender is not specified, it is worth noting what is said by a character in Miriam Tlali's *Amandla* (Soweto: Miriam Tlali, 1986) who, after the Soweto uprising of June 1976, considers leaving high school: "I decided to attend typing classes. Some of my schoolmates who started attending the course last year in August are already employed by IBM." In context, to leave school is a "difficult decision," since completing high school may improve the student's prospects. Tlali, *Amandla*, 121–22.

62. Tlali, *Amandla*, 216–17, 258.

63. Paul N. Edwards and Gabrielle Hecht, "History and the Technopolitics of Identity: The Case of Apartheid South Africa," *Journal of Southern African Studies* 36, no. 3 (2010): 619–39. With Hecht, Edwards continues the work of his pathbreaking

and influential *The Closed World: Computers and the Politics of Discourse in Cold War America* (Cambridge, MA: MIT Press, 1996). Breckenridge, *Biometric State*, 171–75.

64. Morris Kentridge, *I Recall: Memoirs of Morris Kentridge* (Johannesburg: Free Press, 1959), 102–4.

65. Morris Kentridge, 152.

66. Paul de Man, "Aesthetic Formalization: Kleist's *Über das Marionettentheater*," in *The Rhetoric of Romanticism* (New York: Columbia University Press, 1984), 285–86.

67. My study thus situates itself at a different level of analysis than that, say, of Kittler, who, writing in the 1980s, takes digitization as the starting point for his history of media of recording and reproduction: "The general digitization of channels and information erases the differences among individual media. Sound and image, voice and text are reduced to surface effects, known to consumers as interface. Sense and the senses turn into eyewash. Their media-produced glamor will survive for an interim as a by-product of strategic programs. Inside the computers themselves everything becomes a number: quantity without image, sound, or voice." Friedrich A. Kittler, *Gramophone, Film, Typewriter*, trans. Geoffrey Winthrop-Young and Michael Wutz (Stanford, CA: Stanford University Press, 1999), 1.

68. Writing on Kentridge's animated films, Rosalind Krauss terms this a "quasi-automatism." Rosalind Krauss, "'The Rock': William Kentridge's Drawings for Projection," *October* 92 (2000): 6.

Chapter 1

1. *Automation and Technological Change: Hearings Before the Subcommittee on Economic Stabilization of the Joint Committee on the Economic Report, Congress of the United States, Eighty-Fourth Congress, First Session, Pursuant to Sec. 5(a) of Public Law 304, 79th Congress, October 14, 15, 17, 18, 24, 26, 27, and 28, 1955* (Washington, DC: Government Printing Office, 1955), 15–16.

2. See, for instance, Norbert Wiener, "Men, Machines, and the World About," originally published 1954, in *The New Media Reader*, ed. Noah Wardrip-Fruin and Nick Montfort (Cambridge, MA: MIT Press, 2003), 67–68.

3. As Wiener continued, "We communicate with the machine and the machine communicates with us. Machines communicate with one another. Energy and power are not the proper concepts to describe this new phenomenon." Wiener, 71.

4. Wiener, "The First and the Second Industrial Revolution," 162. For discussions of Wiener's position, see Noble, *Forces of Production*, 74–76; and, in a more critical vein, Chude-Sokei, *Sound of Culture*, 82–86; Franklin, *The Digitally Disposed*, 97–103, 112–19.

5. Robert van Houten, Maxwell Dean White, and A. G. Brunt, *Industrial Automation in South Africa: Report on an Investigation* (Pretoria: SACAC, 1973), 3.

6. *National Commission on Technology, Automation, and Economic Progress: Hearings Before the Select Subcommittee on Labor of the Committee on Education and Labor, House of Representatives, Eighty-Eighth Congress, Second Session, on H.R. 10310, and Related Bills to Establish a National Commission on Automation and Technological Progress. Hearings Held in Washington, D.C. April 14, 15, and 27, 1964* (Washington, DC:

Government Printing Office, 1964). This report is referred to in "Toespraak deur sy edele Dr. Carel de Wet tydens die opening van die tweede S.A.R.O.B. konferensie te Kaapstad op 26 September 1967" [Speech by the Honorable Dr. Carel de Wet at the opening of the Second SACAC Conference in Cape Town on 26 September 1967], in SACAC, *Proceedings of Second National Conference on Automation and Computation* (SACAC, 1967), 2. De Wet, however, appears to conflate the 1964 report with the 1955 hearings, referring to it as the recent "Nasionale Kommissie van Ondersoek oor Outomatisasie en Tegnologiese Verandering van die V.S.A." [National Commission of Inquiry on Automation and Technological Change of the U.S.A.], suggesting that he was also familiar with the report of the 1955 hearings.

7. Remarks by Walter S. Buckingham Jr., in *Automation and Technological Change*, 38.

8. At the 1955 congressional hearings, a senator refers to and recommends Kurt Vonnegut's *Player Piano* (1952). See *Automation and Technological Change*, 242, where the title is rendered as "The Piano Player." Vonnegut's novel openly acknowledges its debt to Norbert Wiener, who viewed automation as a "second industrial revolution." Vonnegut, *Player Piano*, 14. Wiener's name appears only once, however, in the record of the congressional hearings.

9. Wiener, "The First and the Second Industrial Revolution," 150.

10. Jan Haak, "Openingsrede deur sy edele, Mnr. Jan Haak, Minister van Ekonomiese Sake, by geleentheid van die derde nasionale SAROB-konferensie te Pretoria op Woensdag, 15 Oktober 1969 om 10. 30 vm" [Opening address by the Honorable Mr. Jan Haak, Minister of Economic Affairs, on the occasion of the Third National SACAC Conference in Pretoria on Wednesday, 15 October 1969 at 10:30 am], in SACAC, *Proceedings of the Third National Conference of the South African Council for Automation and Computation, 15th, 16th and 17th October, 1969 Pretoria South Africa* (Pretoria: SACAC, 1969), 8–9. All translations from the Afrikaans are my own.

11. Republic of South Africa, *Commission of Inquiry into Matters Relating to the Coloured Population Group* (Pretoria: Government Printer, 1976), 519. In 1983, when a new constitution was passed, Coloureds and Indians were given the vote for representatives of their race groups in the so-called Tricameral Parliament. The elections were widely boycotted and the representatives branded as sellouts. The United Democratic Front, a mass-based nonracial alliance of hundreds of different anti-apartheid organizations, was founded partly in reaction against the new constitution, which excluded Africans from direct representation.

12. Erika Theron, "Die vrou in die geldwêreld," *Sarie Marais*, May 12, 1965, 24.

13. On this ideology generally, see Elsabe Brink, "Man-Made Women: Gender, Class, and the Ideology of the *Volksmoeder*," in *Women and Gender in Southern Africa to 1945*, ed. Cherryl Walker (Cape Town: David Philip, 1990).

14. In her Stellenbosch doctoral study, Theron briefly considers the implications of marital status for women factory workers, finding that, whereas Coloured workers were more likely to be married, white workers tended to leave the factory after marrying. Erika Theron, *Fabriekwerksters in Kaapstad: 'n sosiologiese studie van 540 Blanke en Kleurling-fabriekwerksters* [Women factory workers in Cape Town: A sociological study of 540 white and Coloured women factory workers] (Cape Town: Nasionale Pers, 1944), 24–26.

15. See Margaret Hedstrom, *Automating the Office: Technology and Skill in Women's Clerical Work, 1940–1970* (PhD diss., University of Wisconsin–Madison, 1988), 331–86.

16. Although *Sarie* regularly featured articles about white women in the workplace and as owners of small businesses, Erika Theron's appeal is one of the few to address office work as a career (doing so, in part, thanks to the magazine's framing). It may be that the readership of the magazine was divided by class, since there were a series of advice articles in 1967 aimed at married middle-class women whose husbands worked as executives and might have affairs with their secretaries, whereas they themselves were not working outside the household—or, if they were, it was not in an office. See, for example, Margriet Roux, "Die Kantoor-romanse—'n plaag van ons tyd" [The office romance—A plague of our time], *Sarie Marais*, April 26, 1967, 42–44.

17. On this, see, for example, Janet Abbate, *Recoding Gender: Women's Changing Participation in Computing* (Cambridge, MA: MIT Press, 2012), 18–19.

18. In the United States, it was not until the 1960s that significant numbers of black women found work in American offices. For details, see Hedstrom, *Automating the Office*, 363–75.

19. Haak, "Openingsrede," 2.

20. Haak, 3.

21. The best account of how state education policies did and did not change in response to the changing labor demands of urban employers is Jonathan Hyslop, "State Education Policy and the Social Reproduction of the Urban African Working Class: The Case of the Southern Transvaal 1955–1976," *Journal of Southern African Studies* 14, no. 3 (1988): 446–76. Although, in 1970, the government considered strict job reservation measures for commercial and clerical work, it did not follow through with them. See Hyslop, 468.

22. James Boggs, "The Negro and Cybernation," in *The Evolving Society: First Annual Conference on the Cybercultural Revolution—Cybernetics and Automation*, ed. Alice Mary Hilton (New York: Institute for Cybercultural Research, 1966), 169.

23. Miriam Tlali (1933–2017) was the author of three other books: the novel *Amandla* (Johannesburg: Ravan, 1980), referred to previously; a collection of short fiction and reportage, *Mihloti* (Johannesburg: Skotaville, 1984), and a collection of short stories, *Soweto Stories* (London: Pandora, 1989). The latter was published in South Africa as *Footprints in the Quag: Stories and Dialogues from Soweto* (Cape Town: David Philip, 1989). A play by Tlali, *Crimen Injuria*, was published for the first time in Pumla Dineo Gqola, ed., *Miriam Tlali: Writing Freedom* (Cape Town: HSRC Press, 2021), 103–37. As I discuss in chapter 2, Tlali also contributed a column, Soweto Speaking to Miriam Tlali, to *Staffrider* magazine from 1978 to 1979, in which she spoke with Sowetans about their working lives.

24. Miriam Tlali, *Muriel at Metropolitan* (London: Longman, 1979), 15. Over the years, Tlali frequently voiced dissatisfaction with the 1975 Ravan Press edition, and she restored various chapters and passages when she published with Longman. Her novel was later reissued as *Between Two Worlds*, its original title, first by Longman in 1995 and then, with an introduction by the author, by Broadview Press in 2004. For an informative recent intervention in the debate on Tlali's relationship with Ravan,

see Elizabeth le Roux, "Miriam Tlali and Ravan Press: Politics and Power in Literary Publishing During the Apartheid Period," *Journal of Southern African Studies* 44, no. 3 (2018): 431–46.

25. Martine Mariotti and Danelle van Zyl-Hermann, "Policy, Practice and Perception: Reconsidering the Efficacy and Meaning of Statutory Job Reservation in South Africa, 1956–1979," *Economic History of Developing Regions* 29, no. 2 (2014): 202.

26. Mariotti and Van Zyl-Hermann, 202.

27. Mariotti and Van Zyl-Hermann, 204–6.

28. Mariotti and Van Zyl-Hermann, 219.

29. Republic of South Africa, *Report of the Commission of Inquiry into Labour Legislation*, 6 vols. (Pretoria: Government Printer / Directorate of Communication, Department of Labour, 1980).

30. Mariotti and Van Zyl-Hermann, "Policy, Practice and Perception," 206–12.

31. Mariotti and Van Zyl-Hermann, 220, 223.

32. Richard Humphries, "Administrative Politics and the Coloured Labour Preference Policy During the 1960s," in *Class, Caste and Color: A Social and Economic History of the South African Western Cape* (New Brunswick, NJ: Transaction, 1992), 176–79.

33. Mariotti and Van Zyl-Hermann, "Policy, Practice and Perception," 205.

34. T. R. H. Davenport, *South Africa: A Modern History*, 2nd ed. (Toronto: University of Toronto Press, 1978), 298–99.

35. Charles H. Feinstein, *An Economic History of South Africa: Conquest, Discrimination and Development* (Cambridge: Cambridge University Press, 2005), 191.

36. Feinstein, 232–33.

37. Tlali, *Muriel at Metropolitan*, 22, 15. Later in the novel, this fact stymies Muriel when she is offered a job as an office clerk at a scooter repair business. The owner, an Italian immigrant named Saladino, is harassed and intimidated by officials, who use the fact that he does not have a separate toilet or office for black employees to discourage him from hiring her. Tlali, 188–89.

38. For this periodization, I rely on Feinstein, *Economic History of South Africa*, 172–76, 200–203, 211–14. Also see Martine Mariotti, "Labour Markets During Apartheid in South Africa," *Economic History Review* 65, no. 3 (2012): 1100–1122.

39. Department of Labour [South Africa], *Manpower Survey No. 6, 30 April 1965: All Industries and Occupations* (Pretoria: Department of Labour, 1965), and *Manpower Survey No. 9* (Pretoria: Department of Labour, 1971).

40. Tlali, *Muriel at Metropolitan*, 111, 163.

41. Tlali, 188.

42. Pat Fahrenfort, *Spanner in the Works* (Cape Town: Umuzi, 2012), 85–115.

43. *South African Statistics: Compiled by the Bureau of Statistics* (Pretoria: Bureau of Statistics, 1972), G-54. Figures for African clerical workers were not published for those years, and figures for Coloured clerical workers are only given for the Cape Peninsula. The latter are also not disaggregated by gender.

44. This was, in the mid-1960s, evidently the view of business. In an address in August 1966 to the Computer Society of South Africa, A. E. Checksfield, E.D.P. manager with National Cash Register (South Africa), observed that, "with reasonably

inexpensive clerical labour available," in contrast to the United States and Europe, "an extremely unfavorable ratio [of equipment to labor costs] exists. This, in theory, should tend to discourage the acquisition of computers in this country." A. E. Checksfield, "Why Do People Buy Computers, and What Is Involved in Making Them More Effective?," *South African Computer Bulletin* 8, no. 3 (1967): 5.

45. Evidently, wage levels are also not what lead to mechanization in agriculture. See Feinstein, *Economic History of South Africa*, 197.

46. For details on changes in the relevant education policies, see Hyslop, "State Education Policy."

47. Tlali, *Muriel at Metropolitan*, 187.

48. Tlali, 13.

49. Tlali, 80.

50. Tlali, 187.

51. The year 1967 is a guess based on references by characters in the novel to the independence of Lesotho (1966) and the prospective independence of Swaziland (1968), as well as to the visit of Robert F. Kennedy to South Africa (1966). Kennedy is described as "late," making the time of narration later than 1968, the year he was assassinated. Tlali, 136, 139, 161.

52. "Bureau Lessons," *Financial Mail*, February 7, 1969, 398–99. This was evidently also the rule in the United States, at least in the mid-1950s, according to Diebold's congressional testimony. *Automation and Technological Change*, 40.

53. I draw this periodization from Hedstrom, *Automating the Office*, 46.

54. Tlali, *Muriel at Metropolitan*, 44.

55. Tlali, 24.

56. Tlali, 190.

57. As Hyslop shows, this was part of a widespread appeal at that time from businesses for better education for black South Africans. Hyslop, "State Education Policy," 466.

58. Andre Botha, "SA Should Heed This Ominous Threat," *Computerweek*, November 3, 1980, 6. By that time, however, job reservation in the context of a shortage of skilled labor had already done much to "retard the progress of the economy," a situation aggravated and perpetuated by Bantu education. Feinstein, *Economic History of South Africa*, 158.

59. On the government-sponsored Chamdor training center, which had produced six black computer engineers by mid-1978, see David M. Liff, "The Computer and Electronics Industry in South Africa," in *U.S. Business in South Africa: The Economic, Political, and Moral Issues*, ed. Desaix Myers III, Kenneth Propp, David Hauck, and David M. Liff (Bloomington: Indiana University Press, 1980), 201. For initiatives at ICL, see "Black Training in South Africa," *Datarama*, May/June 1978, 9–12; Laura Tatham, "ICL Training in South Africa: Contributing to a Fast-Changing Society," *Datarama*, August/September 1979, 6–8. The programs were also in part a response to pressure from abroad for British and American multinational companies to divest from South Africa and employ Africans, Coloureds, and Indians. For information and observations about training at IBM in the 1980s, see Edwards and Hecht, "History and the Technopolitics of Identity," 634–35.

60. Also see Feinstein, *Economic History of South Africa*, 241. On rising black self-

confidence in this period, which he links to urbanization, education, and literacy, see Tom Lodge, "Resistance and Reform, 1973–1994," in *The Cambridge History of South Africa*, vol. 2, *1885–1994*, ed. Robert Ross, Anne Kelk Mager, and Bill Nasson (Cambridge: Cambridge University Press, 2011), 416–17.

61. "And there are the usual moments of resentment which we all experience when we feel we are being imposed upon, or overworked and underpaid," Roberts continues. "But here the similarity of Muriel's story with any white's shop-talk story ends." Sheila Roberts, foreword to Tlali, *Muriel at Metropolitan* (Johannesburg: Ravan, 1975), n.p.

62. See Feinstein, *Economic History of South Africa*, 237. According to Nattrass and Seekings, "It is likely that widespread underemployment gave way to open unemployment in the early 1970s." Nicoli Nattrass and Jeremy Seekings, "The Economy and Poverty in the Twentieth Century," in *The Cambridge History of South Africa*, vol. 2, *1885–1994*, ed. Robert Ross, Anne Kelk Mager, and Bill Nasson (Cambridge: Cambridge University Press, 2011), 556.

63. Nattrass and Seekings identify a "high-wage institutional framework" whereby, historically, white workers, and then unionized African workers, earned higher wages relative to workers in competitor economies. Nattrass and Seekings, 530, 568–71.

64. Margot Lee Shetterly, *Hidden Figures: The American Dream and the Untold Story of the Black Women Mathematicians Who Helped Win the Space Race* (New York: William Morrow, 2016).

65. See Feinstein, *Economic History of South Africa*, 233. This is registered, in passing, in Trevor Noah's account of his mother's career after she took a secretarial course and typing class: "Under apartheid, if you were a black man you worked on a farm or in a factory or in a mine. If you were a black woman, you worked in a factory or as a maid. . . . By law, white-collar jobs and skilled-labor jobs were reserved for whites. Black people didn't work in offices. My mom, however, was a rebel, and, fortunately for her, her rebellion came along at the right moment. In the early 1980s, the South African government began making minor reforms in an attempt to quell international protest over the atrocities and human rights abuses of apartheid. Among those reforms was the token hiring of black workers in low-level white-collar jobs. Like typists. Through an employment agency she got a job as a secretary at ICI, a multinational pharmaceutical company in Braamfontein, a suburb of Johannesburg." Noah, *Born a Crime*, 23. The idea that white-collar jobs were reserved by law for white people is a commonly received idea and the one with which I began my research for this book. It is clear, however, from the official labor statistics from the 1960s and 1970s, from Miriam Tlali's book, and from the memoir by Pat Fahrenfort to which I referred previously that this was not, in fact, the case, although the barriers, short of an absolute legal prohibition, placed in her and her employers' way would have been significant. Black people *did* work in offices—although, for a long time, black men outnumbered black women in clerical occupations.

66. An exception is research on how television, which was introduced in 1976, related to social and political change during that time. See Ron Krabill, *Starring Mandela and Cosby: Media and the End(s) of Apartheid* (Chicago: University of Chicago Press, 2010).

67. Siegfried Kracauer, *The Salaried Masses: Duty and Distraction in Weimar Ger-*

many, trans. Quintin Hoare (London: Verso, 1998; originally published 1930). For the purposes of my study, the most important work on the United States is Hedstrom, *Automating the Office,* which cites key forerunners such as Margery W. Davies, *Woman's Place Is at the Typewriter: Office Work and Office Workers, 1870–1930* (Philadelphia: Temple University Press, 1982), and Samuel Cohn, *The Process of Occupational Sex-Typing: The Feminization of Clerical Labor in Great Britain* (Philadelphia: Temple University Press, 1985). Kracauer's classic could in some sense be said to have an American counterpart in C. Wright Mills's *White Collar: The American Middle Classes* (New York: Oxford University Press, 1951).

68. Phyllis Altman, *The Law of the Vultures* (London: Jonathan Cape, 1952). The novel also incorporates vignettes of factory work (with unionization), domestic work, and the forced farm labor of pass-law offenders. In a book published around the same time, Peter Abrahams briefly describes working as an "office-boy" at the Bantu Men's Social Centre in Johannesburg in the 1930s. He was then in his late teens and taking correspondence courses to complete high school. Peter Abrahams, *Tell Freedom: Memories of Africa* (New York: Collier, 1970; originally published 1954), 188.

69. As Charles van Onselen observed in the early 1980s, "Viewed historically, the South African labour market has always been dominated by the three major sectors of employment—mining, agriculture and domestic service. The twentieth-century emergence and rise of secondary industry as an employer of labour has supplemented rather than restructured this pattern. In the 1980s, as well as the 1880s, domestic service remains one of the most important sectors of a rapidly developing capitalist economy. Yet, despite this, it is largely in vain that one scans the literature for any reflection of this reality." Charles van Onselen, *New Babylon, New Nineveh,* 205. By "literature," Van Onselen means the research literature, and he notes Jacklyn Cock's pioneering *Maids and Madams: A Study in the Politics of Exploitation* (1980) as a singular exception. Since then, domestic workers have been the subject of numerous academic studies. In imaginative literature, however, examples abound. Among the classics are Elsa Joubert's *Die Swerfjare van Poppie Nongena* (1978; translated as *The Long Journey of Poppie Nongena,* 1980) and Sindiwe Magona's *To My Children's Children* (1990). Doris Lessing's *The Grass Is Singing* (1950) and Nadine Gordimer's *July's People* (1981) are interesting exceptions in that the house servant in these novels is male. For an excellent study of this literature, see Ena Jansen, *Like Family: Domestic Workers in South African History and Literature* (Johannesburg: Wits University Press, 2019).

70. "City of Port Elizabeth: Electronic Computer: City Treasurer's Department," *Eastern Province Herald,* 23 August 1963, 3 PEZ 4/4/1/1/62 1238 Computer File, Western Cape Archives and Records Service, Cape Town, South Africa.

71. "City of Port Elizabeth: Electronic Computer: Conditions of Tender and Specification," 20 August 1963, 1, 3 PEZ 4/4/1/1/62 1238 Computer File, Western Cape Archives and Records Service, Cape Town, South Africa.

72. The CPA first acquired an electronic computer in 1956. "Toespraak deur sy edele Dr. Carel de Wet," 4.

73. "City of Port Elizabeth: Purchase or Rental of Electronic Computer," F. E. Jenvey to Town Clerk, Port Elizabeth, 30 October 1963, 3 PEZ 4/4/1/1/62 1238 Computer File, Western Cape Archives and Records Service, Cape Town, South Africa.

74. "City of Port Elizabeth: Electronic Computer: Schedule of Job Requirements,"

20 August 1963, 1–3, 3 PEZ 4/4/1/1/62 1238 Computer File, Western Cape Archives and Records Service, Cape Town, South Africa.

75. "Report on Schedule of Utilisation for I.B.M.," 17 October 1963, 3, 3 PEZ 4/4/1/1/62 1238 Computer File, Western Cape Archives and Records Service, Cape Town, South Africa.

76. "Report on Visit to Johannesburg and Pretoria: September 4th–8th, 1962," 20 September 1962, 11, 3 PEZ 4/4/1/1/62 1238 Computer File, Western Cape Archives and Records Service, Cape Town, South Africa.

77. Anticipating the installation of the ICT 1500, Bullen describes the Treasury as already "highly mechanised." G. W. Bullen to F. E. Jenvey, 12 January 1964, 3 PEZ 4/4/1/1/63 1239 Computer File, Western Cape Archives and Records Service, Cape Town, South Africa.

78. In a letter, ICT managing director in South Africa H. G. Lederman alludes to a fifteen-year association between the city and ICT (presumably Hollerith prior to the 1959 merger). H. G. Lederman to F. E. Jenvey, 6 December 1963, 3 PEZ 4/4/1/1/63 1239 Computer File, Western Cape Archives and Records Service, Cape Town, South Africa.

79. "Computer Committee: Minutes of Meeting Held in Office of Deputy City Treasurer (Mr. A. S. Aldis) on Friday 5th March 1965"; "Computer Committee: Minutes of Meeting Held in Office of Deputy City Treasurer (Mr. A. S. Aldis) on Monday 29th March 1965"; "Report on Computer Systems and Programs," S. E. Boult to F. E. Jenvey, 8 January 1965, all in 3 PEZ 4/4/1/1/63 1239 Computer File, Western Cape Archives and Records Service, Cape Town, South Africa.

80. P. Gane to F. E. Jenvey, 27 November 1963 and 10 January 1964, 3 PEZ 4/4/1/1/63 1239 Computer File, Western Cape Archives and Records Service, Cape Town, South Africa.

81. B. C. Thurtell to F. E. Jenvey, with enclosed reports, 20 March 1964, 3 PEZ 4/4/1/1/63 1239 Computer File, Western Cape Archives and Records Service, Cape Town, South Africa.

82. F. E. Jenvey to H. MacKinnon, 14 September 1964, 3 PEZ 4/4/1/1/63 1239 Computer File, Western Cape Archives and Records Service, Cape Town, South Africa.

83. "City of Port Elizabeth: I.C.T. Equipment and I.B.M.," memorandum signed by F. E. Jenvey, 4 December 1959, 3 PEZ 4/4/1/1/62 1238 Computer File, Western Cape Archives and Records Service, Cape Town, South Africa.

84. "I.C.T. International Computers and Tabulators S.A. (Proprietary) Limited, Order No. 3929," 27 November 1963, 3 PEZ 4/4/1/1/63 1239 Computer File, Western Cape Archives and Records Service, Cape Town, South Africa.

85. H. G. Lederman to F. E. Jenvey, 31 July 1963, 3 PEZ 4/4/1/1/62 1238 Computer File, Western Cape Archives and Records Service, Cape Town, South Africa.

86. "City of Port Elizabeth: Contracts for Supply and Delivery of Goods: General Conditions of Purchase and Conditions of Tender," 20 August 1963, 11, 3 PEZ 4/4/1/1/62 1238 Computer File, Western Cape Archives and Records Service, Cape Town, South Africa.

87. See Crispian Olver, *How to Steal a City: The Battle for Nelson Mandela Bay: An Inside Account* (Johannesburg: Jonathan Ball, 2017).

88. F. E. Jenvey to H. G. Lederman, 15 August 1963, 3 PEZ 4/4/1/1/62 1238 Computer File, Western Cape Archives and Records Service, Cape Town, South Africa. See also Lederman to Jenvey, 22 October 1964, in which Lederman offers to fly Jenvey or another official to London for a demonstration of the new ICT 1900 computer, an offer that Jenvey appears to have considered but did not take up, citing other commitments on the proposed date. Jenvey to Lederman, 4 November 1964, 3 PEZ 4/4/1/1/63 1239 Computer File, Western Cape Archives and Records Service, Cape Town, South Africa.

89. "S.A.'s Father of Computing," *Computerweek*, May 19, 1978, 9. Punched-card tabulators had been used by the railways since 1911. "South African Railways Install Ten Computers," *South African Computer Bulletin* 8, no. 2 (1967): 5.

90. "S.A.'s Father of Computing."

91. For more details about the company mergers, see "ICL—A Part of Computer History," *Datarama*, October 1977, 13–14.

92. "S.A.'s Father of Computing." These computers were brought into use in 1963. "South African Railways Install Ten Computers," 6–7.

93. On the received genres of computer historiography, and an alternative in the study of discourse, to which my study is indebted, see Edwards, *Closed World*, x–xv.

94. Breckenridge, *Biometric State*, 171–75.

95. Edwards and Hecht, "History and the Technopolitics of Identity," 625–35.

96. J. M. Coetzee, *Youth* (London: Secker & Warburg, 2002), 44.

97. "Laboratory Mystique," *Financial Mail*, February 26, 1965, 475.

98. "'Brains in Competition,'" *Financial Mail*, August 26, 1960, 244.

99. William Beinart and Saul Dubow, *The Scientific Imagination in South Africa: 1700 to the Present* (Cambridge: Cambridge University Press, 2021), 302.

100. "£350,000 Perseus Does Work of 350," *Financial Mail*, December 2, 1960, 692.

101. "Laboratory Mystique."

102. "A Battle of Giants," *Financial Mail*, November 5, 1965, Special Report, 433.

103. P. J. Riekert, "The Computer as a Tool for Increasing National Productivity," *South African Computer Bulletin* 9, no. 8 (1968): 8; G. D. van der Veer, "The South African Scene," *Systems* 4, no. 11 (1974): 10.

104. Gail Purvis, "South African Scenario 1978–1979: A Personalised View of the Year's Computing Scene in South Africa," in *South African Computer Guide* (Johannesburg: Thomson Publications SA, 1981), 16.

105. "NCR 315 Computer for JBS," *South African Computer Bulletin* 7, no. 1 (1965): 12. For a detailed survey of developments in electronic data transmission, see Van der Veer, "The South African Scene." Earlier forecasts may be found in M. C. Strauss, "Communications," *South African Computer Bulletin* 9, no. 2 (1967): 5–9.

106. J. F. Clarke, "Trends in Computing in South Africa—A Review of the Sixties," *South African Computer Bulletin* 11, no. 2 (1970): 16.

107. Percy Tucker, *Just the Ticket!: My 50 Years in Show Business* (Johannesburg: Jonathan Ball, 1997), 257.

108. Tucker, 258, 278. At the end of 1977, Computicket "ceas[ed] to be a bureau customer and was operating its own duplexed Interdata 8/32 machines, the industry's most powerful minicomputers." Tucker, 351.

109. Clarke, "Trends in Computing," 16.

110. "Defence Mode," *Systems* 1, no. 4 (1971): 22.

111. "Bantu Homeland to Get a 2903," *Datarama*, March–April 1975, 14; "Transkei (The World's Newest Nation) and ICL Is There . . . ," *Datarama*, February 1977, 7–9; "Bophuthatswana National Provident Fund: A Computer for the People," *Datarama*, August–September 1980, 14–16.

112. "Government Computers: Too Many?," *Financial Mail*, June 23, 1972, 1010.

113. "IBM Out in Front," *Financial Mail*, March 1, 1968, 665–68.

114. Purvis, "South African Scenario 1978–1979," 15. One result of the restrictions was that ICL regained its market position relative to IBM. See Liff, "The Computer and Electronics Industry," 208–9. Those in the American anti-apartheid movement showed, however, that the trade continued. See *Automating Apartheid: U.S. Computer Exports to South Africa and the Arms Embargo* (Philadelphia: NARMIC / American Friends Service Committee, 1982). For further details, see Edwards and Hecht, "History and the Technopolitics of Identity," 633–35.

115. Purvis, "South African Scenario 1978–1979," 15.

116. Peter Draper, "Disinvestment and the Restructuring of the South African Computer-Hardware Industry," *South African Journal of Economic History* 10, no. 1 (1995): 61; Peter Draper, "The Limits to Indigenous Technological Capacity in the South African Computer-hardware Industry: Company Strategies and the Local Manufacture Campaign of the 1980s," *South African Journal of Economic History* 11, no. 1 (1996): 96–97.

117. R. J. Evans, "Computer Analysis Related to Rock Art," *South African Computer Bulletin* 11, no. 3 (1970): 8–11; J. de Vynck, "Defining the Vague," *Systems* 3, no. 2 (1973): 37.

118. J. M. Coetzee, "Samuel Beckett's 'Lessness': An Exercise in Decomposition," *Computers and the Humanities* 7, no. 4 (1973): 195–98.

119. Pirow, "Use of a Computer for Clerical Procedures," i-8-1-i-8-30. A longer version of Pirow's address appeared as P. C. Pirow, "The Introduction of Automatic Office Facilities for Mines of the Rand Mines Group," *Journal of the South African Institute of Mining and Metallurgy* 63, no. 9 (1963): 453–85. Since it is more easily accessible to readers, I cite the latter, except where Pirow's SACAC address includes passages not included in the *Journal*, and where I cite the SACAC conference discussion, which is found only in the *Proceedings*.

120. Pirow, "The Introduction of Automatic Office Facilities," 471, 479.

121. Pirow, 480.

122. Pirow, 470–71.

123. "Over the years the addition of various benefits, the requirements of the Industry in regard to service increments and First Aid bonus, the payment of incentive, occupational and drilling bonuses and numerous other items have led to considerable complication in the Native payroll, with a resulting increase in the staff required for its preparation." See Pirow, 464.

124. Rosalind C. Morris, "Accounts," in *Accounts and Drawings from Underground: East Rand Proprietary Mines Cash Book, 1906*, ed. William Kentridge and Rosalind C. Morris (Kolkata, India: Seagull Books, 2015), 137–41.

125. Morris, 150.

126. Union of South Africa, *Report of the Low Grade Mines Commission* (Cape Town: Government Printer, 1920), para. 132.

127. The word *mabalana*, probably from Fanagalo, contains the Zulu verb *-bala*, to count or calculate, not to be confused with the verb *-bhala*, to write.

128. Alan Cobley, "'Why Not All Go Up Higher?': The Transvaal Native Mine Clerks' Association, 1920–1925," *South African Historical Journal* 62, no. 1 (2010): 143–61. Cobley notes that the TNMCA also represented hospital attendants and indunas. Cobley, 147, 150.

129. See Pirow, "The Introduction of Automatic Office Facilities," 464.

130. Having been suspended in 1913 because of high death rates due to pneumonia among migrant workers from north of the 22nd parallel, recruitment from Nyasaland, Southern Rhodesia (present-day Zimbabwe), and Northern Rhodesia (present-day Zambia) resumed in 1932. Northern Mozambique also became a source of labor. In the mid-1950s, about 60 percent of African mine workers were recruited from outside of South Africa. Jonathan Crush, Alan Jeeves, and David Yudelman, *South Africa's Labor Empire: A History of Black Migrancy to the Gold Mines* (Boulder, CO: Westview Press, 1991), 34, 232. This changed abruptly in the mid-1970s, as Mozambique, which had gained independence in 1975, and Malawi ended their labor agreements with South Africa. Crush et al., 104–10. At the same time, unemployment in South Africa rose, and, with intensive recruitment in the Bantustans, South African workers began to make up a larger proportion of the workforce (from about 40% in the 1960s to about 60% in the late 1970s). Crush et al., 129–45, 234–35.

131. Union of South Africa, *Report of the Low Grade Mines Commission*, paras. 192, 214–16.

132. Crush et al., *South Africa's Labor Empire*, 71, 234–35.

133. Luís António Covane, *As relações económicas entre Moçambique e a África do Sul, 1850–1964: Acordos e regulamentos principais* (Maputo, Mozambique: Arquivo Histórico de Moçambique, 1989), 106.

134. See Crush et al., *South Africa's Labor Empire*, 122–23.

135. See Jock McCulloch, *South Africa's Gold Mines and the Politics of Silicosis* (Woodbridge, UK: James Currey 2012).

136. Morris shows that it is with accidental death, notably when money was owed the deceased or was found on their body, that the name of the "Native" appears. Morris, "Accounts," 143.

137. "Automation is a means of analyzing, organizing, and controlling our production processes to achieve optimum use of all our productive resources—mechanical and material as well as human." Diebold, in *Automation and Technological Change*, 15.

138. Vonnegut, *Player Piano*, 72–75.

139. Pirow, "The Introduction of Automatic Office Facilities," 478.

140. Pirow, 453.

141. Pirow, 459.

142. Pirow, 460.

143. "£350,000 Perseus Does Work of 350," 692.

144. The corresponding figure in circulation in the United States in 1955 was 150,

presumably because of higher American labor costs. Hedstrom, *Automating the Office*, 168.

145. Pirow, "Use of a Computer," i-8-28.

146. Pirow, "The Introduction of Automatic Office Facilities," 481.

147. Pirow.

148. In the discussion following his address, Pirow identifies the shortage of qualified programmers as a cause for the underutilization of computers: "On the average our aptitude tests have shown that one percent of the population taken as a whole pass our test so that getting a few hundred programmers is an immense personnel selection task." Pirow, "Use of a Computer," i-8-27.

149. Pirow, i-8-16.

150. Pirow, i-8-29. Rand Mines' Harmony gold mine was near Welkom in the Free State.

151. "Opening Address by the Honourable J.F.W. Haak, Deputy Minister of Economic Affairs," in *Proceedings of the First Symposium on Automation and Computation*, 26.

152. "Opening Address by the Honourable J.F.W. Haak."

153. "Reply by the President," in *Proceedings of the First Symposium on Automation and Computation*, 27.

154. At the third SACAC conference, reaction to the government position was more deliberate, with G. S. J. Kuschke, managing director of the Industrial Development Corporation of South Africa, calling for better education and training for Africans, implicitly criticizing the policy of influx control, and pointing to the "conflicting problems" of industrial decentralization in the Bantustans and at their borders. G. S. J. Kuschke, "Automation in the Economic Development of South Africa," in *Proceedings of the Third National Conference of the South African Council for Automation and Computation, 15th, 16th and 17th October, 1969 Pretoria South Africa* (Pretoria: SACAC, 1969), 9–10, 13–16.

155. In his opening speech to the second SACAC conference in Cape Town, the minister of mines and planning, Carel de Wet, was more circumspect, alluding only briefly to "local norms and demands—especially in respect to the peculiar [*eiesoortige*] components and categories of our labor market," to which automation would have to conform. "Toespraak deur sy edele Dr. Carel de Wet," 1. The address was read, in De Wet's absence, by Dr. S. J. P. K. van Heerden, deputy scientific adviser to the prime minister.

156. Brune, who was born in South Africa in 1901, received his doctorate from MIT and worked for many years at General Electric before joining the CSIR, from which he retired in 1966. Ian Craig, *IFAC in South Africa (1961–2005): A Brief History of the South African Council for Automation and Computation* ([Pretoria]: SACAC, 2005), 12.

157. In one of the few references to clerical work in the SACAC proceedings, at the 1969 conference, G. S. J. Kuschke observes that "the increasing demand for trained staff will make it less and less justifiable to waste manpower which has the potential of being trained for the higher skilled functions, on clerical work which can be performed by machines more efficiently, cheaper and faster." Kuschke, "Automation in

the Economic Development of South Africa," 12. In one of the even fewer references to women, "in answer to various questions, Mr. Prinsloo [section head of technical support at ISCOR's data processing services] said that women are outstanding in many aspects of automation-work: 25% of the ISCOR EDP department are women, and they demonstrate a talent for programming." "Bespreking van Referaat B2 deur mnr. G. C. Prinsloo" [Discussion of Address B2 by Mr. G. C. Prinsloo], in *Proceedings of the Third National Conference of the South African Council for Automation and Computation*, 2.

158. Van Houten et al., *Industrial Automation in South Africa*, 7.

159. For an excellent case study, see Gillian Hart, *Disabling Globalization: Places of Power in Post-Apartheid South Africa* (Berkeley: University of California Press, 2002); also see Feinstein, *Economic History of South Africa*, 250.

160. Van Houten et al., *Industrial Automation in South Africa*, 8.

161. Van Houten et al., 5–6, 8–9.

162. Van Houten et al., 2, 11.

163. Van Houten et al., 4.

164. Van Houten et al., 13.

165. Van Houten et al., 13.

166. Van Houten et al., 139.

167. "Computer Survey," *Financial Mail*, November 26, 1971, 784.

168. A shortage was already being predicted for 1973. "Time to Recruit," *Financial Mail*, October 27, 1972, 373.

169. Van Houten et al., *Industrial Automation in South Africa*, 140.

170. Ellen Hellmann and Henry Lever, eds., *Race Relations in South Africa 1929–1979* (London: Macmillan, 1980), 141.

171. Like the regulations contemplated for job reservation in clerical work in 1970, the terms of this law were not enforced after 1971. Hyslop, "State Education Policy," 468.

172. Van Houten et al., *Industrial Automation in South Africa*, 141.

173. Van Houten et al., 140.

174. R. V. Clark, "Non-white Labour in the EDP Industry: Across the Spectrum," *Systems* 2, no. 4 (1972): 2–6. Clark, personnel manager at IBM, South Africa, points to job reservation and discrimination as factors in creating an artificial shortage of labor. See Clark, 6. See also D. Gray, "The Personnel Market 1979/80," in *South African Computer Guide* (Johannesburg: Thomson Publications SA, 1981), 24–25.

175. "Computer Survey," 784.

176. Van Houten et al., *Industrial Automation in South Africa*, 141–43.

177. Van Houten et al., 159.

178. Van Houten et al., 143.

179. Sibusiso Nyembezi, *Learn More Zulu* (Pietermaritzburg: Shuter & Shooter, 1970), 291. Also see Hyslop, "State Education Policy," 457.

180. Van Houten et al., *Industrial Automation in South Africa*, 143, cf. 145–46.

181. Van Houten et al., 155.

182. Van Houten et al., 145.

183. Mariotti and Van Zyl-Hermann, "Policy, Practice and Perception," 220, 223.

184. Van Houten et al., *Industrial Automation in South Africa*, 147, 155.

185. Van Houten et al., 159.

186. Van Houten et al., 146.

187. J. M. Coetzee, "Idleness in South Africa," in *White Writing: On the Culture of Letters in South Africa* (New Haven, CT: Yale University Press, 1988), 12–35.

Chapter 2

1. Rebecca Roach, "J. M. Coetzee's Aesthetic Automatism," *Modern Fiction Studies* 65, no. 2 (2019): 308–37.

2. Personal communication, June 10, 2019.

3. More precisely, March 1962 to May 1963. See J. M. Coetzee, "Form P.86, July 1, 1966," handwritten notes, Container 105.3 Coetzee Personal and Career-Related: International Computers and Tabulators, Ltd., 1963–1965, Harry Ransom Center, Austin, Texas.

4. The two other "Cape Town" writers were Keith Gottschalk and Mothobi Mutloatse, who, identified as being from Pimville, which is part of Soweto, is misplaced.

5. The coincidence of Tlali's and Coetzee's texts being published in the first issue of *Staffrider* is noted by Roach. Rebecca Roach, "Hero and Bad Motherland: J. M. Coetzee's Computational Critique," *Contemporary Literature* 59, no. 1 (2018): 80.

6. The name of the magazine came from the term used to refer to the dangerous practice of riding on the outside of passenger trains. Tlali is told that the women at a Dube self-help club "liked that heading of yours—'Staffrider.' . . . It is frustration which makes our children climb on top of moving trains, isn't it? . . . Will you always call it that? . . . Yes, it's frustration. Have you heard how the prices of things are going up soon?" Tlali, "Soweto Speaking No. 6 / A 'Great Lady' of Soweto / Mrs B. Makau," *Staffrider* 1, no. 3 (1978): 4.

7. J. M. Coetzee, "Hero and Bad Mother in Epic, a Poem," *Staffrider* 1, no. 1 (1978): 36.

8. Miriam Tlali, "Soweto Speaking to Miriam Tlali," *Staffrider* 1, no. 1 (1978): 5. "HP," or hire purchase, is the usual term for buying something on an installment plan.

9. Tlali.

10. Tlali. Tlali's column was a regular feature in *Staffrider* for the first two years, except for a hiatus in early 1979 when Tlali was attending the Iowa International Writers Program (for an account of her experiences in Iowa, see Tlali, "New Horizons," in *Mihloti*, 70–95). Nhlanhla Maake and Joe Masinga contributed to Soweto Speaking in Tlali's absence. After Tlali's column ended, *Staffrider* introduced work by others under a similar rubric—for example, A. Manson and D. Collins, "Voices from the Ghetto: Kwa Mashu Speaking," *Staffrider* 3, no. 1 (1980): 2–3; Joël Matlou, "Voices from the Ghetto: My Lifestyle," *Staffrider* 3, no. 2 (1980): 16–17; Mahlaba Eddie Mhlane, "Voices from the Ghetto: Alexandra Speaking," *Staffrider* 3, no. 3 (1980): 3–4.

11. Adam Cohen, foreword to Studs Terkel, *Working: People Talk About What They Do All Day and How They Feel About What They Do* (New York: New Press, 2004; originally published 1972), ix.

12. Terkel, *Working*, 29.

13. Terkel, xxxiii.

14. A Junior Certificate is a school-leaving qualification awarded after ten years of study. A Senior Certificate would be awarded after twelve years.

15. Tlali, "Soweto Speaking," 4–5. The piece is reprinted as Miriam Tlali, "Leah Koae: The Dressmaker," in *Mihloti*, 44–50.

16. Andrew Godley, "The Sewing Machine," in *The Routledge History of Fashion and Dress, 1800 to the Present*, ed. Véronique Pouillard and Vincent Dubé-Senécal (New York: Routledge, 2024), 31.

17. Godley, 35.

18. Godley, 36.

19. Aimé Césaire, *Notebook of a Return to My Native Land*, trans. Mireille Rosello and Annie Pritchard (Tarset: Bloodaxe Books, 1995), 83. See also Peter Abrahams, *Mine Boy* (London: Heinemann, 1987; originally published 1946), 24–25.

20. In another of her columns, Tlali speaks to Mrs. B. Makau, who helps run a small self-help club, the Soweto Women's Thrift Club. One of the things the club does is teach women to sew by hand and with a machine: "At Dube it's better because we have electricity and we also have two old 'Singer' machines." Tlali, "Soweto Speaking No. 6," 4.

21. Tlali, 5.

22. Coetzee acknowledged that "Hero and Bad Mother" was a computer poem in an interview with David Attwell. J. M. Coetzee, *Doubling the Point: Essays and Interviews*, ed. David Attwell (Cambridge, MA: Harvard University Press, 1992), 22.

23. J. C. Kannemeyer, *J. M. Coetzee: A Life in Writing*, trans. Michiel Heyns (Johannesburg: Jonathan Ball, 2012), 123–25. The poem is also alluded to in Coetzee, *Youth*, 161.

24. The relevant dates are February 1964 to August 1965. See Coetzee, "Form P.86, July 1, 1966."

25. Gqola, *Miriam Tlali: Writing Freedom*, 15.

26. J. M. Coetzee, *White Writing: On the Culture of Letters in South Africa* (New Haven, CT: Yale University Press, 1988), 5.

27. See Isabel Hofmeyr, *Gandhi's Printing Press: Experiments in Slow Reading* (Cambridge, MA: Harvard University Press, 2013).

28. Coetzee, "Idleness in South Africa," 35.

29. I follow the convention, among scholars of Coetzee, of referring to the three-part series, written in the third person and eventually collectively titled "Scenes from Provincial Life," including *Boyhood*, *Youth*, and *Summertime*, under this term, which Coetzee used in an interview with David Attwell in Coetzee, *Doubling the Point*, 394.

30. J. M. Coetzee, *Summertime: Scenes from Provincial Life* (London: Harvill Secker, 2009), 7.

31. Coetzee, *Youth*, 160.

32. Coetzee, 161.

33. Coetzee, 158.

34. Coetzee, 156–58. Having written to various "Provosts, Wardens, and other Heads of Houses" to ask their advice, Jude soon regrets having done so: "I may be an impostor, an idle scamp, a man with bad character, for all that they know to the contrary.... Perhaps that's what I am!" Thomas Hardy, *Jude the Obscure*, ed. Norman Page (New York: Norton, 1978), 93. Studs Terkel dedicated *Working* to Jude Fawley.

35. Coetzee, *Youth*, 157.

36. Christina Lupton, "Workers as Readers: On Coetzee's *Youth* and the Poverty of Time," *Politicsslashletters* 13 (2018), http://politicsslashletters.org/workers-readers-coetzees-youth-poverty-time/.

37. Coetzee, *Youth*, 160–61.

38. Coetzee, 80.

39. Coetzee, 122–23.

40. Coetzee, 136.

41. Coetzee, 98.

42. Coetzee, 44–45, 140.

43. Coetzee, 161.

44. Coetzee, 160.

45. See J. M. Coetzee, "Computer Poem," *The Lion and the Impala* 2, no. 1 (1963): 13; J. M. Coetzee, "Surreal Metaphors and Random Processes," *Journal of Literary Semantics* 8, no. 1 (1979): 24.

46. See Tristan Tzara, "Dada Manifesto on Feeble Love and Bitter Love," originally published 1920, in *Seven Dada Manifestos and Lampisteries*, trans. Barbara Wright (London: Calder, 1977), 39, where the "hat" is in fact a "bag"; Sinclair Beiles, William S. Burroughs, Gregory Corso, and Brion Gysin, *Minutes to Go* (Paris: Two Cities Editions, 1960). A distinction between Tzara's Dadaist experiments and those of the Surrealists is significant for Gysin, who writes that Tzara "might well have burned the Louvre if he hadn't diverted into the Communist Panic by the Art Wing of the Freudian Conspiracy calling itself Surrealism under Andre Breton." See Brion Gysin, "Cut Me Up," in Beiles et al., *Minutes to Go*, 43. I have abbreviated the title of Gysin's essay. For more on Sinclair Beiles, who came from South Africa, and his subsequent career, see Gary Cummiskey and Eva Kowalska, eds., *Who Was Sinclair Beiles?* (Sandton, South Africa: Dye Hard Press, 2009).

47. Coetzee, *Youth*, 160.

48. Howard Nemerov, "Speculative Equations: Poems, Poets, Computers," *American Scholar* 36, no. 3 (1967): 397.

49. Coetzee, "Surreal Metaphors," 22.

50. Coetzee, "Computer Poem."

51. As Hans Magnus Enzensberger writes, regarding his poetry automaton, "Fortunately, it is a matter of activities that are not regulated by wage agreements; otherwise protests against the threatened destruction of jobs could be expected." Hans Magnus Enzensberger, *Einladung zu einem Poesie-Automaten* (Frankfurt: Suhrkamp, 2000), 52.

52. Coetzee, *Youth*, 161. The vocabulary of *The Lion and the Impala* verses does not correspond, however, to that of Neruda's poem, as translated by Tarn. There is also no sign of the "Neruda poems" in the printouts at the Harry Ransom Center. Coetzee, however, identifies the vocabulary of the examples in "Surreal Metaphors" as coming from Neruda.

53. The lines are from Goethe's *West-östlicher Divan* (1819), where they appear in a four-line poem entitled "Besserem Verständniß." They are preceded by the couplet "Wer das Dichten will verstehen / Muß in's Land der Dichtung gehen." Coetzee's elision of these lines suggests that what John may have come to realize in *Youth* is that

one can understand what it is to write poetry (*Dichten*), and even understand what poetry (*Dichtung*) is, without understanding what it means to be a poet (*Dichter*).

54. The latter is something that preoccupies John in Coetzee, *Youth*, 138.

55. Le Roux, "Miriam Tlali and Ravan Press," 445.

56. C. T. Funkhouser, *Prehistoric Digital Poetry: An Archaeology of Forms, 1959–1995* (Tuscaloosa: University of Alabama Press, 2007), 78.

57. In "Surreal Metaphors," Coetzee cites two articles by Samuel R. Levin, including "On the Automatic Production of Poetic Sequences," *Texas Studies in Literature and Language* 5 (1963): 138–46.

58. See Nick Montfort et al., *10 PRINT CHR$(205.5+RND(1)); : GOTO 10* (Cambridge, MA: MIT Press, 2013), 133–42.

59. Theo Lutz, "Stochastische Texte," *augenblick* 4 (1959), https://www.netzliteratur.net/lutz_schule.htm.

60. Coetzee, "Computer Poem," 12.

61. Coetzee.

62. Coetzee.

63. Coetzee.

64. Coetzee, 12–13.

65. Funkhouser, *Prehistoric Digital Poetry*, 36.

66. Coetzee, "Computer Poem," 13.

67. J. M. Coetzee, "Line Generator," 30 May 1963, Computer Poetry 1 folder, osb 143, J. M. Coetzee Papers, Harry Ransom Center, University of Texas, Austin.

68. Coetzee, *Youth*, 81. Those versed in computer lore and popular culture know this to be the same place used as a location for filming an early scene of Stanley Kubrick's *Dr. Strangelove* (1962), in which Peter Sellers as Group Captain Lionel Mandrake is shown at the console of the IBM 7090.

69. See Coetzee, "Form P.86, July 1, 1966."

70. Shetterly, *Hidden Figures*, 206. Enzensberger describes using a computer to generate poetry as "killing a fly with a shotgun" (*Man kann mit Kanonen auf Spatzen zielen*, literally "one can aim cannons at sparrows"). Enzensberger, *Einladung zu einem Poesie-Automaten*, 32.

71. Montfort et al., *10 PRINT*, 135–36. For Noll's program and explanation of how it worked, see A. Michael Noll, "Patterns by 7090," typewritten memorandum, August 28, 1962, http://noll.uscannenberg.org/Art%20Papers/BTL%201962%20Memo.pdf.

72. Coetzee, "Line Generator."

73. Coetzee.

74. "Chronology of *House of Dust*," in Hannah B. Higgins et al., "*The House of Dust* by Alison Knowles," 2016, 8, https://monoskop.org/images/1/15/Knowles_Alison_The_House_of_Dust_Research_Journal_2016.pdf.

75. Janet Sarbanes, "A School Based on What Artists Wanted To Do: Alison Knowles on CALARTS," in Higgins et al., "*The House of Dust* by Alison Knowles," 6.

76. Roach, "Hero and Bad Motherland," 92.

77. To make reading the program easier, I have inserted spaces in some places.

78. See Coetzee, *Youth*, 74.

79. Van Houten et al., *Industrial Automation in South Africa*, 140.

80. See "City of Port Elizabeth: Electronic Computer: Conditions of Tender and Specification," 20 August 1963, 1, 3 PEZ 4/4/1/1/62 1238 Computer File, Western Cape Archives and Records Service, Cape Town, South Africa.

81. *Reference Manual: 709/7090 FORTRAN Programming System* (International Business Machines Corporation, 1961), 10.

82. *Reference Manual: 709/7090 FORTRAN Programming System*, 4.

83. *Reference Manual: 709/7090 FORTRAN Programming System*, 8.

84. *Reference Manual: 709/7090 FORTRAN Programming System*, 3.

85. "That meaning is not what Hopper had in mind," however, as Ceruzzi notes. "For her, a compiler handled subroutines stored in libraries. A compiler method, according to Hopper's definition, was a program that copied the subroutine code into the proper place in the main program where a programmer wanted to use it." Paul E. Ceruzzi, *A History of Modern Computing*, 2nd ed. (Cambridge, MA: MIT Press, 2003), 85.

86. J. M. Coetzee, "Generate Index," 25 March 1965, Computer Poetry 1 folder, osb 143, J. M. Coetzee Papers, Harry Ransom Center, University of Texas, Austin. In *Youth*, Coetzee remarks on John needing to have "a virtuoso command of Atlas's two-level internal language." Coetzee, *Youth*, 144.

87. *Reference Manual: 709/7090 FORTRAN Programming System*, 24, 22.

88. Nick Montfort, *Exploratory Programming for the Arts and Humanities* (Cambridge, MA: MIT Press, 2016).

89. Nick Montfort, "Generator of Five-Word Lines, v1.0: A Speculative Reimplementation, Based on One Page of Output from an Untitled Project by J. M. Coetzee c. 1964–1965, Atlas Autocode," *Memory Slam*, https://nickm.com/memslam/five_word.html.

90. See Abbate, *Recoding Gender*, 81–88.

91. David Link, "There Must Be an Angel: On the Beginnings of the Arithmetics of Rays," in *Variantology 2: On Deep Time Relations of Arts, Sciences and Technologies*, ed. Siegfried Zielinski and David Link (Cologne, Germany: König, 2006), 16–17.

92. David Link, *Poesiemaschinen / Maschinenpoesie: Zur Frühgeschichte computerisierter Texterzeugung und generativer Systeme* (Munich: Wilhelm Fink, 2006), 8.

93. Krauss, "'The Rock,'" 9.

94. For an account of Enigma, see Andrew Hodges, *Alan Turing: The Enigma* (Princeton, NJ: Princeton University Press, 2014; originally published 1983), 273–330.

95. Alan Turing, "Computing Machinery and Intelligence," originally published 1950, in *The New Media Reader*, ed. Noah Wardrip-Fruin and Nick Montfort (Cambridge, MA: MIT Press, 2003), 54.

96. Krauss, "'The Rock,'" 34.

97. Lev Manovich, "New Media from Borges to HTML," in *The New Media Reader*, ed. Noah Wardrip-Fruin and Nick Montfort (Cambridge, MA: MIT Press, 2003), 15.

98. Manovich, 15.

99. Emerson, "Art," 217.

100. For Mak's and others' experiments, see "1401 Movies, Music, Sounds, and Videos," accessed March 13, 2025, https://ibm-1401.info/Movies-n-Sounds.html.

101. Lutz, "Stochastische Texte."

102. J. M. Coetzee, "A Note on Writing," in *Doubling the Point*, 95.

103. See Funkhouser, *Prehistoric Digital Poetry*, 26–27, 35–36.

104. Hannah B. Higgins and Douglas Kahn, eds., *Mainframe Experimentalism: Early Computing and the Foundations of the Digital Arts* (Berkeley: University of California Press, 2012).

105. Hannah B. Higgins and Douglas Kahn, introduction to *Mainframe Experimentalism*, 2–9. See also Funkhouser, *Prehistoric Digital Poetry*, 64.

106. Christoph Klütsch, "Information Aesthetics and the Stuttgart School," in Higgins and Kahn, *Mainframe Experimentalism*, 71.

107. Klütsch, 71–72.

108. Margit Rosen, "'They Have All Dreamt of the Machines—And Now the Machines Have Arrived': New Tendencies—Computers and Visual Research, Zagreb, 1968–1969," in Higgins and Kahn, *Mainframe Experimentalism*, 100.

109. Nemerov, "Speculative Equations: Poems, Poets, Computers," 396.

110. Nemerov, 397.

111. Nemerov, 400.

112. Nemerov, 401.

113. Nemerov, 403–5.

114. Nemerov, 406.

115. Nemerov, 414.

116. Higgins and Kahn, introduction to *Mainframe Experimentalism*, 3.

117. Higgins and Kahn, 4. See also "Chronology of *House of Dust*."

118. Grant Taylor, "The Soulless Usurper: Reception and Criticism of Early Computer Art," in Higgins and Kahn, *Mainframe Experimentalism*, 20.

119. Taylor, 30.

120. Coetzee, *Youth*, 163.

121. Coetzee, *Doubling the Point*, 22.

122. See Coetzee, *White Writing*, 5.

123. John Cage, "Diary: Audience 1966," in *A Year from Monday* (Middletown, CT: Wesleyan University Press, 1967), 50; quoted in Higgins and Kahn, introduction to *Mainframe Experimentalism*, 3.

124. In his testimony before Congress in 1955, James B. Carey, secretary-treasurer of the CIO and president of the International Union of Electrical Workers, calls this a "lot of nonsense." The dominant view is stated by Ralph J. Cordiner, president of General Electric. See *Automation and Technological Change*, 237, 432–33. For a careful tabling of the respective positions of management and organized labor at these hearings, see Hedstrom, *Automating the Office*, 180, 206–7, n95–96. In the art world, the Zagreb New Tendencies group was challenged because of the effects of automation on employment. Rosen, "'They Have All Dreamt of the Machines,'" 106–7.

125. Noah Wardrip-Fruin, "Digital Media Archaeology: Interpreting Computational Processes," in *Media Archaeology: Approaches, Applications, and Implications*, ed. Erkki Huhtamo and Jussi Parikka (Berkeley: University of California Press, 2011), 305.

126. Christopher Strachey, "The 'Thinking' Machine," *Encounter* 3, no. 4 (1954): 26.

127. Strachey's program is discussed in detail by Link, "There Must Be an Angel," 17–24, and Wardrip-Fruin, "Digital Media Archaeology," 307–9.

128. This put him at odds with Turing, who, in 1950, had declared the question "'Can machines think?' . . . to be too meaningless to deserve discussion. Nevertheless I believe that at the end of the century the use of words and general educated opinion will have altered so much that one will be able to speak of machines thinking without expecting to be contradicted." Turing, "Computing Machinery and Intelligence," 55.

129. Strachey, "The 'Thinking' Machine," 31. As Margaret Hedstrom shows, in the United States during the same period, the age and marital status of women performing clerical work was already changing, with more older and married women employed in the context of a post–World War II labor shortage. Hedstrom, *Automating the Office*, 331–86.

130. Strachey, "The 'Thinking' Machine," 26.

131. Wardrip-Fruin, "Digital Media Archaeology," 315–18.

132. Andrew Hodges, *Alan Turing: The Enigma* (New York: Walker, 2000), 478, quoted in Wardrip-Fruin, "Digital Media Archaeology," 306.

133. "The machine room downstairs, dominated by the huge memory cabinets of the 7090, is more often than not empty; he can run programs on the little 1401 computer, even, surreptitiously, play games on it." Coetzee, *Youth*, 81.

134. Coetzee, 168.

135. Coetzee, *Summertime*, 7.

136. Tlali, "Soweto Speaking to Miriam Tlali," *Staffrider* 1, no. 2 (1978): 55.

137. Tlali.

Chapter 3

1. For a detailed discussion of stereoscopy, see William Kentridge and Angela Breidbach, *Thinking Aloud: Conversations with Angela Breidbach* (Johannesburg: David Krut, 2006), 75–84.

2. For discussion and explanation of this effect, see Kentridge and Breidbach, 76–78.

3. Matthew Kentridge, *The Soho Chronicles: 10 Films by William Kentridge* (Kolkata, India: Seagull Books, 2015), 312.

4. For Kentridge himself, before *Stereoscope* is about how one cannot insulate oneself from what is happening in the world outside, the film, which relates to how "[he] was feeling at the time," depicts in its diptychs of Soho Eckstein the struggle to find a balance between a "life [that] was much too complicated" and one that is "simplified and pared-down." Kentridge and Breidbach, *Thinking Aloud*, 74, see also 79–80.

5. For a précis of the narrative arc of the films, see Matthew Kentridge, *The Soho Chronicles*, 5–8. The names Soho Eckstein and Felix Teitlebaum came to Kentridge in a dream. Kentridge, 85. Kentridge had probably also heard of H. Eckstein, the mining company founded in 1887, which took its name from one of its original partners, Hermann Eckstein, whose name, approximately translated from German, was given to the Corner House group of companies. As part of the Corner House, in the early history of gold mining on the Witwatersrand, H. Eckstein is notable for having bought up properties to the south of Johannesburg, where it was one of the first companies to undertake deep-level mining. Subsequently becoming part of Wernher, Beit, & Co.,

H. Eckstein was incorporated into Rand Mines in 1893, the year Hermann Eckstein died, soon after moving to London. Eckstein, who served as the first president of the Transvaal Chamber of Mines, has been described as having been, in his day, the "leading personality of Johannesburg." Cartwright, *Corner House*, 118.

6. Kentridge, however, declares that "the film was not made to be about the nature of stereoscopy." Kentridge and Breidbach, *Thinking Aloud*, 79.

7. This is a simplification. In practice, each alteration becomes three frames. Matthew Kentridge, *The Soho Chronicles*, 25. For a discussion by Kentridge himself of the differences between his technique and cel animation, see the film *William Kentridge: Drawing the Passing*, directed by Maria Anna Tappeiner and Reinhard Wulf (Westdeutscher Rundfunk, 1999). In this film, Kentridge also discusses in detail *Stereoscope*, which he was making at the time.

8. Kentridge and Breidbach, *Thinking Aloud*, 110.

9. Krauss, "'The Rock,'" 6. Kentridge describes his filmmaking technique in "'Fortuna': Neither Program nor Chance in the Making of Images," in *William Kentridge*, ed. Rosalind Krauss (Cambridge, MA: MIT Press, 2017), 26.

10. Matthew Kentridge, *The Soho Chronicles*, 77.

11. Paul E. Ceruzzi, *Computing: A Concise History* (Cambridge, MA: MIT Press, 2012), xi–xiv.

12. Dan Cameron, "Interview with William Kentridge," in *William Kentridge*, by William Kentridge and Neal David Benezra (Chicago: Museum of Contemporary Art and New Museum of Contemporary Art, 2001), 71.

13. Initially composed of Kentridge, Malcolm Purkey, Astrid von Kotze, Pippa Stein, Patrick Fitzgerald, Ari Sitas, and others, when Workshop '71, a group organized by Robert Mshengu Kavanagh, disbanded, several of its members, including Ramolao Makhene, Siphiwe Khumalo, and Arthur Molepo, joined. Martin Orkin, ed., *At the Junction: Four Plays by the Junction Avenue Theatre Company* (Johannesburg: Witwatersrand University Press, 1995), 2.

14. Orkin, 5.

15. William Kentridge et al., *Why Should I Hesitate: Putting Drawings to Work* (Cape Town: Zeitz MOCAA / Koenig Books, 2019), 105.

16. Orkin, *At the Junction*, 56.

17. Orkin, 60.

18. See Mark Sanders, *Complicities: The Intellectual and Apartheid* (Durham, NC: Duke University Press, 2002), 169–74.

19. Kentridge's silkscreened poster for the production, in its first version, featured a portrait of Karl Marx. In its subsequent version, Marx was joined by Jan van Riebeeck and Cecil John Rhodes. Warren Siebrits, ed., *William Kentridge: Prints and Posters 1974–1990* (Göttingen, Germany: Steidl, 2022), vol. 1, pt. 1, 55, and vol. 1, pt. 2, 441–42, 450–51.

20. Kentridge et al., *Why Should I Hesitate*, 104.

21. Orkin, *At the Junction*, 22–23. The play was subsequently published by Ravan Press, along with a foreword by Lionel Abrahams, who also interviewed members of the company. Malcolm Purkey, *The Fantastical History of a Useless Man* (Johannesburg: Ravan, 1978).

22. Sophiatown was home to nearly sixty thousand Africans, Coloureds, Indians,

and Chinese. Its destruction is described in Trevor Huddleston's *Naught for Your Comfort* (London: Collins, 1956), Bloke Modisane's *Blame Me on History* (London: Thames & Hudson, 1963), and other works.

23. For a detailed account of Kentridge's role in the company, and how it influenced his ideas about art making, see Leora Maltz-Leca, *William Kentridge: Process as Metaphor and Other Doubtful Enterprises* (Oakland: University of California Press, 2018), 109–14.

24. "Labour relations, already partly the subject of *Randlords and Rotgut* [1978], again came into focus when it was invited to collaborate in 1982 in the creation of a play for the worker movement, *The sun also rises: Ilanga Lizo Phumela Abasebenzi.* This project subsequently contributed to the emergence of worker theatre in Natal. Ari Sitas and Astrid von Kotze both left the Company at about this time in order to participate in and help facilitate this new phenomenon." Orkin, *At the Junction*, 3. The posters made by Kentridge for these plays are reproduced in William Kentridge and Denis Hirson, *Footnotes for the Panther: Conversations Between William Kentridge and Denis Hirson* (Johannesburg: Fourthwall, 2017), 23, 26. In 1984, Kentridge performed in *A Noose for Scariot Impimpi*, "a play by a shop-stewards' collective aimed at trade union members, performed in community centres around Durban." Kentridge et al., *Why Should I Hesitate*, 113.

25. Kentridge and Hirson, *Footnotes for the Panther*, 22. Kentridge also designed trade union posters. See Kentridge and Hirson, 208.

26. For a long time, Kentridge experimented with ways of representing, in drawings and prints, crowds of people on the move. Kentridge and Breidbach, *Thinking Aloud*, 15. By the late 1980s, Kentridge settled on the procession as one of his signature forms. Ari Sitas accounts for this turn as the oblique but lasting impression on Kentridge of struggle performance culture, including that of trade unions. Ari Sitas, "Processions and Public Rituals," in *William Kentridge*, by William Kentridge and Neal David Benezra (Chicago: Museum of Contemporary Art and New Museum of Contemporary Art, 2001), 63–65. The early wall-mounted arcs described by Sitas evolved into processions in different media, including the film *Shadow Procession* (1999), and sculptures in metal and bronze. Kentridge's more recent processions include the film installation *More Sweetly Play the Dance* (2015) and *Triumphs and Laments* (2016), a large-scale frieze along the bank of the Tiber River in Rome. Parts of *The Head and the Load* (2018), which take the form of a live theatrical panorama, may be seen as an upscaling and culmination of the form. See William Kentridge, "Thirty Thoughts on *The Head and the Load*," in William Kentridge et al., *The Head and the Load* (Munich: Prestel, 2020), 286. For another reading of Kentridge's processions, see Michael Rothberg, *The Implicated Subject: Beyond Victims and Perpetrators* (Stanford, CA: Stanford University Press, 2019), 87–117.

27. In *Ubu Tells the Truth*, for example, which alludes to the animated sequence with the camera and its tripod in *Man with a Movie Camera*. For a commentary on the significance of this allusion, see Mark Sanders, "Anamorphosis: Puppetry, Animation, and Automation in William Kentridge," *Puppetry International Research* 1, no. 2 (2024): 1–31, https://pirjournal.commons.gc.cuny.edu/2024/07/10/anamorphosis-puppetry-animation-and-automation-in-william-kentridge/.

28. Maltz-Leca, *William Kentridge*, 230.

29. I refer loosely to Leon Battista Alberti, *On Painting*, trans. Rocco Sinisgalli (Cambridge: Cambridge University Press, 2011; originally published 1435), 44–73.

30. Morris Kentridge, *I Recall*, 129, 153.

31. "Welcome News for Telephonists," *The South African Telephone and Telegraph Review ("The Live Wire")* 9, no. 4 (1926): 11. The full transcription of Morris Kentridge's question, and the minister's answer, may be found in Union of South Africa, *Debates of the House of Assembly, Third Session, Fifth Parliament 22nd January to 8th June 1926* (Cape Town: Cape Times, 1926), 1356.

32. "Welcome News for Telephonists."

33. Figures for 1930–34 put male operators at about 9–12 percent of all operators represented by the Telephone and Telegraph Association. "Schedules of the Totals of the Various Grades Who Are Members of the Association," *The South African Telephone and Telegraph Review ("The Live Wire")* 17, no. 7 (1934): 10. By 1907, in the United States, out of about 80,000 operators, only about 3,500 were male. Josephine Goldmark, *Fatigue and Efficiency: A Study in Industry* (New York: Charities Publication Committee, 1912), 44.

34. Union of South Africa, *Abridged Annual Report of the Department of Posts and Telegraphs, Year Ended 31st March, 1925* (Pretoria: Government Printer, 1926), 15.

35. Union of South Africa, *Debates of the House of Assembly, Third Session, Fifth Parliament*, 1649–62. In 1928, a decision was taken that when existing switching equipment was replaced in major centers such at the Witwatersrand and the Cape Peninsula, it would be replaced with automatic apparatuses. Union of South Africa, Department of Posts and Telegraphs, *Report of the Postmaster-General for the Financial Year 1928–29* (Pretoria: Government Printer, 1929), 12.

36. For an image of the linocut, with a detailed account of its states and variations, see Siebrits, *William Kentridge: Prints and Posters*, vol. 1, pt. 1, 53, and vol. 1, pt. 2, 439.

37. Matthew Kentridge, *The Soho Chronicles*, 56–59.

38. Smuts called out the air force against a civil uprising for a second time to repress an uprising by the Bondelzwarts in May 1922 in South-West Africa, a formerly German colonial possession then administered by the Union of South Africa under League of Nations mandate. See Union of South Africa, *Report of the Commission Appointed to Enquire into the Rebellion of the Bondelzwarts* (Cape Town: Cape Times, 1923), 24–25.

39. Morris Kentridge, *I Recall*, 103–4.

40. Morris Kentridge, 104, 106, 108–9.

41. Morris Kentridge, 106.

42. Morris Kentridge, 112. For more detail on the Commandos, including their role in racial violence, see Jeremy Krikler, *White Rising: The 1922 Insurrection and Racial Killing in South Africa* (Manchester, UK: Manchester University Press, 2005), 50–77.

43. Morris Kentridge, *I Recall*, 114–18. "It may be of interest," he notes, "that the main reason why, after my arrest, the authorities could not indict me was because I had led the deputation to Tielman Roos's conference, and the police, who were

racking up evidence against strikers and their supporters, took it for granted that they had a case against me for High Treason without further evidence." Tielman Roos, who became minister of justice in the Pact government, was then the leader of the Transvaal National Party. The deputation led by Morris Kentridge presented a resolution passed by a mass meeting of strikers on February 5, 1922, to Roos's conference of "Nationalist and Labour Members of Parliament" that a republican government be established. "We did not press it and the Conference turned down the resolution." Morris Kentridge, 118, 109–10.

44. Krikler, *White Rising*, 39–40, 47–48.

45. Morris Kentridge, *Unemployment in South Africa: A Simple Outline* (Johannesburg: I.S.L. Press, [1922?]), 7. Also see Morris Kentridge, *I Recall*, 94–96.

46. Morris Kentridge, *Unemployment in South Africa*, 7–8.

47. Morris Kentridge, 22.

48. Morris Kentridge, 86–87. For a more detailed account of the arrangement and its history, see Charles van Onselen, *The Night Trains: Moving Mozambican Miners to and from the Witwatersrand Mines, Circa 1902–1955* (Johannesburg: Jonathan Ball, 2019), 50–56.

49. Morris Kentridge, *Unemployment in South Africa*, 86. See also Krikler, *White Rising*, 24.

50. Morris Kentridge, *Unemployment in South Africa*, 26–27.

51. Morris Kentridge, 25–27, 35.

52. Morris Kentridge, 88–89. For a discussion of the significance of this differentiation between proletarian and peasant, in the prelude to the 1922 strike, see Krikler, *White Rising*, 31–32.

53. Morris Kentridge, *Unemployment in South Africa*, 33–34.

54. There is in fact a change in official discourse: "In evidence [before the Commission of Inquiry Regarding Cape Coloured Population of the Union] it was stated that, whereas the civilized labour policy after the year 1924 might be said to be founded upon the wages earned, before that date it was called a white labour policy." Union of South Africa, *Report of Commission of Inquiry Regarding Cape Coloured Population of the Union* (Pretoria: Government Printer, 1937), 37, para. 167.

55. See Krikler, *White Rising*, 110.

56. Stephen Clingman, *Birthmark* (Johannesburg: Jacana, 2015), 173.

57. The words "fight and" are elided in the slogan in the stage directions. Orkin, *At the Junction*, 44. A photograph from the 1976 production confirms that the actual placards used in the play elided the words accordingly. The photograph is reproduced in Maltz-Leca, *William Kentridge*, 88.

58. Orkin, *At the Junction*, 44–45.

59. Krikler, *White Rising*, 130. This is also noted by Morris Kentridge, *I Recall*, 112.

60. Krikler, *White Rising*, 121–26.

61. Morris Kentridge, *I Recall*, 105, 112.

62. Morris Kentridge, 124.

63. Feinstein, *Economic History of South Africa*, 87.

64. Union of South Africa, *Report of Commission of Inquiry Regarding Cape Coloured Population of the Union*, 36, paras. 155 and 160.

65. Union of South Africa, 36, para. 158.

66. Union of South Africa, 37, para. 168.

67. Union of South Africa, 36, para. 156.

68. Union of South Africa, 37, para. 166.

69. Union of South Africa, 38, para. 181; 39, para. 187.

70. Union of South Africa, 39, para. 192; 41, para. 204.

71. Union of South Africa, 43, para. 216; 44, para. 218.

72. As Feinstein drily observes, of the 1924 circular and its definition of "civilized labour," "those who produced this tortuous definition presumably failed to appreciate the irony of issuing it as a *Circular*." Feinstein, *Economic History of South Africa*, 86.

73. Union of South Africa, *Report of Commission of Inquiry Regarding Cape Coloured Population of the Union*, 38, para. 177.

74. Union of South Africa, 41, para. 200.

75. Union of South Africa, 38–39, paras. 182–85. Also see Feinstein, *Economic History of South Africa*, 87.

76. Feinstein, *Economic History of South Africa*, 74.

77. Morris Kentridge, *I Recall*, 152; also see 184, 287; on the National Party's anti-Semitism, see 162–64.

78. Morris Kentridge, 206.

79. Morris Kentridge, 399–400.

80. Ray Alexander and H. J. Simons, *Job Reservation and the Trade Unions* (Woodstock, South Africa: Enterprise, 1959), 25–26.

81. Alexander and Simons, 13.

82. Alexander and Simons, 29–30.

83. "Job reservation describes a system that the Nationalist Government introduced in 1956 to give White wage earners an exclusive or preferred claim to selected occupations in industry, commerce and public services. It amounts to a system of sheltered employment and is operated by statutory and administrative discriminations against Coloured, Indians and Africans." Alexander and Simons, 3. They add, however, "Africans have had much experience of job reservation under the Mines and Works Act of 1911 and of trade union segregation under the Industrial Conciliation Acts of 1924 and 1937. . . . Like many other apartheid laws, the I.C. Act [of 1956] reinforces colour bars that have stood for a long time, but that are being eroded and undermined by industrial expansion and urbanisation." Alexander and Simons, 34.

84. Mariotti and Van Zyl-Hermann, "Policy, Practice and Perception," 220, 223.

85. Alexander and Simons, *Job Reservation*, 6.

86. Alexander and Simons, 8.

87. Morris Kentridge, *Unemployment in South Africa*, 93.

88. Moodie and Ndatshe, *Going for Gold*, 50–51.

89. Paul Stewart, "Safer Underground via Mechanization? The Case of South African Gold and Platinum Mines," *Labour, Capital and Society* 46, no. 1 and 2 (2013): 120.

90. Stewart, 120–23.

91. Morris Kentridge, *Unemployment in South Africa*, 61.

92. Morris Kentridge.

93. See Stewart, "'Kings of the Mine,'" 50–51.

94. See Krikler, *White Rising*, 109–12.

95. Morris Kentridge, *I Recall*, 122.

96. Morris Kentridge, 112–13, 116.

97. The Russian nexus is carefully explored in Jane Taylor, *William Kentridge: Being Led by the Nose* (Chicago: University of Chicago Press, 2017).

98. One can only speculate as to why, for it is not as if the conditions were absent. Sydney Kentridge's bris, in November 1922, the same month as Taffy Long was hanged, was attended by leaders of the Labour Party as well as members of the Zionist Federation and Jewish Board of Deputies. Morris Kentridge, *I Recall*, 122.

99. As Morris Kentridge relates, Arnold, his second son, "proceeded to the [Massachusetts] Institute [of Technology] and became interested in work-study, industrial efficiency and automation. He, and his wife, Marian, are now [i.e., in 1959] resident in England, where he is the Principal of the Work-Study Centre of the British Transport Commission." Sydney, the father of William, was Morris Kentridge's eldest son. His youngest son, Leon, who studied at the University of the Witwatersrand, became a chemical engineer. Morris Kentridge, *I Recall*, 152.

100. Kracauer, *Salaried Masses*, 29.

101. Kracauer, 30. Also see Hedstrom, *Automating the Office*, 2.

102. Alexander and Simons, *Job Reservation*, 9.

103. William Kentridge, "If We Ever Get to Heaven: Occasional Notes on *More Sweetly Play the Dance*," in *More Sweetly Play the Dance*, ed. Marente Bloemheuvel and Jaap Guldemond (Amsterdam: EYE Museum, 2015), 40.

104. Matthew Kentridge, *The Soho Chronicles*, 33.

105. Orkin, *At the Junction*, 65.

106. Orkin, 27.

107. Morris Kentridge, *I Recall*, 115.

108. Kentridge and Hirson, *Footnotes for the Panther*, 158.

109. Kentridge and Hirson, 157.

110. Noah, *Born a Crime*, 23.

111. Some trade union poetry of the 1980s comes from the factory. See Ari Sitas, ed., *Black Mamba Rising: South African Worker Poets in Struggle* (Durban, South Africa: Worker Resistance and Culture Publications, 1986).

112. See, for instance, *The Cape Peninsula Automatic Telephone System and Trunk Exchange* (London: Siemens, 1933). Parts of the switching systems in Johannesburg and Cape Town had been automated by 1925, but Port Elizabeth was the first city to have an automatic exchange. See "'Wetting' the Automatics," *The South African Telephone and Telegraph Review ("The Live Wire")* 8, no. 3 (1925): 9–10. By 1926, Pietermaritzburg evidently also had an automatic exchange. "Praise for Manual Phone System," *The South African Telephone and Telegraph Review ("The Live Wire")* 9, no. 3 (1926): 15. A four-part series of articles describing how automatic exchanges worked appeared in *Live Wire* from May to August 1920. Further discussion of automatic exchanges took place in "A Large Automatic Exchange," "Automatic Telephony: Defining the Trunking Aspect," and "A Telephone Record: Spain's Automatic System," *The South African Telephone and Telegraph Review ("The Live Wire")* 10, no. 2 (1927): 11–13; and, with greater technical detail, "Automatic Exchanges: Maintenance La-

bour Units," *The South African Telephone and Telegraph Review ("The Live Wire")* 17, no. 2 (1934): 12–14.

113. I quote the notice in full, from a summary of matters discussed at the Association's monthly central executive committee meeting: **"Alleged employment of native as 'brush hand.'** . . . That a native is being employed, in the central area as a 'brush hand' to the painter, was a complaint submitted by the Transvaal branch. The divisional engineer, who had been approached, replied that 'the native employed with the painter to carry out his menial work has been with the department some years, and it is not the policy to terminate the services of natives to find employment for Europeans; but should the native leave, the question of his replacement by a European will be dealt with.'

The general secretary said he had learnt that the native was not engaged on 'brush hand' work. The work done by the native was similar to that performed by natives in private shops. It was unskilled.

Although the meeting felt that the work carried out by the native was equivalent to that done by a 'brush hand,' it decided that no action be taken." "Central Executive Meetings," *The South African Telephone and Telegraph Review ("The Live Wire")* 8, no. 12 (1925): 5. Emphasis in the original.

114. "The Government's White Labour Policy: 'An Economic Success,'" *The South African Telephone and Telegraph Review ("The Live Wire")* 8, no. 12 (1925): 7.

115. Among the few published pieces I have found of farm mechanization, the most informative is Michael de Klerk, "Seasons That Will Never Return: The Impact of Farm Mechanization on Employment, Incomes and Population Distribution in the Western Transvaal," *Journal of Southern African Studies* 11, no. 1 (1984): 84–105. Writing in the *Journal of Racial Affairs*, the academic organ of grand apartheid thinking, J. J. Bruwer, director of the Department of Agricultural-Technical Services, presents an argument interesting for paralleling Jan Haak's apartheid-informed outlook for automation in industry and in the office a few years before. Bruwer argues that, by allowing white farmers to do without African labor, or to utilize a smaller African workforce more efficiently, an acceleration in mechanization will contribute to a displacement of African farmworkers to the "homelands." J. J. Bruwer, "Arbeid en meganisasie in die Suid-Afrikaanse landboubedryf" [Labour and mechanization in the South African agriculture industry], *Journal of Racial Affairs* 25, no. 3 (1974): 100–101.

116. The decline, by the late 1960s, in employment of white workers in the manufacture of telecommunications equipment is, however, discussed by David Kaplan, *The Crossed Line: The South African Telecommunications Industry in Transition* (Johannesburg: Witwatersrand University Press, 1990), 31–32.

117. On the convergence, see Ceruzzi, *Computing: A Concise History*, xi–xiv.

118. In contrast to later years, in the early years of computing in the United States and United Kingdom, programming was regarded as women's work. See Abbate, *Recoding Gender*, 24–38.

119. For an account of the strike and its significance, see Joan Sangster, "The 1907 Bell Telephone Strike: Organizing Women Workers," *Labour / Le Travail* 3 (1978): 109–30.

120. "The Strain of Telephone Working," *The South African Telephone and Telegraph Review ("The Live Wire")* 8, no. 3 (1925): 19. William Lyon Mackenzie King, *Industry and Humanity: A Study in the Principles of Industrial Reconstruction* (Toronto: University of Toronto Press, 1973; originally published 1918), 205–6. For ease of reference, I cite a widely available edition of King's book. Apart from a few minor errors in transcription, this passage is quoted in full in *Live Wire* of March 1925. It is quoted again, in condensed form, in the paper's editorial, "More Leave Wanted for Telephonists," *The South African Telephone and Telegraph Review ("The Live Wire")* 9, no. 2 (1926): 1–2.

121. "Because, perhaps, of the comparatively recent introduction of industrial processes such as that of telephone operating, where the motive power is electrical, and where the whole trend of invention has been of a nature to intensify the strain by heightening the possible speed at which operations may be carried on, but little attention has thus far been paid to the possible inimical effects upon the constitutions of women engaged in such callings or the possible deleterious effects upon their offspring." *Report of the Royal Commission on a Dispute Regarding Hours of Employment Between the Bell Telephone Company of Canada, Ltd. and Operators at Toronto, Ont.* (Ottawa, Canada: Government Printing Bureau, 1907), 98.

122. King, *Industry and Humanity*, 205–6.

123. King, 206.

124. King, 206.

125. *Report of the Royal Commission*, 65.

126. King, *Industry and Humanity*, 207. In Weimar Germany, by comparison, the effects of telephone operation on the nervous system would be contested, as laws governing workers' compensation were challenged from the political right. These laws, dating from the 1880s, relied on the concept of "shock" and a notion of the human nervous system as itself electrical and therefore directly affected by electrical charges received by operators. As in North America, South Africa, and elsewhere, the vast majority of telephone operators in Germany were women. Andreas Killen, "From Shock to *Schreck*: Psychiatrists, Telephone Operators and Traumatic Neurosis in Germany, 1900–26," *Journal of Contemporary History* 38, no. 2 (2003): 201–20.

127. The technological novelty and distinctiveness of telephone operating are given greater emphasis in the *Report of the Royal Commission*, 60–61.

128. Kenneth Lipartito, "When Women Were Switches: Technology, Work, and Gender in the Telephone Industry, 1890–1920," *The American Historical Review* 99, no. 4 (1994): 1075–11.

129. King, *Industry and Humanity*, 206. This phrase comes verbatim from the testimony of Dr. Charles Trow, a University of Toronto professor of ophthalmology and otology: "A woman's nature is peculiarly sensitive to reproaches and to words at any time, and that would intensify the nervousness of their calling." *Report of the Royal Commission*, 71.

130. The 1925 *Live Wire* article that quotes Mackenzie King also cites Josephine Goldmark's "standard work," *Fatigue and Efficiency*, which refers to both the 1907 Canadian Royal Commission report and a 1910 US Bureau of Labor report on telephone companies. "The Strain of Telephone Working," 20.

131. "'Those Confounded Girls,'" *The South African Telephone and Telegraph Review ("The Live Wire")* 1, no. 1 (1919): 7; Rupert Hughes, "How She Performed a Miracle," *The South African Telephone and Telegraph Review ("The Live Wire")* 8, no. 12 (1925): 4. The former article also implicitly notes the toll of the 1919 influenza epidemic on operators, referring to the "paralyzing effects of only a partial interruption of the Telephone Service." See "'Those Confounded Girls,'" 7. Infectious disease was not the only extraordinary danger to which South African telephonists were exposed; as Jeremy Krikler relates, during the 1922 Rand Revolt, the central Johannesburg telephone exchange was attacked by a group of female militants, who assaulted some of the operators. Krikler, *White Rising*, 89.

132. *Report of the Royal Commission*, 66–75.

133. King, *Industry and Humanity*, 205.

134. Terkel, *Working*, 29.

135. *Report of the Royal Commission*, 71.

136. On the mnemo-technological machines of this time, see, generally, Kittler, *Gramophone, Film, Typewriter*.

137. Kentridge, *Six Drawing Lessons* (Cambridge, MA: Harvard University Press, 2014), 80–81.

138. For an exhaustive scene-by-scene summary of the film, see Matthew Kentridge, *The Soho Chronicles*, 287–321.

139. Matthew Kentridge writes that Soho must "achieve forgiveness both from his conscience and from others, most notably Mrs Eckstein." He also connects this need to the Truth and Reconciliation Commission, public hearings of which were still taking place when Kentridge made the film, and its amnesty process. *The Soho Chronicles*, 316–19.

140. J. M. Coetzee, *The Pole* (New York: Liveright, 2023), 126.

141. This is an interpretation of the closeup of Soho's face, in semiprofile, in which his left eye occupies the center of the frame, blinking just before the blue pigment flows from the breast and hip pockets of his suit. Matthew Kentridge refers to the resulting flood simply as "water." *The Soho Chronicles*, 312.

142. See Kentridge and Breidbach, *Thinking Aloud*, 92.

143. As Kentridge tells Angela Breidbach, "it partly has to do with choosing images of those obsolete technologies, like this switchboard, in which those strings of lines and vectors going in are part of the actual world, so it becomes a kind of naturalism; but it also refers to something that we know but do not see in the world now—where in fact there are infinitely more lines of contact, connecting us." Kentridge and Breidbach, 74.

144. "That's for experts," Kentridge remarks. Kentridge and Breidbach, 80.

145. Matthew Kentridge, *The Soho Chronicles*, 310.

146. Cameron, "Interview with William Kentridge," 71.

147. Cameron.

148. Cameron. See also Kentridge and Breidbach, *Thinking Aloud*, 74.

149. For observations on how modernist literature could still rely on this visibility, see Hugh Kenner, *The Mechanic Muse* (New York: Oxford University Press, 1987), 5–15.

150. See, generally, Sigmund Freud, *From the History of an Infantile Neurosis*, originally published 1918, in *The Standard Edition of the Complete Psychological Works of Sigmund Freud*, ed. James Strachey et al. (London: Hogarth, 1953–74), 17:7–122; Melanie Klein, *Narrative of A Child Analysis: The Conduct of the Psycho-analysis of Children as Seen in the Treatment of a Ten Year Old Boy* (London: Hogarth, 1961).

151. Krauss, "'The Rock,'" 34–35.

152. Kentridge and Breidbach, *Thinking Aloud*, 66.

153. Catherine Kentridge, *The Book of Cathy: A South African Childhood* (Middletown, DE: Davies Slate, 2013), 96.

154. Significantly, Muizenberg is also the site of a childhood memory associated with anamorphosis. Kentridge, *Six Drawing Lessons*, 15.

155. Freud, *From the History of an Infantile Neurosis*, 43n.

156. According to Catherine Kentridge, William Kentridge's elder sister, remembering impressions from her childhood, "Morris had written his memoirs when he was in his 70s and gave an autographed copy to each of his grandchildren. He had been a well-known politician, and the walls of his flat were covered in framed cartoons of Morris by famous political cartoonists such as Bob Connolly. These had appeared in the local papers over the years. They always emphasized the large nose, the monocle, and the striped double-breasted suit. . . . The flat also contained a gloomy bronze bust of Morris. I tried not to see it as it gave me the creeps with its blind and hollow eye sockets." Catherine Kentridge, *The Book of Cathy*, 8–11. Oedipal aggression is close to the surface of these descriptions, with the phallic nose juxtaposed in the cartoons with the grandfather's weak eyes, which are, symbolically, taken out in the bronze bust. When Morris Kentridge died in 1964, his grandchildren were "11, nine, two, and two-months-old." See Catherine Kentridge, 7. It therefore seems likely that he autographed his book, published in 1959, only for the two eldest grandchildren, Catherine and William, and not also for Eliza and Matthew, the two youngest. In any case, the first few lines of Morris Kentridge's *I Recall* emerge in a 1989 silkscreen by Kentridge entitled *Six Russian Writers*, suggesting a mediation of the grandfather through the book, if not simply as writing, then as pre-text to be written and drawn on. The image is reproduced in Maltz-Leca, *William Kentridge*, 94.

157. Matthew Kentridge, *The Soho Chronicles*, 56.

158. William Kentridge, *Lecture, Triennale, Milan*, in *Facts and Fiction: Arte e narrazione*, ed. Roberto Pinto (Milan: Commune di Milano, 1998), quoted in Carolyn Christov-Bakargiev, *William Kentridge* (Brussels: Société des Expositions du Palais des Beaux-Arts, 1998), 28–29.

159. Freud, *From the History of an Infantile Neurosis*, 29–47. A different interpretation of the "co-articulation . . . of the forensic and the erotic" in this interview is provided by Taylor, *William Kentridge: Being Led by the Nose*, 106.

160. Klein, *Narrative of a Child Analysis*, 20–26.

161. Sydney Kentridge, "A Barrister in the Apartheid Years," in *Free Country: Selected Lectures and Talks* (Oxford: Hart, 2012), 174.

162. Sydney Kentridge, "Evil Under the Sun: The Death of Steve Biko," in *Free Country*, 160.

163. Sydney Kentridge, "The South African Bar: A Moral Dilemma?," in *Free Coun-*

try, 26–27; see also 175–76. He also cites the work of the Legal Resources Centre (LRC) and explains how it litigated "within the limits of the existing legal system," achieving notable successes in the *Komani* (1980), *Rikhoto* (1983), and *Mthiya* (1983) decisions, which invalidated crucial elements of apartheid influx control in a prelude to its full abolition by the state in 1986. Sydney Kentridge, "A Barrister in the Apartheid Years," 178–79. As early as 1973, Felicia Kentridge, who founded the LRC, had embraced the approach to public interest law pursued in the United States whereby cases would be taken on for their potential to change the way the law was applied. Stephen Ellmann, *And Justice for All: Arthur Chaskalson and the Struggle for Equality in South Africa* (Montgomery, AL: NewSouth, 2020), 228–29. Community legal aid clinics, which existed before the LRC came into being, were another aspect of Felicia Kentridge's work. Felicia Kentridge, "Law Clinics," *De Jure* 9, no. 1 (1976): 120–24.

164. In fact, this is almost precisely the expression used by Kentridge: "I think that one of the mysteries I uncovered as a boy was that my father was an impossible act to follow. I wasn't going to do it better." Robert Enright and William Kentridge, "Achievements of Indecision: The Art of William Kentridge," *Border Crossings*, February, 2002, 24, quoted in Maltz-Leca, *William Kentridge*, 343n17.

165. Kentridge and Breidbach, *Thinking Aloud*, 70. See also William Kentridge, *Six Drawing Lessons*, 14–15. He speaks to Denis Hirson of "strong fathers, when the opinions around one are too strong." Kentridge and Hirson, *Footnotes for the Panther*, 81. For an interesting discussion of the implications of Kentridge's quest for an alternative path to his father's legal reasoning, see Maltz-Leca, *William Kentridge*, 38–40.

166. This is the single biographical fact about her mentioned by her father-in-law: "Sydney, and his wife Felicia—both Advocates in the Supreme Court of the Transvaal." Morris Kentridge, *I Recall*, 66. As for Felicia's parents, "Mr. Max Geffen was, for many years, the Chairman of the Jewish Historical Society, and his wife, Irene, was the first woman advocate in South Africa." Morris Kentridge, *I Recall*, 375.

167. Although it is stated that she was a lawyer. Kentridge, *Six Drawing Lessons*, 58.

168. Kentridge, 98.

169. Morris Kentridge is not mentioned by Michael Rothberg, who identifies the parents. Rothberg, *Implicated Subject*, 222–23n6. Leora Maltz-Leca, who attaches some importance to the parental generation, especially the father, cursorily mentions Morris Kentridge and his role in the 1922 revolt. Maltz-Leca, *William Kentridge*, 38–40, 95. Maltz-Leca does, however, briefly mention William Kentridge's maternal grandmother and her distinction of having been "the first female barrister in South Africa and the second in the British Empire." Maltz-Leca, 38. Perhaps the most suggestive remarks on the relation of grandson and grandfather come from Jane Taylor, who, arguing that the story of Perseus and Acrisius functions as an "Ur-myth" in certain of Kentridge's works, writes that "a grandchild is born to displace, and to do so in a more radical way even than a child, because the action is more displaced, further removed, and thus less motivated than the intimate conflict between parent and child. This remoteness is evident in the story of Perseus and Acrisius, where the old man is slain by a discus thrown into the air: the missile is not directed at the grandfather but finds its own mark, as it were. . . . Of course, this does not rule out the Oedipal

conflict between father and son." Taylor, *William Kentridge: Being Led by the Nose*, 85n11. Taylor does not, however, elaborate on the ways this conflict plays out when Kentridge's work is read in the context of labor politics.

Chapter 4

1. Kohler, "Thinking Through Puppets," in *Handspring Puppet Company*, ed. Jane Taylor (Johannesburg: David Krut, 2009), 42.

2. For a commentary on this body of work, see Andreas Huyssen, "The Shadow Play as Medium of Memory in William Kentridge," in *William Kentridge*, ed. Rosalind Krauss (Cambridge, MA: MIT Press, 2017), 77–98.

3. "Büchner's Woyzeck is a German soldier in [the] 1800s, but in this version, Woyzeck is a migrant worker in 1950s Johannesburg, a landscape of barren industrialisation." Handspring Puppet Company, *Woyzeck on the Highveld*, accessed March 13, 2025, https://www.handspringpuppet.com/handspring-puppet-company-productions.

4. Georg Büchner, *Werke und Briefe: Münchner Ausgabe*, ed. Karl Pörnbacher, Gerhard Schaub, Hans-Joachim Simm, and Edda Ziegler (Munich: dtv, 1988), 613–22.

5. Büchner, 623–24.

6. My discussion is based on the film made of a performance in February 2008 at the Market Theatre in Johannesburg. Handspring Puppet Company, *Woyzeck on the Highveld*, dir. William Kentridge, video of 2008 production, accessed March 13, 2025, https://www.handspringpuppet.com/handspring-puppet-company-productions.

7. I am assuming that the English translation that Handspring used evokes, in some measure, the Barker's low German and borrowed French words.

8. Basil Jones, "Puppetry and Authorship," in Taylor, *Handspring Puppet Company*, 254. Jones also refers to Victoria Nelson for how "our instinct for the supernatural—our animist beliefs—have been repressed and displaced from their religious origin, resulting in a welling up of dark imaginings in popular culture." Jones, 255.

9. Kohler, "Thinking Through Puppets," 137.

10. Adrian Kohler and Basil Jones, "The Magical Life of Objects: An Interview with Adrian Kohler and Basil Jones," *Lincoln Center Theater Review* 55 (2011): 14.

11. Gerhard Marx, "A Matter of Life and Death: The Function of Malfunction in the Work of Handspring Puppet Company," in Taylor, *Handspring Puppet Company*, 242.

12. Jane Taylor entertains this briefly but without pursuing the implications. Taylor, *Handspring Puppet Company*, 34. There has been much valuable work that explores with greater specificity how cybernetics and theories of the mind and brain developed reciprocally in the heyday of cybernetics in the 1950s and 1960s. In *The Closed World*, Paul Edwards brilliantly shows how, in Cold War–era American popular culture, the emergence of the cyborg, which developed in tandem with theories of cognition based on information theory, was the counterpart to the "closed world" discourse of computing. In a more recent work, Lydia Liu's exploration of the links among psychoanalysis, theories of language and writing, cybernetics, and cognitive science stands out. Lydia Liu, *The Freudian Robot: Digital Media and the Future of*

the Unconscious (Chicago: University of Chicago Press, 2010). On the history of cybernetics, see Kline, *The Cybernetics Moment*.

13. See, for example, Jennifer Parker-Starbuck, "Animal Ontologies and Media Representations: Robotics, Puppets, and the Real of 'War Horse,'" *Theatre Journal* 65, no. 3 (2013): 373–93.

14. There is evidence too for arguing that, in the nineteenth century, the *but* was, for some observers, also the soul. See, generally, Victoria Nelson, *The Secret Life of Puppets* (Cambridge, MA: Harvard University Press, 2001).

15. As with "diceromaton," my rendering is a best guess. The point is that, in his second naming of the beast, Handspring's Barker uses a slightly different word. This evokes the parodic use, in Büchner's text, of French terms and a wordplay that, although not negligent of meaning, sometimes exceeds it.

16. Handspring Puppet Company, *Woyzeck on the Highveld*, video of 2008 production. Italicized text are lines addressed to the rhino by the Barker. The Barker also appears at the start of the play, when, in a preview medley, some of the words from the scene in Büchner's text are spoken, along with some from other scenes.

17. Büchner, *Werke und Briefe*, 237. Although the diglossia of the Barker's language is not apparent from it, I quote in what follows from the English text of *Woyzeck* in Georg Büchner, *Complete Plays, Lenz and Other Writings*, trans. John Reddick (London: Penguin, 1993), 109–38.

18. Büchner, *Werke und Briefe*, 237 / *Complete Plays*, 116–17.

19. This is the upshot of how Kentridge figures the rhinoceros in his production of Mozart's opera, *The Magic Flute*, in which a sequence from a German colonial film from 1911 of a rhinoceros hunt forms a part, and in other works. See Kate McCrickard, "I Am the Bird Catcher," in *Flute*, by William Kentridge, ed. Bronwyn Law-Viljoen (Johannesburg: David Krut, 2007), 150–52; Maria-Christina Villaseñor, "Constructions of a Black Box: Three Acts with Prologue," in *Black Box/ Chambre Noire*, by William Kentridge (Berlin: Deutsche Guggenheim 2005), 85–87, 95. The rhino, more recently, makes an appearance in Kentridge's drawings for *Triumphs and Laments* and *The Head and the Load*.

20. Büchner, *Complete Plays*, 116.

21. Büchner, 116.

22. Büchner, 117.

23. Büchner, *Werke und Briefe*, 238.

24. Büchner, *Complete Plays*, 116; translation modified.

25. Büchner, 117; translation modified. Relating the scene to notes made by Büchner on Descartes, Günter Oesterle writes, "This comic proceeding allows philosophical-historical conclusions about the fund of ideas from which—or rather against which—it is spoken here. The thrust of the animal-human comparison in both market scenes is directed against Descartes' dualism of animal and human, body and soul. Büchner makes an entry in his reading notes on Descartes' views: 'The animals are nothing other than soulless machines, automata; the main reason that they may be denied a soul lies in their lack of speech. Animals would find and connect signs for their thoughts if they had a soul.' This explains why the proof of the Barker ends with the problem of speech." Büchner, *Werke und Briefe*, 655. It should be clear, however,

that I read the Barker's words not as simply repeating the idea that animals are defi-
cient because they lack the ability to use signs, which establishes a dualism of animal
and human being that Oesterle says Büchner is against, but that the Barker seems to
ask, given that an animal has reason, how a human is anything but a calculating animal. The objection to the Barker would thus be against the implication that, if reason
as calculation is the criterion, like animals, human beings may as well be machines or
automata. This objection is, in fact, consistent with Descartes's argument in *A Discourse on the Method*, where he concludes, regarding animals, "so that what they can
do better than us does not prove that they have any mental powers, for it would follow
from this that they would have more intelligence than any of us, and would surpass us
in everything. Rather, it shows that they have no mental powers whatsoever, and that
it is nature which acts in them, according to the disposition of their organs; just as we
see that a clock consisting only of ropes and springs can count the hours and measure
time more accurately than we can in spite of all our *wisdom*." René Descartes, *A Discourse on the Method*, trans. Ian Mclean (Oxford: Oxford University Press, 2006), 48.

26. Hugh Kenner, *The Counterfeiters: An Historical Comedy* (Bloomington: Indiana University Press, 1968), 25–26, 131–38.

27. E. T. A. Hoffmann, "Automata," trans. Alexander Ewing, in *The Best Tales of
Hoffmann*, ed. E. F. Bleiler (New York: Dover, 1967), 71–103. This translation, however, elides the phrase that contrasts the "speaking Turk" in the story with "all similar
dalliances, as are so often exhibited at fairs" (*allen ähnlichen Tändeleien, wie sie wohl
öfters auf Messen und Jahrmärkten gezeigt werden*). E. T. A. Hoffmann, "Die Automate," in *Die Serapionsbrüder*, ed. Wulf Segebrecht and Ursula Segebrecht, in E. T. A.
Hoffmann, *Sämtliche Werke in sechs Bänden*, ed. Hartmut Steinecke et al. (Frankfurt:
Deutscher Klassiker Verlag, 2001), 4:396.

28. Chude-Sokei, *Sound of Culture*, 22–24.

29. "A 'uman he is, a 'uman being in animal form, but a beast, an animal all the
same. [*The horse disgraces itself.*]" (*Ei Mensch, ei tierische Mensch und doch ei Vieh, ei
bête. [Das Pferd führt sich ungebührlich auf.]*). Büchner, *Complete Plays*, 117.

30. John Reddick, *Georg Büchner: The Shattered Whole* (Oxford: Clarendon,
1994), 303.

31. This was a debate among Büchner scholars in the decade leading up to Handspring's production. See Büchner, *Werke und Briefe*, 589–95.

32. Taylor, *Handspring Puppet Company*, 70.

33. For a long time, black men outnumbered black women in domestic service.
It was only in 1932 that census figures showed more black women in domestic work
in Johannesburg than men. Jansen, *Like Family*, 71. "Up until the 1980s, older male
'houseboys' were still fairly common in smart Johannesburg neighborhoods such as
Westcliff, Houghton and Parktown." Jansen, 202. For the definitive study of changes
in employment patterns in domestic work in Johannesburg in the late nineteenth
and early twentieth centuries, see Van Onselen, *New Babylon, New Nineveh*, 205–74.

34. The ambiguity is palpably expressed, and multiplied, when, in the 2008 revival, Woyzeck says to himself that, having been born in 1962, he is thirty-six years
old. Breaking with strict verisimilitude, the play is thus both set in 1998 and is a period piece set in the 1950s.

35. Mr Drum [Henry Nxumalo], "Bethal Today," *Drum*, March 1952.

36. It is important to note that, despite the improvement in their relative position by the late 1980s, the wages of unskilled black mine workers still placed them below the poverty line. V. L. Allen, *Organise or Die: The History of Black Mineworkers in South Africa*, vol. 3, *1982–1994* (Keighley, UK: Moor Press / Merlin, 2005), 452–58.

37. By the 1970s, African men were leaving white-owned farms to seek higher wages in manufacturing and mining. Women tended to remain on the increasingly mechanized farms, where their real earnings showed a rise from a low base, although those earnings declined relative to real wages in mining, manufacturing, and construction. During the same period, farm employment declined. De Klerk, "Seasons That Will Never Return," 91–93, 99–100.

38. Jeremy Baskin, *Striking Back: A History of COSATU* (London: Verso, 1991), 224–39.

39. South Africa, *Manpower Survey 1994: Occupational Information* (Pretoria: Central Statistical Service, 1997), 39–41. In *Faustus in Africa* (1995), another Handspring adaptation directed by Kentridge, however, the "Prologue in Heaven" takes place in a 1920s-style office where a switchboard operator connects Mephistopheles with God, as filing clerks and typists work. For these details, I draw on two different video recordings: Handspring Puppet Company, *Faustus in Africa*, 13 minutes and 41 seconds, https://www.youtube.com/watch?v=bZt718purgA&ab_channel=HandspringPuppetCompany; artvideotv, "Faustus in Africa by William Kentridge excerpt," 14 minutes and 18 seconds, https://www.youtube.com/watch?v=6sLGwUaY150&ab_channel=artvideotv. For commentary on the scene, see Lalu, *Undoing Apartheid*, 73.

40. Taylor, *Handspring Puppet Company*, 70.

41. Taylor, 70.

42. Büchner, *Werke und Briefe*, 691. On Freud, see Ernest Jones, *The Life and Work of Sigmund Freud*, vol. 1 (New York: Basic Books, 1953), 46–50.

43. Reddick, *Georg Büchner*, 15–16.

44. Büchner, *Complete Plays*, 183.

45. Reddick, *Georg Büchner*, 39.

46. Büchner, *Complete Plays*, 183.

47. Büchner, 118.

48. Büchner, *Werke und Briefe*, 636–37.

49. Büchner, *Complete Plays*, 122.

50. It is worth knowing that such a theory is summarized, and argued to be immaterial to the court's judgment, by E. T. A. Hoffmann in his brief in the case of Daniel Schmolling, who, in 1817, had committed a similar crime to Johann Christian Woyzeck, and the documentation of whose case was one of Büchner's sources. Büchner, *Werke und Briefe*, 627, 679. Hoffmann cites Reil, citing Pinel, on the question of an "only momentary or partial" (*nur momentan oder teilweise*) mental disturbance or "partial insanity, which an idée fixe produces" (*partielle Wahnsinn, den eine fixe Idee erzeugt*). "Ausführung des Criminal-Senats des Kammer-Gerichts," in *Zeitschrift für die Kriminal-Rechts-Pflege in den Preußischen Staaten mit Ausschluß der Rheinprovinzen*, ed. Julius Eduard Hitzig, vol. 1, bk. 2 (Berlin: Ferdinand Dümmler, 1825),

292–93. In the years before his death in 1822, Hoffmann served as Kammergerichtsrath (Counsel to the Superior Court) in Berlin. For a careful elucidation of Hoffmann's position in the Schmolling case, see Rüdiger Safranski, *E.T.A. Hoffmann: Das Leben eines skeptischen Phantasten* (Munich: Carl Hanser, 1984), 425–35.

51. "The human being is therefore irresistibly captivated by their intention, and just as irresistibly held by it. Here therefore the blind drive, an automatic urge [*ein automatischer Drang*], would cancel the moral freedom of the will, without a mental breakdown otherwise being indicated." See "Ausführung des Criminal-Senats des Kammer-Gerichts," 291. A psychoanalytic interpretation of the killing might relate this automatism to the doubling of Woyzeck's given names in those of Woost.

52. Büchner, *Werke und Briefe*, 696.

53. Büchner, 607.

54. Büchner, *Complete Plays*, 118. *Der Hessische Landbote* proclaims, "The life of the peasant is one long work-day; strangers devour his land in his presence, his whole body is a callus, his sweat is the salt on the gentry's table." Büchner, 168.

55. Büchner, 119–20.

56. Kentridge, "If We Ever Get to Heaven," 25–26.

57. Hoffmann, "Automata," 78–79, where the words *das Kunstwerk* and *der Künstler* are translated as "the figure" and "the exhibitor," respectively.

58. Büchner, *Complete Plays*, 105.

59. Büchner, 38.

60. Büchner, 171; translation modified.

61. Büchner, 118. In Lehmann's ordering, this scene follows the one with the Barker and horse.

62. Heinrich von Kleist, *Sämtliche Werke und Briefe*, ed. Helmut Sembdner (Munich: dtv, 2008), 930.

63. "The actor must go, and in his place comes the inanimate figure—the über-marionette we may call him, until he has won for himself a better name." Edward Gordon Craig, "The Actor and the Über-Marionette," *The Mask* 1, no. 2 (1908): 11.

64. Heinrich von Kleist, "The Puppet Theatre," in *Selected Writings*, ed. and trans. David Constantine (London: J. M. Dent, 1997), 412.

65. De Man, "Aesthetic Formalization," 285–86.

66. Jurgis Baltrušaitis, *Anamorphoses; ou Thaumaturgus opticus: Les perspectives dépravées—II* (Paris: Flammarion, 1996). This work was originally published in 1984 as the third and expanded edition of a book first published in 1955. The use of ana-morphosis as a concept-metaphor had become widespread in French thought by the 1960s, according to Baltrušaitis, *Anamorphoses*, 291–305. Two examples are Jacques Lacan, *The Four Fundamental Concepts of Psycho-Analysis*, trans. Alan Sheridan (Harmondsworth: Penguin, 1979), 85–89, 92, and Jean-François Lyotard, *Discourse, Figure*, trans. Antony Hudek and Mary Lydon (Minneapolis: University of Minnesota Press, 2011), 378–80.

67. De Man, "Aesthetic Formalization," 285.

68. Martin Heidegger, *Parmenides*, in *Gesamtausgabe*, pt. 2, vol. 54 (Frankfurt: Klostermann, 1982), 119.

69. See Matthew B. Kirschenbaum, *Track Changes: A Literary History of Word*

Processing (Cambridge, MA: Harvard Belknap, 2016), 5, who draws here on Michael Heim's pathbreaking *Electric Language: A Philosophical Study of Word Processing* (New Haven, CT: Yale University Press, 1987).

70. J. M. Coetzee, *In the Heart of the Country* (London: Vintage, 2004), 80. Also see Mark Sanders, "Automatic Writing, Automatic Reading: Programming and Labor in Two Novels by J. M. Coetzee," *Modern Fiction Studies* 71, no. 2 (2025): 286–311.

71. Nemerov, "Speculative Equations," 404. Although Kirschenbaum, following Heim, sees the computer as fundamentally different from the typewriter, in that they "reduce all of their input and output to symbolic tokens that are themselves numeric—mere indicators of discrete physical events like voltages and currents and magnetic polarities" (ibid.), it should be noted that one of the developments in the history of the Chinese typewriter involved input mediation in which a given key brought up an array of characters from which the user would choose—hence a switch, mechanical in operation, that anticipates the electronic switching of the computer and its keyboard. See Thomas S. Mullaney, *The Chinese Typewriter: A History* (Cambridge, MA: MIT Press, 2017), 239–47.

72. On PRINT before screens, see Nick Montfort, "Continuous Paper: The Early Materiality and Workings of Electronic Literature," MLA Convention, Philadelphia, PA, December 28, 2004, https://nickm.com/writing/essays/continuous_paper _mla.html.

73. Elsewhere I have explored this conversion with reference to photorealist painting, albeit without reference to computing. Mark Sanders, "Mimesis, Memory, Memorandum," *Journal of Literary Studies* 25, no. 3 (2009): 106–23.

74. Cameron, "Interview with William Kentridge," 71.

75. Kentridge, *Six Drawing Lessons*, 15.

76. Kentridge and Breidbach, *Thinking Aloud*, 41.

77. One example is the following: "I walk backward and film myself walking backward, so I can project it forward. It is clearly wrong. The lean is in the wrong direction. . . . I lean forward as I walk backward, an unnatural action, to make a natural illusion." Kentridge, *Six Drawing Lessons*, 107. For a detailed exploration of the parallels, see Sanders, "Anamorphosis."

78. There is a similar scene in *Ubu and the Truth Commission*, in which an unnamed man sets out various wares on a table.

79. Handspring recently adapted Coetzee's novel *Life & Times of Michael K*. It would be possible to make the same arguments about the techniques in that production as in *Woyzeck on the Highveld* and *Ubu and the Truth Commission*.

80. Mark B. N. Hansen proposes a comparable theorization, taking up Alfred North Whitehead's "neutral theory of experience in order to decenter—*but not to dispense with*—the perspective of the human." See Mark B. N. Hansen, *Feed-Forward: On the Future of Twenty-First-Century Media* (Chicago: University of Chicago Press, 2015), 15.

81. Lalu, *Undoing Apartheid*, 26.

82. Lalu, 158. By "protension," Lalu probably refers to how expectation is elaborated in the phenomenology of time consciousness. As Husserl writes, "If we relate the use of the word 'perception' to the differences in givenness with which temporal

objects present themselves, the antithesis of perception is the primary memory and the primary expectation (retention and protention) that occur here." Edmund Husserl, *On the Phenomenology of the Consciousness of Internal Time (1893–1917)*, trans. Rudolf Bernet (Dordrecht: Springer Netherlands, 1992), 41.

83. Lalu, *Undoing Apartheid*, 114.

84. Lalu, 132.

85. Hendrik Frensch Verwoerd, *Verwoerd aan die woord: Toesprake 1948–1962*, ed. A. N. Pelzer (Johannesburg: Afrikaanse Pers-Boekhandel, 1964), 77–78.

86. See Lodge, "Resistance and Reform," 416–24.

87. Lodge, 419.

88. Lalu, *Undoing Apartheid*, 165.

89. "CUTS TDP Project Case Study: The Clothing Industry in South Africa (First Draft)," Institute for Global Dialogue (IGD), n.d., 3–4, accessed March 14, 2025, https://cuts-citee.org/pdf/Case_Study-The_Clothing_Industry_in_South_Africa.pdf.

90. For an example, see Fahrenfort, *Spanner in the Works*. During the period on which I concentrate, however, a Coloured labor preference, instituted in 1962, made it more difficult for black African women to find work in either factories or offices in the Western Cape. One reads, in another autobiography, of how the loss of a white-collar position—as a school teacher—forced one educated black woman into domestic work after she was unable to find other work: "I phoned, in response to advertisements in newspapers: hotels, hospitals, restaurants and factories. No luck. I could not get a job as a waitress or scullerymaid. I could not find one as a nurse-aid or cleaner. Jobs as a tea-girl eluded me. Eventually, desperate, I resorted to domestic work." Sindiwe Magona, *To My Children's Children* (New York: Interlink, 1994), 107. The year is, incidentally, 1962. See Magona, 96. For more on the peculiar way in which the Western Cape labor market was racialized, see Humphries, "Administrative Politics and the Coloured Labour Preference Policy."

91. See, for instance, Kentridge, "If We Ever Get to Heaven," 40.

92. For an image of the sculpture, and a discussion, see Jane Taylor, "The Shadow of the Object May Be a Sound Seeing Voices in William Kentridge," *ArtAfrica*, September 26, 2019, https://artafricamagazine.org/the-shadow-of-the-object-may-be-a-sound-seeing-voices-in-william-kentridge/.

93. Karl Marx, *Capital: A Critique of Political Economy*, vol. 1, trans. Ben Fowkes (New York: Vintage, 1977), 548. "All work at a machine," Marx writes, "requires the worker to be taught from childhood upwards, in order that he may learn to adapt his own movements to the uniform and unceasing motion of an automaton." Marx, 546.

94. Büchner, *Complete Plays*, 119–20.

95. See Kline, *The Cybernetics Moment*. Although cybernetics was not a general feature of the South African moment, as the SACAC conference proceedings from the late 1960s, to which I refer in chapter 1, show, computer scientists and policymakers were abreast of the relevant American developments.

96. Moodie and Ndatshe, *Going for Gold*; Stewart, "'Kings of The Mine'"; Van Onselen, *The Night Trains*.

97. See Von Schnitzler, *Democracy's Infrastructure*; Ballim, *Apartheid's Leviathan*.

98. It would be unfair not to note a single exception in telephony, namely Kaplan, *Crossed Line*, which provides a brief history of telecommunications in South Africa in the context of its analysis of how the economics of manufacturing of telephone equipment in South Africa was affected when a decision was made in 1977 to move from analog to digital equipment, making the country an early adopter.

99. See Sanders, "Anamorphosis."

100. As Breckenridge observes of African science and technology studies, "People line up on either side of big themes—the economic and political effects of colonialism, demography or disease, for example—and they then assemble their historiographical allies and their enemies rather than choose a more specific problem." Serlin, "Confronting African Histories of Technology," 93–94.

101. Vladímir Propp, *Morphology of the Folktale*, 2nd ed., trans. Laurence Scott (Austin: University of Texas Press, 1968), 39–50.

102. Martin Heidegger, "The Question Concerning Technology," in *The Question Concerning Technology and Other Essays*, trans. William Lovitt (New York: Harper, 1977), 34.

Conclusion

1. One finds different estimates on the internet, ranging from around 35 percent to over 100 percent, when subscriber lines are divided by total population. I use a conservative estimate.

2. Ceruzzi, *Computing: A Concise History*, xi–xiv.

3. See, for example, Union of South Africa, *Debates of the House of Assembly, Third Session, Fifth Parliament 22nd January to 8th June 1926*, 1649–62.

4. See Strachey, "'Thinking' Machine," 31; Terkel, *Working*, xxxiii.

5. Tlali, "Soweto Speaking to Miriam Tlali," *Staffrider* 1, no. 1 (1978): 4–5.

6. Another way of putting this is in terms of so-called technological leapfrogging. See Serpell, *The Old Drift* (New York: Hogarth, 2019), 457.

7. Serpell, *Old Drift*, 457, 424, 507–8.

8. Serpell, *Old Drift*, 484.

9. Serpell, *Old Drift*, 438.

10. Serpell, *Old Drift*, 442.

11. Serpell, *Old Drift*, 444, 161. Serpell also writes about Nkoloso in "The Zambian 'Afronaut' Who Wanted to Join the Space Race," *New Yorker*, March 11, 2017.

12. Willem Anker, *Skepsel* (Cape Town: Queillerie, 2020), 286–87.

13. Karel Čapek, *R.U.R. (Rossum's Universal Robots)*, trans. Claudia Novack (London: Penguin, 2004; originally published 1921).

14. Anker, *Skepsel*, 191–92, 198, 201–2, 206.

15. Anker, 201–2.

16. Anker, 201.

17. Anker, 315.

18. See, for example, Maria Mies, *Patriarchy and Accumulation on a World Scale: Women in the International Division of Labour* (London: Zed, 1986).

19. Dinesh C. Sharma, *The Outsourcer: The Story of India's IT Revolution* (Cambridge, MA: MIT Press, 2015), 31–33.

20. Sharma, 15–17, 20–21.

21. "At the CSIR, which installed its first digital computer, code-named ZEBRA, in 1958, computing was also becoming a focus of interest. The organization sought to take the lead as the national centre of computing, and from 1967 an IBM 360 mainframe platform was installed and regularly updated." Beinart and Dubow, *The Scientific Imagination in South Africa*, 302.

22. Draper, "Disinvestment," 61; Draper, "The Limits," 96–97.

23. Sharma, *The Outsourcer*, 105–29.

24. Sharma, 184.

25. Sharma, 94.

26. Assa Doron and Robin Jeffrey, *The Great Indian Phone Book: How the Cheap Cell Phone Changes Business, Politics, and Daily Life* (Cambridge, MA: Harvard University Press, 2013).

27. See, for example, Serpell, *Old Drift*, 425.

28. Heidegger, "Question Concerning Technology," 34.

29. Thomas S. Mullaney, *The Chinese Computer: A Global History of the Information Age* (Cambridge, MA: MIT Press, 2024).

30. Mullaney, *The Chinese Typewriter*, 17.

31. Mullaney, *The Chinese Computer*, 87.

32. For a detailed account of how, drawing on Chinese telegraphy, the typewriter was adapted, see Mullaney, *The Chinese Typewriter*.

33. Mullaney, 237–81.

34. Mullaney, *The Chinese Computer*, 155–83.

35. Mullaney, 7.

36. Mullaney, 5.

37. Predictive text works in a similar way. Mullaney, 185–214.

38. Mullaney, 20–28.

39. Mullaney, 217.

40. Mullaney, 223.

41. Mullaney, *The Chinese Typewriter*, 316.

42. Mullaney, *The Chinese Computer*, 227–29.

43. "Without Input Method Editors, contextual shaping, dynamic ligatures, rendering engines, layout engines, adaptive memory, contextual analysis, autocompletion, predictive text, the 'modding' of the BIOS; the hacking of printer drivers, 'Chinese-on-a-chip,' and, above all, an embrace of hypography, no Western-built computer could have achieved a meaningful presence in the world beyond the Americas and Europe. Today, hypography is the global norm. Hypography made global computing possible." Mullaney, 230.

44. Li Yuan, "What Chinese Outrage over '3 Body Problem' Says About China," *New York Times*, April 8, 2024, https://www.nytimes.com/2024/04/08/business/3-body-problem-china-reaction.html?searchResultPosition=2.

45. Cixin Liu, *The Three-Body Problem*, trans. Ken Liu (New York: Tor, 2019). Liu's novel was published in Chinese in 2006. On computing, also relevant is Liu's "The Poetry Cloud," trans. Chi-yin Ip and Cheuk Wong, *Renditions* 77/78 (2012): 87–113. For another notable, and more extensive, literary treatment of Von Neumann, see Benjamín Labatut, *The Maniac* (New York: Penguin Press, 2023).

46. Liu, *The Three-Body Problem*, 211–12.
47. Liu, 213.
48. Liu, 215.
49. Liu, 219–23.
50. Liu, 223.
51. Ceruzzi, *History of Modern Computing*, 21–24.
52. Liu, *The Three-Body Problem*, 208.
53. Liu, 217, 219.
54. Liu, 217–18.
55. See, for example, Shetterly, *Hidden Figures*.
56. Liu, 218.
57. Liu, 228.

Selected Bibliography

Abrahams, Peter. *Tell Freedom: Memories of Africa*. New York: Collier, 1970. Originally published 1954.

Alexander, Ray, and H. J. Simons. *Job Reservation and the Trade Unions*. Woodstock, South Africa: Enterprise, 1959.

Altman, Phyllis. *The Law of the Vultures*. London: Jonathan Cape, 1952.

Automation and Technological Change: Hearings Before the Subcommittee on Economic Stabilization of the Joint Committee on the Economic Report, Congress of the United States, Eighty-Fourth Congress, First Session, Pursuant to Sec. 5(a) of Public Law 304, 79th Congress, October 14, 15, 17, 18, 24, 26, 27, and 28, 1955. Washington, DC: Government Printing Office, 1956.

Ballim, Faeeza. *Apartheid's Leviathan: Electricity and the Power of Technological Ambivalence*. Athens: Ohio University Press, 2023.

Baltrušaitis, Jurgis. *Anamorphoses; ou Thaumaturgus opticus: Les perspectives dépravées—II*. Paris: Flammarion, 1996.

Baskin, Jeremy. *Striking Back: A History of COSATU*. London: Verso, 1991.

Beiles, Sinclair, William S. Burroughs, Gregory Corso, and Brion Gysin. *Minutes to Go*. Paris: Two Cities Editions, 1960.

Breckenridge, Keith. *Biometric State: The Global Politics of Identification and Surveillance in South Africa, 1850 to the Present*. Cambridge: Cambridge University Press, 2014.

Bruwer, J. J. "Arbeid en meganisasie in die Suid-Afrikaanse landboubedryf" [Labour and mechanization in the South African agriculture industry]. *Journal of Racial Affairs* 25, no. 3 (1974): 88–102.

Büchner, Georg. *Complete Plays, Lenz and Other Writings*. Translated by John Reddick. London: Penguin, 1993.

Büchner, Georg. *Werke und Briefe: Münchner Ausgabe*. Edited by Karl Pörnbacher, Gerhard Schaub, Hans-Joachim Simm, and Edda Ziegler. Munich: dtv, 1988.

Cameron, Dan. "Interview with William Kentridge." In *William Kentridge*, by William Kentridge and Neal David Benezra. Chicago: Museum of Contemporary Art and New Museum of Contemporary Art, 2001.

The Cape Peninsula Automatic Telephone System and Trunk Exchange. London: Siemens, 1933.

Cartwright, A. P. *The Corner House: The Early History of Johannesburg.* Cape Town: Purnell, 1965.

Ceruzzi, Paul E. *A History of Modern Computing.* 2nd ed. Cambridge, MA: MIT Press, 2003.

Cobley, Alan. "'Why Not All Go Up Higher?': The Transvaal Native Mine Clerks' Association, 1920–1925." *South African Historical Journal* 62, no. 1 (2010): 143–61.

Coetzee, J. M. "Computer Poem." *The Lion and the Impala* 2, no. 1 (1963): 12–13.

Coetzee, J. M. *Doubling the Point: Essays and Interviews.* Edited by David Attwell. Cambridge, MA: Harvard University Press, 1992.

Coetzee, J. M. "Hero and Bad Mother in Epic, a Poem." *Staffrider* 1, no. 1 (1978): 36–37.

Coetzee, J. M. "Idleness in South Africa." In *White Writing: On the Culture of Letters in South Africa.* New Haven, CT: Yale University Press, 1988.

Coetzee, J. M. "Line Generator," May 30, 1963. Computer Poetry 1 folder, osb 143. J. M. Coetzee Papers. Harry Ransom Center, University of Texas, Austin.

Coetzee, J. M. "Surreal Metaphors and Random Processes." *Journal of Literary Semantics* 8, no. 1 (1979): 22–30.

Coetzee, J. M. *Youth.* London: Secker & Warburg, 2002.

Crush, Jonathan, Alan Jeeves, and David Yudelman. *South Africa's Labor Empire: A History of Black Migrancy to the Gold Mines.* Boulder, CO: Westview Press, 1991.

De Klerk, Michael. "Seasons That Will Never Return: The Impact of Farm Mechanization on Employment, Incomes and Population Distribution in the Western Transvaal." *Journal of Southern African Studies* 11, no. 1 (1984): 84–105.

De Man, Paul. "Aesthetic Formalization: Kleist's *Über das Marionettentheater.*" In *The Rhetoric of Romanticism.* New York: Columbia University Press, 1984.

Diebold, John. *Automation: The Advent of the Automatic Factory.* New York: Van Nostrand, 1952.

Edwards, Paul N. *The Closed World: Computers and the Politics of Discourse in Cold War America.* Cambridge, MA: MIT Press, 1996.

Edwards, Paul N., and Gabrielle Hecht. "History and the Technopolitics of Identity: The Case of Apartheid South Africa." *Journal of Southern African Studies* 36, no. 3 (2010): 619–39.

Ellmann, Stephen. *And Justice for All: Arthur Chaskalson and the Struggle for Equality in South Africa.* Montgomery, AL: NewSouth, 2020.

Emerson, Ralph Waldo. "Art." In *Essays and Representative Men.* London: Collins Clear-Type Press, n.d.

Enzensberger, Hans Magnus. *Einladung zu einem Poesie-Automaten.* Frankfurt: Suhrkamp, 2000.

Feinstein, Charles H. *An Economic History of South Africa: Conquest, Discrimination and Development.* Cambridge: Cambridge University Press, 2005.

Freud, Sigmund. *Standard Edition of the Complete Psychological Works of Sigmund*

Freud. 24 Volumes. Edited by James Strachey, Anna Freud, Alix Strachey, and Alan Tyson. London: Hogarth Press, 1953–74.

Funkhouser, C. T. *Prehistoric Digital Poetry: An Archaeology of Forms, 1959–1995*. Tuscaloosa: University of Alabama Press, 2007.

Goldblatt, David, and Nadine Gordimer. *On the Mines*. Cape Town: Struik, 1973.

Gqola, Pumla Dineo, ed. *Miriam Tlali: Writing Freedom*. Cape Town: HSRC Press, 2021.

Guy, Jeff, and Motlatsi Thabane. "Technology, Ethnicity and Ideology: Basotho Miners and Shaft-Sinking on the South African Gold Mines." *Journal of Southern African Studies* 14, no. 2 (1988): 257–78.

Hedstrom, Margaret. *Automating the Office: Technology and Skill in Women's Clerical Work, 1940–1970*. PhD diss., University of Wisconsin–Madison, 1988.

Higgins, Hannah B., and Douglas Kahn, eds. *Mainframe Experimentalism: Early Computing and the Foundations of the Digital Arts*. Berkeley: University of California Press, 2012.

Hodges, Andrew. *Alan Turing: The Enigma*. Princeton, NJ: Princeton University Press, 2014. Originally published 1983.

Hyslop, Jonathan. "State Education Policy and the Social Reproduction of the Urban African Working Class: The Case of the Southern Transvaal 1955–1976." *Journal of Southern African Studies* 14, no. 3 (1988): 446–76.

IBM. *Reference Manual: 709/7090 FORTRAN Programming System*. International Business Machines Corporation, 1961.

Kannemeyer, J. C. *J. M. Coetzee: A Life in Writing*. Translated by Michiel Heyns. Johannesburg: Jonathan Ball, 2012.

Kaplan, David. *The Crossed Line: The South African Telecommunications Industry in Transition*. Johannesburg: Witwatersrand University Press, 1990.

Kentridge, Catherine. *The Book of Cathy: A South African Childhood*. Middletown, DE: Davies Slate, 2013.

Kentridge, Felicia. "Law Clinics." *De Jure* 9, no. 1 (1976): 120–24.

Kentridge, Matthew. *The Soho Chronicles: 10 Films by William Kentridge*. Kolkata, India: Seagull Books, 2015.

Kentridge, Morris. *I Recall: Memoirs of Morris Kentridge*. Johannesburg: Free Press, 1959.

Kentridge, Morris. *Unemployment in South Africa: A Simple Outline*. Johannesburg: I.S.L. Press, [1922?].

Kentridge, Sydney. "A Barrister in the Apartheid Years." In *Free Country: Selected Lectures and Talks*. Oxford: Hart, 2012.

Kentridge, William. "'Fortuna': Neither Program nor Chance in the Making of Images." In *William Kentridge*, edited by Rosalind Krauss. Cambridge, MA: MIT Press, 2017.

Kentridge, William. "If We Ever Get to Heaven: Occasional Notes on *More Sweetly Play the Dance*." In *More Sweetly Play the Dance*, edited by Marente Bloemheuvel and Jaap Guldemond. Amsterdam: EYE Museum, 2015.

Kentridge, William. "In Praise of Shadows." In *William Kentridge*, edited by Rosalind Krauss. Cambridge, MA: MIT Press, 2017.

Kentridge, William. *Six Drawing Lessons*. Cambridge, MA: Harvard University Press, 2014.

Kentridge, William, and Angela Breidbach. *Thinking Aloud: Conversations with Angela Breidbach*. Johannesburg: David Krut, 2006.

Kentridge, William, and Denis Hirson. *Footnotes for the Panther: Conversations between William Kentridge and Denis Hirson*. Johannesburg: Fourthwall, 2017.

Kentridge, William, and Rosalind C. Morris. *Accounts and Drawings from Underground: East Rand Proprietary Mines Cash Book, 1906*. Kolkata, India: Seagull Books, 2015.

King, William Lyon Mackenzie. *Industry and Humanity: A Study in the Principles of Industrial Reconstruction*. Toronto: University of Toronto Press, 1973. Originally published 1918.

Kleist, Heinrich von. "The Puppet Theatre." In *Selected Writings*, edited and translated by David Constantine. London: J. M. Dent, 1997.

Kline, Ronald R. *The Cybernetics Moment; Or Why We Call Our Age the Information Age*. Baltimore: Johns Hopkins University Press, 2015.

Kracauer, Siegfried. *The Salaried Masses: Duty and Distraction in Weimar Germany*. Translated by Quintin Hoare. London: Verso, 1998. Originally published 1930.

Krauss, Rosalind. "'The Rock': William Kentridge's Drawings for Projection." *October* 92 (2000): 3–35.

Krauss, Rosalind, ed. *William Kentridge*. Cambridge, MA: MIT Press, 2017.

Krikler, Jeremy. *White Rising: The 1922 Insurrection and Racial Killing in South Africa*. Manchester, UK: Manchester University Press, 2005.

Lalu, Premesh. *Undoing Apartheid*. Cambridge: Polity, 2023.

Le Roux, Elizabeth. "Miriam Tlali and Ravan Press: Politics and Power in Literary Publishing During the Apartheid Period." *Journal of Southern African Studies* 44, no. 3 (2018): 431–46.

Link, David. *Poesiemaschinen / Maschinenpoesie: Zur Frühgeschichte computerisierter Texterzeugung und generativer Systeme*. Munich: Wilhelm Fink, 2006.

Link, David. "There Must Be an Angel: On the Beginnings of the Arithmetics of Rays." Translated by Gloria Custance. In *Variantology 2: On Deep Time Relations of Arts, Sciences and Technologies*, edited by Siegfried Zielinski and David Link. Cologne, Germany: König, 2006.

Liu, Cixin. *The Three-Body Problem*. Translated by Ken Liu. New York: Tor, 2019.

Lupton, Christina. "Workers as Readers: On Coetzee's *Youth* and the Poverty of Time." *Politicsslashletters* 13 (2018). http://politicsslashletters.org/workers-readers-coetzees-youth-poverty-time/.

Lutz, Theo. "Stochastische Texte." *augenblick* 4 (1959). https://www.netzliteratur.net/lutz_schule.htm.

Maltz-Leca, Leora. *William Kentridge: Process as Metaphor and Other Doubtful Enterprises*. Oakland: University of California Press, 2018.

Manovich, Lev. "New Media from Borges to HTML." In *The New Media Reader*, edited by Noah Wardrip-Fruin and Nick Montfort. Cambridge, MA: MIT Press, 2003.

Mariotti, Martine. "Labour Markets During Apartheid in South Africa." *Economic History Review* 65, no. 3 (2012): 1100–1122.

Mariotti, Martine, and Danelle van Zyl-Hermann. "Policy, Practice and Perception: Reconsidering the Efficacy and Meaning of Statutory Job Reservation in South Africa, 1956-1979." *Economic History of Developing Regions* 29, no. 2 (2014): 197–233.

Marx, Leo. *The Machine in the Garden: Technology and the Pastoral Ideal in America*. New York: Oxford University Press, 1964.

Mavhunga, Clapperton Chakanetsa. *Transient Workspaces: Technologies of Everyday Innovation in Zimbabwe*. Cambridge, MA: MIT Press, 2014.

Mavhunga, Clapperton Chakanetsa, ed. *What Do Science, Technology, and Innovation Mean from Africa?* Cambridge, MA: MIT Press, 2017.

Montfort, Nick, Patsy Baudoin, John Bell, Ian Bogost, Jeremy Douglass, Marc C. Marino, et al. *10 PRINT CHR$(205.5+RND(1)); : GOTO 10*. Cambridge, MA: MIT Press, 2013.

Moodie, T. Dunbar, and Vivienne Ndatshe. *Going for Gold: Men, Mines, and Migration*. Berkeley: University of California Press, 1994.

Mullaney, Thomas S. *The Chinese Computer: A Global History of the Information Age*. Cambridge, MA: MIT Press, 2024.

Nemerov, Howard. "Speculative Equations: Poems, Poets, Computers." *American Scholar* 36, no. 3 (1967): 394–414.

Noah, Trevor. *Born a Crime: Stories from a South African Childhood*, paperback ed. New York: Spiegel and Grau, 2019.

Orkin, Martin, ed. *At the Junction: Four Plays by the Junction Avenue Theatre Company*. Johannesburg: Witwatersrand University Press, 1995.

Pirow, P. C. "The Introduction of Automatic Office Facilities for Mines of the Rand Mines Group." *Journal of the South African Institute of Mining and Metallurgy* 63, no. 9 (May 1963): 453–85.

Reddick, John. *Georg Büchner: The Shattered Whole*. Oxford: Clarendon, 1994.

Report of the Royal Commission on a Dispute Regarding Hours of Employment Between the Bell Telephone Company of Canada, Ltd. and Operators at Toronto, Ont. Ottawa, Canada: Government Printing Bureau, 1907.

Republic of South Africa. *Commission of Inquiry into Matters Relating to the Coloured Population Group*. Pretoria: Government Printer, 1976.

Roach, Rebecca. "Hero and Bad Motherland: J. M. Coetzee's Computational Critique." *Contemporary Literature* 59, no. 1 (2018): 80–111.

Roach, Rebecca. "J. M. Coetzee's Aesthetic Automatism." *Modern Fiction Studies* 65, no. 2 (2019): 308–37.

Ross, Robert, Anne Kelk Mager, and Bill Nasson, eds. *The Cambridge History of South Africa*. Vol. 2, *1885-1994*. Cambridge: Cambridge University Press, 2011.

SACAC. *Proceedings of the First Symposium on Automation and Computation*. Johannesburg: SACAC, 1965.

SACAC. *Proceedings of Second National Conference on Automation and Computation*. [Pretoria]: SACAC, 1967.

SACAC. *Proceedings of the Third National Conference of the South African Council for Automation and Computation, 15th, 16th and 17th October, 1969 Pretoria South Africa*. Pretoria: SACAC, 1969.

Sangster, Joan. "The 1907 Bell Telephone Strike: Organizing Women Workers." *Labour / Le Travail* 3 (1978): 109–30.

Schreiner, Olive. *The Story of an African Farm*. Harmondsworth: Penguin, 1993. Originally published 1883.

Schreiner, Olive. *Woman and Labour*. London: Virago, 1978. Originally published 1911.

Sharma, Dinesh C. *The Outsourcer: The Story of India's IT Revolution*. Cambridge, MA: MIT Press, 2015.

Shetterly, Margot Lee. *Hidden Figures: The American Dream and the Untold Story of the Black Women Mathematicians Who Helped Win the Space Race*. New York: William Morrow, 2016.

Sitas, Ari. "Processions and Public Rituals." In *William Kentridge*, by William Kentridge and Neal David Benezra. Chicago: Museum of Contemporary Art and New Museum of Contemporary Art, 2001.

Stewart, Paul. "'Kings of the Mine': Rock Drill Operators and the 2012 Strike Wave on South African Mines." *South African Review of Sociology* 44, no. 3 (2013): 42–63.

Strachey, Christopher. "The 'Thinking' Machine." *Encounter* 3, no. 4 (1954): 25–31.

Taylor, Jane, ed. *Handspring Puppet Company*. Johannesburg: David Krut, 2009.

Terkel, Studs. *Working: People Talk About What They Do All Day and How They Feel About What They Do*. New York: New Press, 2004. Originally published 1972.

Theron, Erika. "Die vrou in die geldwêreld." *Sarie Marais*, May 12, 1965, 24–25, 41, 44.

Tlali, Miriam. *Muriel at Metropolitan*. London: Longman, 1979.

Tlali, Miriam. "Soweto Speaking No. 6 / A 'Great Lady' of Soweto / Mrs B. Makau." *Staffrider* 1, no. 3 (1978): 4.

Tlali, Miriam. "Soweto Speaking to Miriam Tlali." *Staffrider* 1, no. 1 (1978): 2–6.

Tlali, Miriam. "Soweto Speaking to Miriam Tlali." *Staffrider* 1, no. 2 (1978): 55.

Turing, Alan. "Computing Machinery and Intelligence." Originally published 1950. In *The New Media Reader*, edited by Noah Wardrip-Fruin and Nick Montfort. Cambridge, MA: MIT Press, 2003.

Union of South Africa. *Debates of the House of Assembly, Third Session, Fifth Parliament 22nd January to 8th June 1926*. Cape Town: Cape Times, 1926.

Union of South Africa. *Report of Commission of Inquiry Regarding Cape Coloured Population of the Union*. Pretoria: Government Printer, 1937.

Union of South Africa. *Report of the Low Grade Mines Commission*. Cape Town: Government Printer, 1920.

Van Houten, Robert, Maxwell Dean White, and A. G. Brunt. *Industrial Automation in South Africa: Report on an Investigation*. Pretoria: SACAC, 1973.

Van Onselen, Charles. *New Babylon, New Nineveh: Everyday Life on the Witwatersrand 1886–1914*. Johannesburg: Jonathan Ball, 1982.

Van Onselen, Charles. *The Night Trains: Moving Mozambican Miners to and from the Witwatersrand Mines, Circa 1902–1955*. Johannesburg: Jonathan Ball, 2019.

Vilakazi, B. W. "In the Gold Mines." Translated by A. C. Jordan. *Africa South* 1, no. 2 (1957): 115–19.

Vonnegut, Kurt. *Player Piano*. New York: Dial Press, 2006. Originally published 1952.

Wardrip-Fruin, Noah. "Digital Media Archaeology: Interpreting Computational Processes." In *Media Archaeology: Approaches, Applications, and Implications*, edited by Erkki Huhtamo and Jussi Parikka. Berkeley: University of California Press, 2011.

Wardrip-Fruin, Noah, and Nick Montfort, eds. *The New Media Reader*. Cambridge, MA: MIT Press, 2003.

. "Welcome News for Telephonists." *The South African Telephone and Telegraph Review ("The Live Wire")* 9, no. 4 (1926): 11.

Wiener, Norbert. "The First and the Second Industrial Revolution." In *The Human Use of Human Beings: Cybernetics and Society*. New York: Da Capo, 1988. Originally published 1954.

Wiener, Norbert. "Men, Machines, and the World About." Originally published 1954. In *The New Media Reader*, edited by Noah Wardrip-Fruin and Nick Montfort. Cambridge, MA: MIT Press, 2003.

Index